HOW ABOUT THAT!

THE LIFE OF MEL ALLEN

STEPHEN BORELLI

www.SportsPublishingLLC.com

ISBN: 1-58261-733-3

Publishers: Peter L. Bannon and Joseph J. Bannon Sr.
Senior managing editor: Susan M. Moyer
Acquisitions editor: Mike Pearson
Developmental editor: Regina D. Sabbia
Art director: K. Jeffrey Higgerson
Project manager: Greg Hickman
Dust jacket and insert design: Joseph Brumleve
Imaging: Heidi Norsen and Dustin Hubbart
Photo editor: Erin Linden-Levy
Vice president of sales and marketing: Kevin King
Media and promotions managers: Courtney Hainline (regional),
        Randy Fouts (national), Maurey Williamson (print)

Printed in the United States of America

Sports Publishing L.L.C.
804 North Neil Street
Champaign, IL 61820

Phone: 1-877-424-2665
Fax: 217-363-2073
Web site: www.SportsPublishingLLC.com

For Mom and Dad,
who have never thrown me a pitch I couldn't hit

CONTENTS

PART IV—REDEMPTION (1965–1996)

PREFACE

As an Oklahoma farmer tuned his television to Edward R. Murrow's *Person to Person* in April 1957, he nearly shot out of his easy chair.

"Johnny! Johnny!"

A 10-year-old boy appeared in the den just as Murrow, a cigarette in hand and plumes of smoke surrounding him, looked into his in-studio television screen, which revealed a lake on a large homestead. A man rowed into the picture.

"That's Mel Allen," the father said eagerly.

Some 25 years later, a boy in Pelham, New York, sat in a sofa chair like his grandfather's, similarly glued to a TV set. A catchy jingle sounded. *Dunnt-dunnt, Dunnt-dunnt. Dun dun … dun dun dun …*

"Hello there everybody, this is Mel Allen," a familiar voice said. "Welcome to *This Week in … Baseball … "*

For the next 30 minutes, I drifted into a desirable daze listening to the voice, much like my father and grandfather had back in Oklahoma. This book is nearly 50 years in the making. I was part of the generation that grew up learning baseball from Mel. A Yankees fan in the New York City area, I religiously watched *T.W.I.B.* before Saturday's *Game of the Week* on NBC. I loved the highlights but also just listening to the voice. To paraphrase announcer Bob Costas, it put me in a baseball frame of mind.

The spark that started this project came when I wrote a sports column for USATODAY.com about Mel in August 2000. I focused on how much I missed him as a part of *T.W.I.B.* The response I received from readers of my column was overwhelming. Roy Epstein, a former *T.W.I.B.* producer, was especially moved because Major League Baseball, which owns the right to the show, had dismissed Epstein and many of his *T.W.I.B.* co-workers after Mel died.

"Please know that your column touched more people than you realize and believe me they all applaud you," Epstein wrote.

Epstein put me in touch with Geoff Belinfante, the former executive producer of *T.W.I.B.*, and the book was born. I spent the morning of January 2, 2001, interviewing Belinfante and former *T.W.I.B.* writer John Bacchia at their office in South Hackensack, New Jersey, and didn't look back.

I accomplished a large portion of my research thanks to the gratitude of Mel's family: his brother and sister-in-law, Larry and Margie Allen; his sister, Esther Kaufman; and his nieces and nephews—Risa Frackman, Bill Kaufman, Carolyn Bern and Andy Allen. They spent endless hours of interview time with me in person and over the phone and endured my constant callbacks and e-mails. Larry allowed me to look through boxes and boxes of Mel Allen memorabilia in Alabama. The boxes contained thousands of newspaper clippings arranged by year; scrapbooks of Mel's early New York career; old audio and video of Mel; piles and piles of letters and other correspondence; and countless other gems. Larry pored over stories, letters and other documents with his keen eye to help me verify facts, giving me more than a hint of how thorough he once was as Mel's assistant.

The family didn't have to help me. I came to them, and I cherish the experiences of learning about these kindhearted people. They were all candid and honest with me, discussing subjects that must have been unpleasant to them. In lighter moments, Larry would say that when he brought up the idea of writing a book to Mel, his brother said, "Why don't you do a book?"

In many ways, Larry did.

ACKNOWLEDGMENTS

In addition to Mel's family, I would like to thank my interviewees: Maury Allen, Marty Appel, Luis Arroyo, John Bacchia, Hank Bauer, Easter Bellamy, Geoff Belinfante, Bob Berger, Aaron Bern, Yogi Berra, John Blackburn, Johnny Blanchard, Bob Bodziner, Jim Bouton, Andy Carey, Jerry Coleman, E. Culpepper Clark, Richard Ben Cramer, Bob Dolgan, Mark Durand, Elmo Ellis, Rabbi Joseph Ehrenkranz, Len Faupel, Warner Fusselle, Joe Gallagher, Joe Garagiola, Curt Gowdy, Bill Guilfoile, Ernie Harwell, Tommy Henrich, Mickey Herskowitz, Ralph Houk, Bill Israel, Bill Kane, Blanche Klar, Leonard Koppett, Bonnie LaBresh, Jack Lang, Joe Lavine, Robert Lipsyte, Robert Merrill, Heather Mitchell, Edward Mullins, Bobby Murcer, Phil Pepe, James Permutt, Arthur Richman, Bobby Richardson, Phil Rizzuto, Jim Rogal, Jeff Scott, Vin Scully, Jody Shapiro, Ouisie Shapiro, Charlie Silvera, Moose Skowron, Curt Smith, George Steinbrenner, Charley Steiner, John Sterling, Bert Sugar, Mike Torrez, Suzyn Waldman, Willie Weinbaum, Clark Whelton and Bob Wolff.

Without these generous people, I wouldn't have been able to describe Mel in detail in significant spots of this book. Not mentioned on this list are countless others who helped make my project possible, including: William Gildea, the great *Washington Post* sportswriter who read my proposal before I sent it around to publishers; Jerry Izenberg, the classic Newark *Star-Ledger* columnist who has been a lasting mentor for me; Mike Dodd, the amiable *USA TODAY* sportswriter who told me about my publisher; Glen Elsasser, an eloquent cousin and journalist who has encouraged me throughout my career; Tom Bird, a family friend and expert on Jewish culture who helped me sort out some terms; Mary Clark, the librarian for the University of Alabama's College of Communication and Information Sciences who allowed me to watch videos in her library on nights and weekends; David Sager, who permitted me to manually forward and rewind through Mel's audiocasts at the Library of Congress; Tom McEwen, who provided me with numerous Yankees-related phone numbers; Steve Gietschier, who mailed me crucial Mel-related *Sporting News* clippings; Charles Kuykendall, who helped acquaint me with Cordova, Alabama; Noah Gordon and Dave Kaplan, who set up key interviews for me; and Matthew Tosiello, for his scanning expertise.

I would also like to thank: The Miley Collection for the use of the audio of some of Mel's greatest games; the New York Public Library-American Jewish Committee Oral History Collection, Dorot Jewish Division, and The New York Public Library, Astor, Lenox and Tilden Foundations, for providing me with interview transcripts with Mel from February 8 and 24, 1979; the Associated Press, CBS, ESPN, the former *Look* magazine, Major League Baseball

Productions, NBC, the former *TV Radio Mirror* magazine, *Sports Illustrated*, SportsChannel, *The Birmingham News*, *The Crimson-White*, the Mutual Broadcasting System, *The New York Times*, *The Sporting News* and *Yankees Magazine* for their especially telling accounts of Mel and his family and the issues surrounding them; the W.S. Hoole Special Collections Library at the University of Alabama and its extremely friendly and helpful staff; the Museum of Television & Radio in New York and its warm and informative staffers; the entire New York Public Library System and Library of Congress for their comprehensive audio, video, microfilm and other printed materials concerning Mel; the Paul W. Bryant Museum in Tuscaloosa, Alabama, for its facts and figures about Alabama football; and the A. Bartlett Giamatti Research Center at the Baseball Hall of Fame in Cooperstown, New York, and its passionate employees and volunteers.

Thanks also to authors Curt Smith (*Voices of the Game*), David J. Halberstam (*Sports on New York Radio*) and Peter Golenbock (*Dynasty*) for writing telling accounts of radio, baseball and the Yankees that gave me a solid framework to write this book. Other especially helpful books to me were Charles Edward Adams's *Blocton: The History of an Alabama Coal Mining Town*; Sally Bedell Smith's *In All His Glory: The Life of William S. Paley*; Richard M. Cohen and David S. Neft's *The World Series: Complete Play-By-Play of Every Game*; editor Leonard Dinnerstein and editor Mary Dale Palsson's *Jews in the South*; Keith Dunnavant's *Coach: The Life of Paul 'Bear' Bryant*; John Dunning's *On the Air: The Encyclopedia of Old-Time Radio*; Glenn Feldman's *Politics, Society and the Klan in Alabama 1915-1949*; Gilbert Geis and Leigh B. Bienen's *Crimes of the Century*; Curt Gowdy and Al Hirshberg's *Cowboy at the Mike* and Gowdy and John Powers's *Seasons to Remember*; Ben A. Green's *A History of Tuscaloosa, Alabama 1816-1949*; David Halberstam's *Summer of '49* and *October 1964*; Joe Hendrickson's *Tournament of Roses: The First 100 Years*; Seymour M. Hersh's *The Dark Side of Camelot*; Mickey Mantle and Mickey Herskowitz's *All My Octobers*; Ted Patterson's *The Golden Voices of Baseball;* Jon D. Swartz and Robert C. Reinehr's *Handbook of Old-Time Radio*; and Suzanne Rau Wolfe's *The University of Alabama, A Pictorial History.*

Finally, I would like to thank: those numerous others who helped me along the way whom I may have left out; my friends, who haven't seen me for months; my co-workers, who adjusted their schedules on multiple occasions to accommodate my writing; my acquisitions editor, Mike Pearson, for his vision; my content editor, Gina Sabbia, for her patience and attention; my family for their constant love and support; and Colleen, for putting up with my writing moods. She is the love of my life, and without her, I couldn't have done this.

—Stephen Borelli
February 2005

INTRODUCTION

"Hello there everybody. This is Mel Allen ... "

The voice, laced with a lilting Alabama drawl, was once as recognizable as the president's and as familiar as a friend's. It meant only the most majestic teams and events: the New York Yankees, the World Series, the Rose Bowl. It invited you to huddle by your radio and listen, assuring you it would do the rest. Inflecting with the roars and deflating with the groans of the crowd, the voice took you on a journey with a line drive down the left-field line, following the ball as it knocked around in the outfield corner and made its way back to second base to almost nail the runner. The voice carried you from a jarring block to a touchdown scamper. It gave you a ringside seat as a boxer's knees wobbled from a right cross.

It broadcast the DiMaggio and Mantle Yankees dynasties that spanned the late 1930s through mid-1960s, peppering games with shouts of "How about that!" and "Going ... going ... gone!" It painted picture-perfect nicknames of Yankees greats: The graceful "Joltin' Joe" DiMaggio could turn a game with a smash to the gap or a running catch; "Old Reliable" Tommy Henrich and Hank "Man of the Hour" Bauer were men the Yankees wanted at bat in the clutch; "Steady Eddie" Lopat was a confident, consistent winner on the mound.

An article once tagged Allen as "the Homer of Homers." He was indeed a sports bard, loyal to his Yankees but always poised to praise the opposition. "His mellifluous tones make a lineup sound like a soliloquy from *Hamlet*," late *Los Angeles Times* sportswriter Jim Murray once wrote.

Allen, who studied dramatics in college, thought of himself as a narrator and the players as actors. His voice brought sporting venues into listeners' living rooms well before televisions existed, making the ball players, the ballparks and the games seem larger than life. Longtime author and *New York Times* writer Robert Lipsyte, a native New Yorker who used to drift off to sleep listening to Allen's broadcasts, realized this phenomenon upon his first trip to Yankee Stadium.

"I was overwhelmed at how small the park was, how dull the grass was," Lipsyte says. "I was amazed at how less grand it was than what he had led me to believe."

Richard Sandomir, a *New York Times* sportswriter, wrote shortly after Allen died in 1996 that "he was everything a sportscaster should be: quick, smart, descriptive and exuberant."

Says Curt Gowdy, another sportscasting giant: "There was nobody better than Mel Allen."

Says Bob Wolff, the former voice of the Washington Senators: "Mel was born with or acquired a voice which is so warm and homey and distinctive that all the announcers who came along after him could never emulate him."

Says Jerry Coleman, the voice of the San Diego Padres who worked with Allen on Yankees broadcasts in the mid-1960s: "Mel had that great quality in his voice that made him the perfect broadcaster. It made him overpowering."

During his prime, Allen repeatedly topped the national polls that named a "best sportscaster," but he was so much more than that. In an era before teams had armies of announcers and cable television broadcasts, he was the primary voice and face of the love-'em or hate-'em Yankees, the most powerful and recognized organization in sports.

"No man in the history of the Yankees has ever meant more to the Yankees than Mel Allen," George Steinbrenner says.

Over the team's "Home of Champions" radio network, Allen was the soundtrack of Yankees success. At Yankee Stadium, he charmed crowds as master of ceremonies for Old Timers' Day and for tributes to the team's superstars. On Broadway, his voice played from a tape recording during performances of the musical *Damn Yankees*. In Hollywood, his voice called Babe Ruth's 60th home run in *The Babe Ruth Story*, a 1948 movie starring William Bendix as the Babe. Never mind that Allen was only 14 years old in 1927 when the Ruth actually swatted No. 60.

Allen was so identified with the Yankees that their fans credited him for unparalleled success and their detractors blamed him for relentlessly winning. As the Yankees claimed pennant after pennant, Allen's voice became synonymous with the World Series, too. He broadcast 20 Series on radio or television.

"He was Mr. October long before Reggie," says Joe Garagiola, the Baseball Hall of Fame broadcaster who had the unenviable task of taking Allen's place in the Yankees broadcast booth. "You don't fill Mel Allen's shoes," he says. "I was the next broadcaster." Merv Griffin, whose television program NBC once preempted for two weeks in favor of Allen's coverage of the World Series, introduced himself upon his return to the air as "Mel Allen's winter replacement."

A 1950s *Variety* magazine poll identified Allen as one of the "25 most recognizable voices" in the world. Allen was the only sportscaster on a list that included Winston Churchill and Franklin Delano Roosevelt. Another American president, Dwight Eisenhower, received six fewer lines than Allen for his entry in a late-1950s edition of *Who's Who in America*. *Who's Who* repeatedly ran Allen's biography as his voice and face overwhelmed the country. In movie theaters, Allen was the sports voice of Fox Movietone News, narrating highlights from Pasadena to Churchill Downs to West Point. On commercials, he hawked Ballantine beer, White Owl cigars and Gillette razor blades, sometimes with Yankees stars like Whitey Ford. In person, he appeared in celebrity charity benefits with Bob Hope and Perry Como.

Allen was a comic book hero and a frequent member of the White House guest list. A tall, commanding presence who wore a wide smile, he met swarms of young male admirers seeking his autograph and hordes of older female ones seeking his hand in marriage when he emerged from Yankee Stadium. Allen was one of the "10 Sexiest Bachelors on Earth" to five 1950s glamour girls, including Joan Collins and Zsa Zsa Gabor, who compiled a list of leading men.

"In New York City, his base of operations, Mel Allen has a following that only a politician, which Allen in some ways is, could love," *Sports Illustrated*'s Huston Horn wrote in 1962. "There are people to whom his voice is a comfort, his handshake, a benediction, his autograph, an heirloom."

Allen earned around $200,000 a year for his broadcasting work during the 1950s and 1960s, then an unheard-of figure for a sportscaster. He had a greater income than the athletes he described.

"Well, he deserved it," Yogi Berra says. "He had that voice. I loved to hear it."

Behind that voice is an untold story of a boy raised by Jewish immigrants whose families fled czarist Russia to escape the brutal pogroms. Allen's parents stood up to the Ku Klux Klan in Alabama and survived the throws of the Great Depression. Their boy reached the bright lights of New York and the pinnacle of his profession, sacrificing his personal life along the way. Allen stayed a lifelong bachelor but remained a devoted family man.

Spurned by the Yankees in 1964, he all but disappeared from the public eye for over a decade. But he re-emerged to broadcast games for Steinbrenner, extending his Yankees net from the Lou Gehrig to Don Mattingly eras. He became one of the first two voices enshrined in the Baseball Hall of Fame and hosted the groundbreaking television highlight show, *This Week in Baseball*. *T.W.I.B.* anointed Allen as the voice for a sport once again, this time for a brand new generation of adoring fans.

PART I

DIXIE
(1913–1936)

CHAPTER 1

Valentine's Day

William Israel was known as "Wolf." His appearance justified such a fierce-sounding surname. He stood over six feet tall and wore a thick, black beard. A self-made Jewish merchant, Israel escaped from Russia to America with his wife and children during the pogroms, a period of mass murdering of Jews. At the time, Russia was enduring enormous political unrest that historians link to the 1917 revolution. In 1881, terrorists killed Czar Alexander II. Jews had had unprecedented rights under the emperor, but his successors, Alexander III and Nicholas II, were anti-Semitic. The faltering czarist regimes identified Jews as revolutionaries and persecuted them with an ideology that mirrored that of Nazi Germany.

Before coming to the United States, Wolf Israel and his family lived in Kobrin, an agricultural town near Poland that was part of Imperial Russia. (Today, Kobrin is in Belarus.) In 1884, Israel, then 29 years old, made his way to England and sailed across the English Channel to Scotland. He traveled aboard the *State of Nevada* to New York Harbor, where he arrived on November 14, 1884. Israel went through the immigration port at Castle Garden, an island off the southwest tip of Manhattan.

Israel journeyed to Baltimore, where he knew of a *landsman*, a Yiddish term meaning someone from your part of the country. Jacob Epstein, a young Lithuanian immigrant, had started the Baltimore Bargain House in 1882. Operating from the city's Inner Harbor area in a facility that took up two city blocks, Epstein outfitted fellow immigrants and sent them all over the United States. Because Jews were oppressed in Russia, many of them weren't qualified to do much more than peddle. But Epstein provided them with counsel and supplies and aided them in getting their families across the Atlantic. Epstein helped thousands of aspiring storeowners, and their Southern businesses began in canvas peddling backpacks.

Epstein pointed Israel toward Birmingham, Alabama. With its plentiful surrounding mineral region, the "Magic City" had sprouted up after the Civil War amid a coal, iron and steel boom. Epstein gave Israel merchandise, money to buy a horse and wagon and instructions to sell his goods to farmers. Israel peddled his wares despite not knowing how to speak English. He found no anti-Semitism in the bucolic Southern communities he traversed. The farmers knew nothing about it. Regardless of their race or creed, peddlers overjoyed these rural families upon arriving at their homes. Families pushed back their tables, beds and chairs to give the peddlers an honorary place in the middle of the floor. Peddlers learned to pack their brightest-colored cloths in the first bags they opened to entice their audience. Then they overwhelmed their customers with a rush of smells: cheap perfumes, soap, leather goods, and spices. For these isolated people, a country store had opened in their living room.

Farmers found Israel to be an honest man. He often shared the supper table with his Gentile customers, using his own glass dishes. Because he kept kosher, Israel wouldn't eat the farmers' meat, but he happily accepted their eggs, cheese and coffee. Sometimes, Israel stayed overnight and farmers gave him their best bedrooms. As Israel traveled from farm to farm, he began to pick up the English language and save some money. He returned to Russia, where he went into the timber business, but his partner turned out to be a crook who ran off with his money.

In need of a second start amid the mounting pogroms of Russia, Israel came back to the United States in 1888 at age 33 along with his brother, Samuel Abraham Israel. Back in Russia, his fifth child, Julius Allen Israel, Mel Allen's father, was born in 1889. Julius had a twin sister who died of an ailment in infancy. In 1891, Wolf Israel sent for his family. By this time, he had established a personal relationship with Epstein, who facilitated the arrival of his wife, Ethel, and their five children in Baltimore and then their journey to Alabama.

The family settled in Bibb County, a once-poor area that began to thrive in the 1880s when miners struck coal. In 1892, Israel opened a department store on Main Street in West Blocton, located about 35 miles southwest of Birmingham, along with partner H. Weinstein. Weinstein and Israel sold clothing, furniture, mining tools, groceries, "all dry good cheaper than can be bought in New York," they bragged in an advertisement in the *Blocton Courier*. Israel eventually took over sole possession of the business, and his store became the largest in the county. He and Ethel, who was originally from Austria, raised eight children, and Israel ensured that scores of other members of his extended family also reached America and West Blocton. Israel took his family very seriously. If you were related to him, he treated you like you were his own child or sibling. Before Israel died in 1930, he left a clause in his will that funded more relatives' entrée to the United States.

❉ ❉ ❉ ❉ ❉ ❉ ❉

The Tennessee Coal, Iron, and Railroad Company controlled the mines of Blocton, the company town adjacent to West Blocton that housed them. The TCI brought in experienced miners from Pennsylvania, West Virginia and Ohio. As droves of immigrants also settled in the area in the 1890s, West Blocton became Bibb County's largest municipality. The town's Main Street merchants served a population of close to 12,000.

Wolf Israel was beloved among his customers, whom he allowed to buy goods on credit. Speaking in his broken English, he told them to come back and settle up on their weekly paydays. Many of them were Russians, Poles, Germans, Italians and other immigrants who worked in the mines. Compatriots lived together in sections of shacks built against hills such as Little Italy. West Blocton also had a Wild West flavor to it. Gangs, outlaws and bandits roamed freely, stealing cotton and cattle, robbing people of their valuables and killing anyone in their way. Some crimes were race related, as West Blocton had a sizeable black population during this Jim Crow era. Sometimes drunken brawls broke out thanks to unlawful saloons known as Blind Tigers. For its disorder, Bibb County became saddled with the moniker "Bloody Bibb." Bibb was notorious for jail-breaks. The *Bibb Blade* once mockingly reported: "Five prisoners have escaped jail and four more were put in. The Sheriff should fix the fence."

One of the most feared outlaws around West Blocton was the aptly named Bart Thrasher, who carried a hefty price on his head. West Blocton shopkeepers locked their doors when they saw Thrasher entering town. In 1896, seven-year-old Julius Israel nearly had an encounter with Thrasher in the woods near West Blocton, where he would often go to hunt and fish. Julius was with a boy named Saul, who was several years older than him. Julius watched cautiously as Saul, a roughneck who carried a gun, pointed his weapon at a bird in a tree. Suddenly, Saul dropped the gun and fell flat on the ground.

"Get down quick!" he yelled to Julius.

Julius dove into the grass. He saw two men clad in overalls with guns slung over their shoulders pass on a nearby road.

"What's the matter?" Julius asked Saul. "What did you do that for?"

"Did you know that was Bart Thrasher?" Saul replied.

Thrasher and a sidekick were headed into West Blocton, where they killed Griff Bass, West Blocton's first policeman. Thrasher reportedly shot Bass at Harvey's Drug Store because Bass was part of a posse that had killed a member of Thrasher's outlaw family. After taking out Bass, the pair went around to homes of various sheriffs, constables and deputies and left notes pinned to their pillows saying they were next.

Vigilance groups called "beat clubs" had emerged in each of Bibb County's voting precinct in an attempt to combat such lawlessness. In addition, West Blocton's citizens were permitted to carry guns in their hip pockets, provided they were not concealed. To take on Thrasher, however, the town called upon Henry Cole, a strikebreaker known throughout the state. Cole, who had been deputized, was a tough customer with 16 notches in his gun, one for each man he had killed, so the story went. Cole hid under a bridge, and when Thrasher and his sidekick got halfway across it, he shot them both in the back, killing them on the spot.

There was a strange paradox at play between West Blocton's outlaws and citizens. The town was crawling with outlaws, but they usually didn't bother the general population. Instead, they waged vendettas against the law, which was invariably responsible for the deaths of some of their "family" members. West Blocton's residents usually felt they could leave the doors to their homes and businesses unlocked in good faith. As an adult, Julius Israel had a nostalgic remembrance of the Wild West element in his hometown. He loved the television show *Gunsmoke* because it reminded him of West Blocton.

Wolf Israel upheld the virtues of *Gunsmoke*'s fictional residents of Dodge City, Kansas: Hard work and clean, honest, orderly living. He served West Blocton's Jewish congregation as devoutly as *Gunsmoke*'s no-nonsense marshal, Matt Dillon, protected Dodge City. Israel was considered the patriarch of West Blocton's Jewish community. The earliest written record of a Jewish religious rite in West Blocton was the marriage of Annie Israel, Wolf's eldest child, to Israel Kronenberg in 1896. The town's Jewish community organized its congregation and built its first synagogue in 1905. The congregation's bylaws, largely the work of Israel's eldest son, Sam, also called for a shochet, a Jew who performed the ritual slaughter of animals that became kosher meat, and a Hebrew school.

The Jewish congregation of West Blocton was small, rising to only six or seven families at its peak. Wolf Israel worked tirelessly to see that the Jewish community not only survived, but that it remained strictly orthodox. Because Israel's was the first Jewish family in town, the patriarch was known to jump in a horse and buggy and ride 10 miles to round up the 10 adult males required for a minyan at temple services. Years later, when his grandson, Mel Allen, attended the University of Alabama in Tuscaloosa, located about 25 miles northwest of West Blocton, he would bring a carload of Kappa Nu fraternity brothers to help his Uncle Sam ensure a minyan on Jewish High Holy Days.

Before West Blocton's synagogue was built, Jewish peddlers flocked to West Blocton and gathered in a loft above a drug store that was converted into a place of prayer. Wolf and Ethel Israel would let these peddlers stay at their home, lining up feather beds in their living and dining rooms. Wolf Israel made his children stand and participate in the loft on Holy Days. Yom Kippur was a long day of standing, praying and fasting, and Jews would inhale snuff as a pick me up when they felt faint. Young Julius noticed the snuff made some of the people sneeze, which gave him an idea. He snuck out to the drug store, where a friend of his filled prescriptions, and asked his friend for something stronger than snuff. The guy gave him cayenne pepper. Julius returned to the loft and stirred the pepper into the ritual snuffbox. The whole congregation broke into such a sneezing fit that it couldn't carry on the services. When he found out who the culprit was, Wolf Israel grabbed Julius by the ear and dragged him out of the room.

Mel Allen's father grew up living the American dream. He and his Christian friends leisurely ran barefoot in the summertime and played pranks on one other. Julius fished, hunted, shot marbles and played baseball with a stick. When he got older, he dated Christian girls. Wolf Israel saw Julius's activities as a waste of time. Wolf hadn't played games as a boy. Instead, he pitched in to help his family survive in Russia. In West Blocton, Wolf worked from early in the morning until late into the evening, and he expected his children to help him in the store when they weren't in school.

Julius was the family's Tom Sawyer. When his friends stopped outside his father's store on the way to the ball field, he couldn't resist the temptation to go with them, even if a licking awaited him upon his return. Ethel Israel would try to stand up to her husband on behalf of her son, Julius, but to no avail. Nevertheless, Julius's mother was a strong influence on him. She was a sweet, gentle, nurturing woman who rarely raised her voice.

"Every noble thought I ever had came from my mother," Julius said late in his life.

Wolf Israel might have had such thoughts if he wasn't always working at his store, where Sam, his eldest son, also spent most of his time. Wolf saw Sam, who was about three years older than Julius, as the model son. Unlike Julius, who was always out playing, Sam was preparing for a career, as Wolf Israel felt any young man should do. When he retired, Wolf Israel thought about how Julius was never where he was supposed to be while Sam was keeping the books in the store. The father divided his business into shares of 51 and 49 percent, in favor of Sam. Julius turned down his portion. "If you can't treat me like an equal son, I don't want it," he told his father. Relatives thought he was crazy. Ike Nathews, the husband of Julius's younger sister, Esther, got the 49 percent and he and Sam operated the family business as the I&N Quality Store.

❈ ❈ ❈ ❈ ❈ ❈ ❈

Like Wolf Israel, Abraham Leibowitz, a rabbi and cantor in Russia, evacuated his family to America. The Leibowitzes got out in 1905 to avoid the pogroms and a call for Abraham to serve in the czar's army. Abraham Leibowitz, his wife, Risa Pearl, and their children settled in Louisville, Kentucky, where a relative had gotten Abraham the position as cantor in a small synagogue.

Abraham was a gentle man who was neat, proper and extremely learned. Mel Allen's mother's people were educators and scholars. They were relatives of Shmarya Levin, who sat on the first Russian Duma of legislators in 1906, and Simon Dubnow, the famous Jewish historian and intellectual active in Russia in the Zionist movement for establishment of a Jewish state.

Anna Leibowitz, Mel Allen's mother and the eldest of seven Leibowitz children, was in her late teens when the family arrived in America. She had gone to a school for Jewish children that Levin ran in Yekaterinoslav, a picturesque city built on the Dnieper River to honor 18th Century Russian empress Catherine the Great. (Today the city is located in the Ukraine and known as Dnepropetrovsk.) In czarist Russia, Jewish children weren't permitted to attend public schools, so Anna embraced her new opportunities in America, taking night classes to learn English.

The Israel and Leibowitz families were brought together when Wolf Israel was helping to establish a Birmingham congregation, which called upon Abraham Leibowitz to be its rabbi and cantor. At a Purim party, amid the celebration of Queen Esther's rescue of the Jews from the clutches of the evil Haman, Julius Israel and Anna Leibowitz met and fell in love. Even after Abraham Leibowitz took another position at a synagogue in Minneapolis, Julius and Anna stayed in touch.

This relationship didn't please Wolf Israel. The Leibowitzes were fine people, but they were dreamers, not merchants. Anna's five brothers were classical musicians and she loved to sing. She had masterfully stepped into the lead female role in a Birmingham rendition of Solomon Anski's classic Yiddish play, *The Dybbuk*, when the lead actress in a Jewish acting group visiting from New York had fallen sick. After the performance, Anna's parents quickly pulled her from the stage. They thought it wasn't appropriate for a rabbi's daughter to perform with this band of strange people who traveled from town to town.

Wolf Israel shared the moral standards of Abraham Leibowitz, but he thought that the Leibowitz family didn't possess much earning power. Abraham Leibowitz made about $1,200 a year. How would his daughter help Julius become a successful businessman? What Wolf Israel didn't know was that the Leibowitz brothers, who later shortened their last name to "Leib" for show business purposes, could always find work, even when the Great Depression set in. When the family later lived in Detroit, the brothers played together professionally as "The Four Leibs."

Wolf Israel also took personal issue with Anna Leibowitz, a spitfire who talked back to him—in Russian, no less. The Israel patriarch liked to approve, if not arrange his children's unions to ensure that their families had the potential to earn successful livings. Wolf Israel had selected a woman for Julius from another tiny Alabama town. She was a widow who had inherited a store from her late husband. Wolf Israel knew Julius wasn't a businessman at heart, and here was a lady who was running a store all by herself.

Julius crossed his father once again. In February 1912, he left Alabama on a train, departing his home state for the first time since entering it as a babe in his mother's arms. Julius Israel and Anna Leibowitz were married on February 25, 1912, in Minneapolis. He was 23, she was 21. Because Wolf Israel opposed the union, not a single member of Julius's family attended the wedding.

❖❖❖❖❖❖❖

Julius planned to open a general store in Johns, Alabama, a primitive mining town about 20 miles southwest of Birmingham. The situation presented a potential problem. Julius was now married to a sophisticated city girl who had lived on a boulevard in Yekaterinoslav in Russia. But he was taking her to a town where she would have to use an outhouse.

Luckily, Julius's sister and brother-in-law, Rosa and Joe Sachs, already lived in Johns. Joe Sachs ran a large, successful business, selling everything from furniture to caskets. (His motto, naturally, was "From the cradle to the grave.") Rosie, as his wife was known, showed Anna how to be a distinguished Southern woman. Rosie had golden fingers, working her wizardry with everything from a needle and thread to cooking utensils. She imparted her wisdom onto Anna, who became a splendid cook and an immaculate housekeeper. Anna always said she couldn't have endured Johns without Rosie.

On the Israels' first Valentine's Day together as a married couple (February 14, 1913), Anna gave birth to a boy. According to his birth certificate, the baby's name was Mordecai Israel. Julius and Anna actually named him Melvin Israel, and he will forever be remembered as Mel Allen after changing his last name when he entered the radio business. There were no hospitals in Johns, so the Israels had to take their horse and buggy to Birmingham to have Mel. In adulthood, Allen would use the scenario as fodder for a good joke when he gave a speech.

"If my mother hadn't had the foresight of going to Birmingham," he would say, "I would have had to say I was born in Johns."

Mel was a hazel-eyed, brown-haired bundle of energy. He could walk at nine months, and Anna was careful not to turn her back on him after that. He broke his leg as a toddler when he tripped and fell trying to stand up in his stroller. Another time, Mel walked up to the family cow and stood underneath it, bouncing and smiling. His mother was terrified that her baby would get kicked or crushed. Anna Israel, a woman known for her dramatic mannerisms and expressions, got down on all fours, making funny faces and motioning her son toward her. Finally, Mel ran into her arms.

As Julius listened to his son form words at one year old, he yearned to introduce little Mel to one of his favorite pastimes. When he would ride into Birmingham for buying trips, Julius liked to catch the Birmingham Barons of the Southern League at Rickwood Field. He wished he could take Mel to a baseball game with him sometime, but Anna balked at the idea.

"He's still a baby," said his wife, a strong-willed woman who always spoke her mind. "He's too young to take to the ballpark."

When Mel was two and a half years old, Julius brought his son with him on a buying trip to Birmingham. Breaking a promise to his wife, Julius took Mel to a Barons game. On the way home, father turned to son and said, "Don't tell Mom." His son didn't, although Julius was cooked when Anna asked her boy what they did in Birmingham. "I had peanuts and soda pop!" he said.

Honesty was usually very important to Mel's parents. Julius told his children that if you lied to someone, you were underestimating him and you risked losing his respect. When Mel was very young, he was walking with his parents and swiped an apple from a nearby fruit stand. Julius and Anna noticed their son munching on the piece of fruit but didn't say anything to him until they were home. Julius then sternly asked Mel where he had gotten the apple. Mel was afraid of his father, who looked like a giant to him. At close to six feet tall, Julius had a strong chest, broad shoulders and weighed 190 pounds. Julius took off his belt and smacked the tip of it against his hands, which immediately prompted Mel to tell him he had picked the apple off the fruit stand.

Mel never stole again.

Julius possessed a booming voice that Mel would inherit. When his children acted up, Julius often stood up, stomped his foot, clenched his fists, put on a mean face and roared some Russian phrases. Julius was actually a mild-tempered man who knew only a few words of Russian. All his kids knew, though, was that they had better behave.

Julius was a respected family man in Johns. When the town's mines closed and a panic had set in, an unemployed black miner thought highly enough of Julius to offer him his 12-year-old son, Joe. The man explained that the boy's mother had died and that he had no way of feeding him. The miner pleaded with Julius, saying the boy could do chores to earn his keep. Julius and Anna gave Joe a place to sleep, fed him, sent him to school and raised him like one of their own children until he went off to fight in World War I.

Racism was never an issue with the Israels, even as they lived in the deep South. Julius and Anna told their children to treat all people as they wanted to be treated themselves. When the family lived in nearby Bessemer, Alabama, a few years later, Anna threw a wedding for a black woman who worked as her housekeeper. The racial climate outside was so heated that the Israels pulled down the shades for fear townspeople would turn against the family and Julius's business. But the Israels provided the woman with a gown and held a ceremony in their living room. Decades later, when the family lived in the New York City area, they had a black live-in housekeeper, Easter Bellamy, who was an honorary member of the family. (Easter sat with the family in the front of the temple at Mel's funeral in 1996.)

After Johns' mines closed, Julius moved his wife and child to Sylacauga, Alabama, located about 50 miles to the southeast. In Sylacauga, Anna bore Mel a sister, Esther, who was 19 months younger than their first child. Julius later moved the family to Bessemer, an industrial center 13 miles southwest of Birmingham. There he ran a women's clothing store called The Parisian, an ancestor of what is today a large Southern department store chain. Bessemer had vast mines, mills and plants producing everything from steel to red ore to bituminous coal to limestone to pipe works, but the town had a charming feel. Honeysuckles grew beside the Israel house, and on summer afternoons, the air was intoxicatingly sweet.

Mel and Esther played freely outside the Israel home, for automobiles weren't commonplace yet. Mel would ride his tricycle to Julius's store, which was only a few blocks away, with Esther tagging along beside him. One day brother and sister were on their way when Mel pulled ahead of Esther and coasted toward a blind alley. At the same instance, a truck appeared, slamming into Mel and the tricycle. The truck demolished the tricycle and pinned Mel underneath its wheel. A terrible racket brought screaming people rushing from storefronts. Hearing the commotion, Julius sprinted from one direction, Anna from the other. Julius got there first and, with the help of policemen, pried Mel out from under the truck. Julius ran with his limp son in his arms to the hospital, which was two blocks away, as Esther watched, sobbing uncontrollably. Mel broke the leg that was left unscathed in his stroller accident as a baby, but was otherwise OK. Anna sat by her son's side day and night as he recovered. She and Julius talked about suing the truck company, but they agreed that they didn't want blood money. They were just happy that Mel was alive.

Julius and Anna knew they had one gifted child. When he was four years old, Mel would flip through the pages of Sears and Roebuck catalogues while using the outhouse. When he came inside, he had his parents explain the words that went with the pictures. His progress improved rapidly. Before the age of five, he could take on newspaper articles. His father was so proud he would stand Mel on the counter of his store and have him read the sports page to customers. Julius soon began to challenge his son with more difficult reading material. By the time Mel was seven and less than a month enrolled in school, he gave his father goosebumps by reading an editorial in the *Birmingham Age-Herald* endorsing the presidential candidacy of James M. Cox, Ohio's Democratic governor. Julius had known Mel was bright, but he was also modest and quiet. When Mel came home from school, threw down his things and ran out to play, Julius sometimes saw different books than his son had the day before.

"Those are not your books," Julius said. "Whose books did you take?"

"Nobody's," Mel said, shrugging.

Mel had been skipped to a higher grade, something that happened frequently during his childhood. When he was an adult, Mel credited his precocity to learning to read at an early age. Throughout his life, he would devour anything he could get his hands on. As a boy, he particularly liked the tales of Frank Merriwell, a Yale-educated hero who outwitted his adversaries on the fields of sport and life as often as he overpowered them. That sounded familiar to his family. The spotlight naturally shone on Mel, who starred in school and just about everywhere else. When he acted in children's plays, Mel, like Frank Merriwell, always ended up in the hero's role.

CHAPTER 2

Obey Our Parents

Tragedy struck Mel's family in 1918, when Anna's brother, Isadore, died of influenza at age 23. Isadore, who was two years younger than Anna, was concertmaster of the Minneapolis Symphony Orchestra. A brilliant musician, he was also mild-tempered and a perfect gentleman. Julius put Anna, Mel and Esther on a train for Toledo, Ohio, where Anna's family lived at the time. Anna cried the whole way. Mel attended school in Toledo as Anna and children remained there for about six months before returning to Bessemer.

Times would improve temporarily for the family. World War I officially ended on November 11, 1918, when the Allies and Germans signed their armistice. Flags waved and bands blared as Mel and Esther marched proudly in a Bessemer parade. Mel was dressed as a doughboy, his sister as a Red Cross nurse as Julius and Anna watched proudly. They had found their niche in the ladies' ready-to-wear business. Anna, lovely and artistic, made hats and modeled dresses for customers at their store, The Parisian. When singer and actress Lillian Russell was touring the South, she even wore one of Anna's finely crafted hats for a Birmingham performance.

The owner of The Parisian Company, Laurens Bloch, was fond of the hardworking Israels. Bloch operated a store similar to Julius's in Birmingham and wanted to expand to Atlanta, hoping Julius could run the Birmingham store. But Bloch died before he and Julius could sign a contract, and his nephew took over in Birmingham. Still, Julius and Anna thought Bloch had been so good to them that they named their third child, Laurens Israel, after him. Larry, as he was known, arrived in 1920.

Bloch's death marked another bad break indicative of Julius Israel's up-and-down career, which was dogged by prejudice, poor economic times and even worse luck. In a similar twist of fate, a farmer who had not been able to make a payment to Julius offered him the deed to some property on Miami Beach as collateral. At the time, the offer wasn't enticing, as the area was undeveloped and crawling with mosquitoes. But sympathy got the better of Julius and he took the deed anyway, sliding it under his cash register. "Who would want to go down to malaria-infested Miami?" Israel said. He lost the deed.

Matters would get worse for the Israels in Bessemer as the city's economy collapsed amid postwar depression, crippling business at Julius's Parisian store and forcing him to sell. He managed to make a meager $20,000 for it. In 1922, the Israels moved north about 25 miles to the Walker County mining and mill town of Cordova, Alabama, where Julius opened another general store at the tip of Main Street. The store was a couple of doors down from the Dixie Theater, where Julius paid the owner a monthly fee to let Mel and Esther have unlimited access to movies. Julius would give his children a nickel to buy ice cream and Coca-Cola, and they would stay there all day.

As Mel got older, he found something else even more enticing than movies. He woke up every day for sports, especially baseball. Mel began following box scores at age five and, by the time he was eight, had memorized batting averages of Southern League players and prominent major leaguers. He loved to play outside with his friends, who were often older than him because he skipped ahead in school, in fields and sandlots until his mother called him for dinner. Dinner was at 12 o'clock and supper was promptly at six. Mel was usually late.

Anna Israel hoped Mel's sports passion was just a phase. She wanted her son to be a concert violinist like her brother, Max. Anna's hopes were dashed forever one night while Mel was out playing with friends after supper. He brought a peach outside and wanted to divide it among his friends. He took out a pocketknife and began to cut the piece of fruit. He also sliced into the first joint of his right forefinger, causing blood to spurt out. From that day on, he couldn't move the joint. Because he was right-handed, his violin-playing days were over. Mel's mother made a desperate move—she figured he could at least blow a horn, so she gave him cornet lessons. But Anna soon realized she would have to live with sports for the rest of her life, for better or for worse. "Sometimes I think Mel was born with a baseball in his mouth," she once said wryly.

Mel continued skipping grades in Cordova and entered high school at age 11, yet he still carried many qualities of an adolescent. He would lie awake scared as a distant freight train sounded its horn in the middle off the night. *Woooooooooooooo.*

Mel was also freaked by a chilling murder case that he overheard adults discussing. On May 21, 1924, Nathan Leopold and Richard Loeb, both well to do, well-educated college-aged boys from Chicago with gleaming academic records, murdered 14-year-old Bobby Franks. Leopold and Loeb picked out Franks, a handsome Jewish boy like themselves, at random while he was walking home from a schoolyard and clubbed him to death with a chisel. "They killed as they might kill a spider or a fly, for the experience," Leopold and Loeb's lawyer, Clarence Darrow, would say later.

The story profoundly affected Mel, Esther suspects. "Mel got the notion that he was a special person, that they were out to get him," she says today. Esther remembers one night in particular when Mel couldn't sleep. Mel and little Larry were in a double bed, while Esther had a single in the same room.

"Esther? Esther? Do you hearsomething?" Mel asked.

"I don't hear anything," she said.

"Shhhh … ! Listen," he said. "Don't you hear that?"

"No, I don't hear it."

"I think somebody's trying to get in here," Mel said. "I'm getting out of here."

Mel jumped out bed, dragging Esther and Larry with him into his parents' room.

"Run!" Mel screamed. "I think somebody's trying to kidnap me!"

❁ ❁ ❁ ❁ ❁ ❁ ❁

Mel wasn't the only exquisitely talented member of the family. His uncle in Detroit, Max Leibowitz, who shortened his name to Max Leib for the music business, was a gifted violinist. Max was probably the most talented of all his musical brothers. Max played his first solo on a real violin as a five-year-old. He went on to study with Maurice Warner of the Detroit Symphony. Warner was a pupil of Leopold Auer, the great violin virtuoso. Max's teachers told him that if he worked extremely hard, he could become a world-class violinist. They suggested he go to Europe for training for the concert stage. The pogroms fresh in her mind, Max's mother, Risa Pearl Leibowitz, blocked that endeavor.

"I was able to get my family to America," she said. "I will not send my baby son back to Europe for any reason. He'll make a living here."

Instead, Max was picked to play in the National High School Orchestra in Chicago, where he was named concertmaster.

Like his nephew Mel, Max would much rather play baseball that do just about anything else. Max, Anna Israel's baby brother, was only about two years older than Mel and more like a brother than an uncle. When they were boys, Max interrupted a family gathering by choking Mel and yelling, "Don't call me uncle! I'm not your uncle!" But the two would grow to share a special bond over baseball. During several summers of Mel's youth, Anna would prepare baskets of her delectable Southern fried chicken, pack Mel, Esther and later Larry with her into a Pullman car and they would head north to Detroit, where her parents moved from Toledo when Max was 12. Mel and Max played endless hours of softball in a paved alley across the street from the Leibowitz's house on Martindale Avenue. Both could knock the stuffing out of the ball. Occasionally, Max's mother would pop her head outside and yell, "Watch your hands, Max! That's your future!"

Max's parents saw his musical talent as a source of income during trying economic times. Risa Pearl Leibowitz used to chase him around the house with a broom to make him practice his violin. Max's parents took him on a Southern tour while the Israels were living in Cordova, and Mel and Max attended high school there together in Cordova. Here was a plump, northern Jewish boy who played the violin in the heart of Ku Klux Klan territory.

❈ ❈ ❈ ❈ ❈ ❈ ❈

Cordova was a picturesque town on the Warrior River surrounded by plush green hills. But it had a dark side: It was infested by the Klan. The Klan had always been all around the Israels. Alabama's Klan's membership was 115,000 strong in 1925. The secret society existed everywhere in the state that the family lived. In Jefferson County, which housed Birmingham, Bessemer and Johns, 30 or 40 Klansmen decked out in full regalia of white masks and sheets regularly interrupted Protestant church services by walking the center aisle to hand the pastor a donation. In Sylacauga, Klansmen donated large American flags to the town's public schools, where they staged elaborate ceremonies. In Tuscaloosa, where Mel attended the University of Alabama, three blacks were arrested in the rape and murder of a 21-year-old white woman in 1933. A mob with apparent Klan complicity shot, beat and burned the men alive, killing two of them.

The Klan was likely to force itself upon anyone who wasn't a white, moral, upstanding, temperate American-born Protestant. Public enemy No. 1 were blacks, but immigrants and Jews were not far down its hit list. In 1920, Jews made up less than one percent of Alabama's 2.35 million people. Though a part of a distinct minority group, the Israels were openly religious in Cordova. Rabbi Leibowitz and his wife had raised Anna as an orthodox Jew. Julius, who had grown up among Christian friends in West Blocton, could have done without being orthodox. He hadn't spent too much time in synagogues and, unlike Anna, he couldn't even read Hebrew. But Julius called himself a "patriotic Jew." He was proud of his religious heritage and tried any way he could to make Anna happy in her religion.

Anna was content when she could have a kosher home, and so Julius would get kosher meat in Birmingham, which was 30 miles southeast of Cordova. Julius would also pack the nine or so Jewish children who lived in Cordova into his car and drive to nearby Jasper or even to Birmingham for Sunday school. Still the Cordova years also marked one of the only periods of Mel's life when anti-Semitism directly affected his family. Max, his chubby Jewish cousin visiting on his Southern concert tour, was an easy target for insults in a schoolyard among the blue-collar children of mill workers in heart of Klan country. Mel had his own problems. Because he was frequently moved up in school, he was always one of the smallest kids in his class. A bigger boy mercilessly picked on Mel before and after school.

The bully hurled racial slurs at Mel like "kike" and "Jew baby" while pushing him around.

When Julius saw his son moping around the house, he asked him what was wrong. Mel told him.

"Mel, you're gonna have to face up to him," his father said.

"But you always told me not to fight," Mel replied.

"No, you misunderstand me, son," Julius continued. "I always told you never to start a fight, but if someone starts a fight with you and there is no way of stopping it with dignity, then you fight back."

Mel thought about his father's words. The next time the bully approached him, he decked him to gain his much-coveted schoolyard respect. Years later, when Mel was established as the voice of the New York Yankees, he found out that the old Cordova bully was working in Connecticut and called him. When his old nemesis answered, he said, "You want another lickin'!" The two laughed and Mel took him to lunch.

Mel's mother stood up to the Klansmen of Cordova in her own way. The Klan normally treated women as second-class citizens and was known to whip them for speaking out. Stubborn Anna Israel wasn't going to let anyone marginalize her. When a Klansman shopped in the Israel store, she said to him: "Mr. Nelson, I'll sell you these piece goods, but if I see you in that [Klan] parade, I'm going to quit coming into your grocery store." Another time, Anna was shopping for Passover in Nelson's store, where about a dozen Klansmen were having an open meeting around his potbelly stove, spitting tobacco juice in between sentences. "I'll fix them," she thought. She told Nelson she needed the best steaks he had, and quickly.

"Why Mrs. Israel? You expecting company?" Nelson asked.

"I sure am, I'm expecting some very important company," she said. "I want you to cut them special. I need to have them just perfect."

Anna Israel had the Klansmen mesmerized by her story.

"Well, who's coming?" Nelson asked

"Jesus Christ," she said calmly. "And he has nowhere he can stay in this town except in my house."

The men laughed. Most of the Klansmen in town found Anna Israel endearing. "One of these days, Mrs. Israel, we're gonna come after you," one would say to her.

"Oh yeah?' she fired back. "You try that. I have a big gun at home. And before you reach me, you're gonna have some dead Ku Kluxers to cover."

The Alabama Klan of the 1920s had as much to do with power as persecution. The organization was so deeply rooted in the state—the *New York World* called Alabama "Klan-ridden"—that if a person wanted to succeed in business or politics, he had better align himself. Two of the state's most noted liberals, governor Bibb Graves and Hugo Black, a U.S. senator who went on to become a Supreme Court justice, used their Klan membership to further their own careers.

Julius Israel even worked on Black's Democratic campaign in 1926. After he was elected, Black wrote a secret letter of Klan resignation.

The Israels didn't see the Klan's cross burnings and lynchings that are played out on television and in movies. Still, when the local kleagle (Klan attorney), a large, intimidating man, walked into the Israel store whittling on a stick with a knife and demanding to see young Mel, Anna was nervous.

"What do you want with Melvin?" Anna Israel asked. "What did he do?"

"He didn't do nothin'," the Klansman replied. "We just need him to settle a bet a friend and me have about what was Babe Ruth's earned-run average in 1916."

The Cordova Klansmen genuinely liked the Israels. Julius and Anna were light-skinned and neither one of them spoke with a foreign accent. In fact, Julius, a lifelong Southerner, had a heavy Southern drawl. But the Israels found out that a passive aggressive Klan could also be destructive. Solely because Julius and Anna were Jewish, Cordova's citizenry began boycotting their store, as well as those of other Jewish merchants in town. The Israels lost their business and moved to Greensboro, North Carolina.

❈ ❈ ❈ ❈ ❈ ❈ ❈

In Greensboro, Mel got close to the game he loved as a batboy for the local Patriots of the Piedmont League, one of baseball's top minor leagues. (Future Yankees Hall of Famers Phil Rizzuto, Yogi Berra and Johnny Mize would all play in it.) Mel learned how to curse from hanging around the Piedmont League players and befriended a Patriots pitcher named Jim Turner. Turner was an easygoing Southerner who noticed Mel's keen interest in baseball. He and Mel met again in New York in the 1940s when Turner was a Yankees pitcher and Mel the team's top broadcaster. Turner later became the Yankees' pitching coach.

Mel spent his Saturday afternoons in Greensboro at a corner cigar store posting baseball scores on a blackboard as men gathered around. The boy gave inning-by-inning updates as he got the information from telegraph reports. The cigar shop was down the street from Julius's store, Tipp's Ready-To-Wear, which specialized in women's clothing.

Mel excelled at Greensboro High School, unbeknownst to his mother. All Anna Israel saw was her boy rushing off to his baseball jobs or to the sandlot. The melodramatic mother had a vision of her son being sent home from school, all of his books in hand, rejected because he didn't study enough. One morning around 10 a.m., Anna looked out the front window and there was Mel, toting a pile of schoolbooks. "It was a beautiful sun shining day just like I prophesized," Anna recounted for *Sports Illustrated* in 1962. "I see the school principal coming up the walk. My God, he's been expelled, I thought. My God, let me fall down dead on this spot and I welcome it, I thought."

Mel's principal was actually bringing him home to tell to tell Anna that her son had the best grades in his class. Because of Mel's scholastic accomplishments, the Civitan Club selected him to serve as North Carolina's lieutenant governor for a day. Mel and a group of other honored schoolmates were driven on the country roads of North Carolina to Raleigh, then treated to a luncheon. In the afternoon, they toured the state prison, where a bug-eyed Mel got to sit in the Tar Heel electric chair.

Mel, who was a sophomore, was written up in a Greensboro High School newsletter after delivering one of his papers to the student body at an assembly. "We have a very promising student in our school, Malvin Israel," the newsletter read, "and we had the opportunity of hearing his own paper on 'About Our Souls.' Your future looks promising, Malvin!" The school newsletter also published an essay "Malvin" wrote entitled "Why We Should Love and Obey Our Parents":

> There is a great number of reasons why we should love and obey our parents, for instance, they suffer for us, have us educated and provide for us. But, there is one main reason—to form our character.
>
> Character leads to success and high ideals of life. Character is the result of a faithful performance of duty. To obtain a good character we must possess the knowledge of right and wrong. This knowledge must first be acquired from our parents. In order that a child may be trained to the habits of duty that they shall become virtues in his character, it is necessary to enforce obedience. In order that the lesson of obedience be learned, love for our parents should be present to make the conditions pleasanter.
>
> The lack of reverence for our parents is a disagreeable exhibition. It indicates ignorance and selfishness. It leads to evil doings. Our criminal records show that the most terrible crimes have been committed by boys under nineteen years of age and these boys end up with death in the electric chair or a life sentence in the penitentiary. The reason for these crimes is disrespect for our parents.
>
> A few good maxims to remember are:
>
> "Whom will he help that does not help his mother?"
>
> "There is not fear for any child who is frank with his father and mother."

Julius and Anna had taught their children to respect their elders, a trait Mel upheld his entire life. Even as an adult, he lived with his parents, taking care of them until their deaths. "Mel is the best Christian I know," Julius used to say. "He treats people like he wants to be treated."

Mel took Hebrew lessons in Greensboro from a man named Mr. Sinai. Every day, the two would go over characters, which become words, which eventually become the text of the Mel's bar mitzvah speech. The speech, delivered completely in Hebrew, caught the eye of a wealthy Jew in the Israels' Greensboro community who offered to pay Mel's way to study and become a rabbi.

Mel had a different calling, which he would realize more when the family headed to Detroit for his junior year of high school. The Israels were enduring financial hardship and moved in with Anna's parents until they could get back on their feet. Mel attended Central High School, where he was vice president, and found himself drawn to Navin Field, the famous home of the Tigers on the corner of Michigan and Trumbull. Mel had grown up a Tigers fan because he frequently visited his relatives in Detroit. He saw his first major league game at Navin Field when he was 12 years old. Shortly before he and Julius left for the game, Mel tore his finger on a rusty nail and had to get an injection of anti-tetanus serum. Father and son still made it to Navin Field, but when Mel witnessed his first home run, the cocktail of medicine and excitement caused him to faint.

Mel returned to Navin Field with his Uncle Max, who concocted a plan: the boys would become soda vendors and watch games for free. The case of Coke bottles he toted around was heavy for small, lanky Mel, but he didn't care. The boy's head snapped around when Tigers first baseman Johnny Neun turned an unassisted triple play. Mel would quickly sell his quota, then sit down and take in more action. He watched so much on the field that his supervisor got annoyed and promptly fired him after he had worked at just one game. But that didn't keep Mel away from Navin Field, where he would also experience the majesty of Babe Ruth. The Bambino was larger than life, an oversized, cartoonish man who riveted crowds with his behemoth blows. When Mel saw Ruth hit one of his moonshots to dead center to crown a Yankee win, he became a fan for life.

When he wasn't at Navin Field, Mel listened to Ty Tyson, the voice of the Tigers, on radio station WWJ. Tyson was a rookie during the 1927 season, which began when Mel and his family were temporarily living in Detroit. Tyson was accurate and knowledgeable, and his descriptive, easygoing style made Tigers games easy to follow. "I said, 'Now there is the ideal life,' Mel told *The Sporting News* in 1948. "'You talk and talk and folks listen and you get aid. In addition, you are in and out of baseball.'" Mel was unknowingly already embarking on a career.

❋ ❋ ❋ ❋ ❋ ❋ ❋

Julius moved the family to Birmingham after he was unsuccessful finding work in Detroit. Back in Alabama, he got a job as a traveling salesman of men's clothing. This second phase of his career would last about 10 years. He sold shirts, ties, caps and more and often made good commission. Mel attended Birmingham's Phillips High, his fourth high school in four years, for his senior year, and again got excellent grades.

In Phillips High's 1928 annual, *The Mirror*, Mel listed his senior ambition as: "To be high up in the world [aviator]." Mel was petrified of flying. When the Israels lived in Bessemer, Julius took him to an airfield and Mel saw a man killed when he was sucked into a plane's propeller. The statement "to be high up in the world" involved conquering fears. The scrawny, 14-year-old Mel needed courage as he tried his hand at baseball, basketball and football at Phillips High. He was no match for his older classmates, who towered over him. One of them, Ben Chapman, would be a New York Yankees outfielder just two years later.

Mel was most successful at the game of love. During his senior year of high school in Birmingham, he became smitten with the plumber's daughter, neighborhood beauty Sophie Silver. Sophie was two years younger than Mel and an eighth grade classmate of Esther's. Unlike Mel's sister, who was tall and thin, Sophie had already blossomed into womanhood. She had killer curls and even better curves, which she showed off with a little strut. Mel and Sophie were virtually inseparable that year. Young and carefree, they liked to play teen kissing games in the Silver living room.

Mel had another female admirer up north. Blanche Lesnick, who lived around the corner from Mel's grandparents in Detroit, would watch Mel and his Uncle Max play ball during the summertime. Blanche loved looking at Mel, who was tall, dark and dreamy.

"The minute I saw him, I liked him," Blanche Klar, married for nearly 60 years, says today. "He was so polite. He called his mother 'ma'am,' which I loved."

Growing up in the South, Mel never said "yes" or "no" without a "ma'am" or "sir" after it. Mel's Southern accent intrigued Blanche, who was about five and a half years younger than he was. "He was the first boy I ever liked," she says. "He was my summer boyfriend."

After spending several summers in Detroit with Blanche during his teenage years, Mel told her he wouldn't be seeing her anymore. He would be staying in Alabama to concentrate on his college studies. That was okay with her.

"I had other boyfriends during the year," she says. "I didn't wait for him." Blanche was much more troubled when Mel told her he was going to take speech classes at the University of Alabama. "What are you taking speech for!" she said, alarmed that he might lose that charming Southern accent.

Blanche and Sophie were the first of many beauties whom Mel would leave behind in his quest for professional success, which began west of Birmingham in Tuscaloosa.

CHAPTER 3

The Capstone

Mel was a mere 15 years old when he set foot on the campus of the University of Alabama in the fall of 1928. He looked every bit the part. He had a boyish face that sharply contrasted with the stubbly mugs of fraternity brothers when they posed for a picture in front of the Kappa Nu house. A cousin had given Mel the nickname "Mutt" because he was tall and lanky like the character in the popular comic strip *Mutt and Jeff*. Mel was so skinny that he didn't have enough flesh to hold his bones in place. His knees would come out of his joints and a doctor would have to pop them back in. This became such a problem that Mel had to wear bandages on his knees in order to secure the joints.

Mel reported to baseball tryouts at a spindly 130 pounds. He was a slow runner after breaking both legs as a child. (One of the legs hadn't set properly, making Mel bow-legged.) A boy among bigger, stronger and faster men, Mel was quickly cut. As if that wasn't bad enough, Wallace Wade, the famous Alabama football coach, was helping out with tryouts when Mel let ground ball after ground ball roll through his legs at second base.

"I wanted to be a big league ballplayer," he said later. "Well, I just wasn't good enough. I couldn't have made the big leagues in 500 years of trying."

His aspirations for a baseball-playing career squashed, Mel sought to satisfy his love for sports elsewhere. Mel played intramural baseball, basketball and football and joined the staff of *The Crimson-White*, the student newspaper, as a sportswriter. He initially approached this position casually. Covering men's and women's summer baseball and volleyball leagues in June of 1930 under the byline "Melvin Israel," he wrote the following lead: "The fair sex, not to be outdone, took part last week in the masculine games of baseball and volleyball. It is quite a treat to watch the girls prancing to and fro in a wild frenzy, greatly excited—also to watch a feminine 'legging' it around the sacks for a home run. Yes, sir! It's fun." Later in the article, Mel commented on why he thought the women only played a five-inning baseball game: "Being the weaker sex, they can't very well last the 'whole five innings.' "

Ah, Mel loved university life. He strode proudly down University Avenue, lined with its grand oak trees, wearing button-down collared shirt and slacks like the other college men. He listened to the Denny Chimes, a monument erected along University Avenue in honor of University President George Hutcheson Denny, play cheerful hymns as he walked in and out of the Alabama Union building at the corner of University and Colonial Place.

A couple of miles down University Avenue, at the corner of Broad Street and Greensboro Avenue in downtown Tuscaloosa, Mel had a Saturday job at Brown's Dollar Store selling shoes. The work was thankless. Mel started out fitting the smelly feet of farmers in the bargain basement, where a pair of shoes cost less than a dollar. He eventually graduated to the more upscale ground floor. On a good day, he took home $5.

Mel, like Esther and Larry after him, viewed working at Brown's with a strong sense of obligation to his hard-working parents. Julius had moved the family to Tuscaloosa because he couldn't pay to board Mel in a dormitory. About all he could afford was a roof over the family's head. Mel's work at Brown's helped pay his way through school. America was in the throws of the Great Depression, but in-state students could attend the University of Alabama for less than $100 a year. Tuscaloosa was peppered with boarding houses that took in cash-strapped students. Lurie's on Eighth Street charged $20 a semester for lodging and two meals a day. Several other spots had similarly reasonable rates.

As banks and businesses failed and bread lines grew after the infamous stock market crash of 1929, Julius continued selling men's clothing on the road. He was never away for long periods of time, but Julius worked hard, always ensuring his family was well fed and well clothed, even through his toughest financial straits. He managed to move his family into a comfortable, two-level house on Alaca Place, which was within walking distance of the University.

The Israel home was nestled in a pleasant, middle-to-upper class neighborhood. The paved street was lined with oak trees crawling with squirrels and large, black ants. The wealthy Rosses, who lived across the street, owned the only ice plant in town. On sweltering Alabama summer afternoons in these days before air conditioning, the Rosses would give the Israels extra chips of ice from their mule-pulled wagon. Mrs. Ross also scolded Larry, who was eight years old when the family moved to Tuscaloosa, for playing football with black boys who lived in the alleys behind the whites' houses. Another neighbor, Mrs. Perkins, gave Esther piano lessons. Esther worked Saturdays at Brown's Dollar Store starting at age 14, and the $2 she made each week went toward the lessons. Anna Israel was going to make a pianist out of one of her children if it killed her.

❄ ❄ ❄ ❄ ❄ ❄ ❄

In the early 1930s, Tuscaloosa was a cozy town of about 21,000 with a touch of culture. The local 'Bama theater ran the latest from Hollywood: Fred Astaire and Ginger Rogers in *Swing Time*; Clark Gable and Myrna Loy in *Men in White*; Shirley Temple in *Now and Forever*; Stan Laurel and Oliver Hardy in *Babes in Toyland*. As Mel drifted off to sleep at night, he would listen on the radio to the dance bands of Glenn Miller, Benny Goodman and Tommy Dorsey performing "for the late dancers" in New York. Such big-name bands would play at the University of Alabama on occasion.

Mel lived comfortably and happily during his early college years. His life was consumed by the Capstone. That was the nickname president George Hutcheson Denny gave to his University.

"The University of Alabama is the capstone of the public school system of the state," Denny wrote. "Its work is based on the work of affiliated schools which in turn rest upon the public elementary schools. Through this chain of schools, elementary and secondary, the University is within reach of every youth in Alabama."

Denny, who served as Alabama's president from 1912 to 1936 and briefly in 1941, adroitly steered the University through Depression years. The ravaging effects of the Civil War still damaged the South. The North had never bothered to properly rebuild a region it had pulverized. The state of Alabama and the rest of the mostly rural South lagged behind the North in everything from industry and innovations to educational systems. But Denny didn't let that reality reach his beloved Capstone, which he changed dramatically during his presidency. The campus he inherited contained nine major buildings, including classrooms and dormitories. Meanwhile, only 400 students were enrolled. When Denny retired, the university had 23 major buildings, 22 fraternity houses, 13 sorority houses and a football stadium (Denny Stadium, naturally) and nearly 5,000 students enrolled.

Denny was beloved by students, who affectionately referred to him by the nickname of "Mike" when he emerged from the president's mansion on University Avenue smoking his pipe.

"A great privilege is yours," Denny wrote in a welcome to students published in *The Crimson-White* on September 9, 1932. "The opportunity to secure a college education, with all that it affords of worthwhile associations and of study under the direction of well-trained and experienced men and women, is an opportunity denied to many and available to comparatively few. For this reason you should remember always that much is expected of you by those at home as well as by us, and you should strive with all of your strength to live up to these expectations."

Denny piled money and resources behind athletics, for he felt they were one of the best ways to enhance the reputation of the University and establish a strong sense of pride among students. Denny brought in Wallace Wade, a Tennessee-born football coach from Vanderbilt University. Wade quickly built Alabama into a national power to rival those of the North and West. Under his guidance, the Crimson Tide became the first team from the South to receive an invitation to the Rose Bowl. As a heavy underdog on New Year's Day 1926, Wade's team toppled Washington 20-19 on college football's grandest stage. With Civil War bitterness still widespread in the South, a band of Southern boys had finally beaten those damn Yankees.

As Alabama football became Southern football, an institution around which the entire region could rally, Mel became imbued with Crimson Tide pride. He began voraciously writing football articles so he could get closer to the team. By his senior year of 1931-32, Mel was sports editor of *The Crimson-White* and of the school's yearbook, *Corolla*. Mel didn't just cover football. He wrote about basketball in a listless era of one-handed jump shots and final scores of 36-29 and punned and clichéd while handling the "twin killings" of the baseball diamond. But during his time at the University of Alabama, the sport Mel most enjoyed writing about was "King Football," as he referred to it numerous columns.

By the fall of 1931, when Mel was a senior, *The Crimson-White's* football beat was his. That season, Alabama was coming off a 24-0 clobbering of Washington State in the 1931 Rose Bowl, crowning another perfect season for the Crimson Tide. Wade, who had taken Alabama to three Rose Bowls, winning two of them and tying one, had left Alabama to take the head coaching job at Duke University. The campus was practically in tears.

"Alabama will be welcome at the colorful Tournament of Roses classic any time the Crimson Tide can muster another great team," wrote the *Los Angeles Times'* Braven Dyer, later a Rose Bowl booth partner of Mel's. "But it won't seem like old times with Wallace Wade gone. Wade belonged to Alabama and 'Bama belonged to Wade."

Denny hired a virtual unknown as Wade's replacement. Thirty-two-year-old Frank Thomas had been a college assistant at Georgia and head coach at Chattanooga. Thomas grew up in the tough industrial town of East Chicago, Indiana, and played under the legendary Knute Rockne at Notre Dame. A third-string Irish quarterback, he was a teammate of the vaunted "Four Horsemen" (right halfback Don Miller, fullback Elmer Layden, left halfback Jim Crowley, quarterback Harry Stuhldreher) and roommate of George "The Gipper" Gipp. But for such pedigree, Thomas, a small man with a roly-poly face and potbelly, looked like a plumber. He also sometimes seemed rather aloof. Once as President Denny watched football practice, he said to Thomas, "Are we going to have another unbeaten team and go to the Rose Bowl?"

"No," Thomas replied. "We don't have a triple-threat back who can do everything well. We won't make it."

Denny glared at Thomas. "Mr. Thomas," he said, "you knew we were going to have a football team, didn't you?"

Thomas (or "Tommy" as he became affectionately known around campus) turned out to be a perfect fit in Tuscaloosa. He stressed fundamentals, defense, preparation and repetition of his complicated Notre Dame box offense, which, when run to perfection, rendered opponents helpless.

"Keep the players high," he once said about his coaching philosophy, "and make practice a pleasure but not a lark. Be a disciplinarian, but not a slave driver."

Thomas compiled a 115-24-7 record at Alabama and would later be inducted into the College Football Hall of Fame. He won two national championships, made three Rose Bowl appearances (winning twice), had three undefeated seasons and claimed four titles in the new Southeastern Conference. Most importantly, Thomas maintained the astronomical level of success and enthusiasm under which Alabama basked with Wade.

The Crimson Tide coaching job was a position of national prominence, and Wade had spared little time for college reporters. But when an 18-year-old *Crimson-White* sports editor sought Thomas out for the first time, the coach gave Mel Israel a 30-minute interview and more than enough information for his column. When the interview ended, Mel, astounded by Thomas's generosity, thanked the coach for his time.

"Now, do you have all you want?" Thomas asked him. "Are you sure you understand what you've got?"

Through the successes and failures of "the Thomasmen," which Mel called Thomas's Alabama teams in his columns, writer and coach developed a lifetime friendship. Thomas made Mel his protégé, schooling him on football philosophies and strategies. Tommy bought Mel a suit from Black's, a distinguished men's store in Tuscaloosa, and invited him over to his home. Before big games, Mel would sit with Thomas as the coach frantically paced the room and repeatedly looked at his pocket watch. "Coach, it ain't been but 30 seconds," Mel would joke. "The time hasn't changed that much." Mel would call Thomas "the greatest friend I ever had."

Thomas's first teams at Alabama featured Johnny "Hurri" Cain, a spectacular left-footed punter and runner; Millard "Dixie" Howell, a glamorous strong-armed passer; Don Hutson, a fleet-footed end who jumped, dove and somersaulted to get to any ball thrown from his shoelaces to several feet above his head; and Paul "Bear" Bryant, the tough-as-nails "other end" to Hutson who became legendary for his coaching. Mel had the privilege of teaching Bryant, a man who later was known for his gruff growls at players, in freshman speech class. During the spring semester of 1932, when Mel was in his senior year of undergraduate studies, he filled in as a speech and debating instructor when a professor fell ill. Just 19 years old at the time, Mel had a reputation around campus as an easygoing guy. Friends and athletes took his class thinking it would be a breeze, but Mel refused to be a pushover.

"Anybody in here can make an 'A' in this course if you work," he told his students on the first day of class, "but otherwise you're all gonna fail."

Printing neatly in his blue, hardcover grade book between the names Craig Boyce and Joseph Busch, Mel wrote a number of lower-cased A's next to the name "Bryant, Paul W." Bryant actually scored a 70 in the class, good for a "C." The little A's stood for absences. Years later, Mel wouldn't let Bryant forget it. "No wonder you mumble so much," Mel would say. "You made too many A's!"

******

In October 1933, the Crimson Tide made its first appearance in New York, taking on Fordham at the Polo Grounds. "Sleepy" Jim Crowley, Frank Thomas's former Notre Dame teammate, coached the vaunted Rams. Mel, who didn't often travel with Alabama's team, stayed in Tuscaloosa. The Polo Grounds, where Mel would cover Fordham games in 1937 for a New York radio station, was in a distant land to Mel in 1933. These Yankees were the enemy. "The Dixie boys are now looking for an Eastern scalp!" *The Crimson-White* proclaimed on its front page. Mel picked Alabama to win by six points. "We are confident that they will afford the Fordham Rams plenty of trouble throughout the afternoon, and if Crowley's men should win, they will know that they have worked hard for the victory," he wrote in his "Around the Conference" column. The Tide lost 2-0 before 60,000 in New York, but 'Bama pride remained high.

Alabama's greatest rival of the day was Tennessee. General Robert Neyland, a strict, West Point-educated proponent of the single-wing offense, built the Volunteers into a national power soon after Wade made Alabama dominant. Alabama and Tennessee locked in a ferocious battle every third Saturday of October. The game was the most anticipated in the South, almost always deciding the SEC championship. After Alabama lost to Tennessee 7-3 in 1932, Mel wrote in "Around the Conference": "Despite the loss of the game, Coaches Thomas, Crisp, Drew, et al, and the team are to be commended on the great game which they put up against the Vols and let it be said right here that rather than Tennessee taking the 'Bam' out of 'Bama, the Tide came nearer to taking the 'Nocks' out of Knoxville."

By the fall of 1934, anticipation of a season with boundless promise gripped the Capstone. Thomas had lost only four games in his first three years at Alabama and he returned an experienced 11, led by Howell and Hutson.

"Coach Frank Thomas will send a squad onto the field that many consider the best in the Southeastern Conference," Mel wrote in a front-page story in *The Crimson-White* ahead of Alabama's traditional season opener against Howard College of Birmingham. "All authorities are unanimous in their belief that the Crimson will finish close to the top of the conference chase." Mel called the Tide's ends of Hutson and Bryant the "best in the South."

Tennessee and Alabama both reached their showdown undefeated and collided at Birmingham's Legion Field before an overflow crowd. "It's here at last!" Mel proclaimed to begin "Around The Conference" the day before the big event. "ALABAMA vs. TENNESSEE!" That night, Alabama students flooded the steps of the Union Building for what *The Crimson-White* billed as "the greatest pep meeting ever planned for the University." Players and coaches spoke amid cheer-leaders' cries and beats from the band as Alabama's student body ushered its heroes off in style. Then everyone headed to Legion Field.

The next day, the Tide trampled Tennessee 13-6 and Rose Bowl dreams filled the minds of Alabama's faithful. In November 1934, the month in which the New York Yankees signed a San Francisco minor league baseball phenom named Joe DiMaggio, Mel was following the Tide's pounding of Kentucky (34-14), Clemson (40-0), Georgia Tech (40-0) and Vanderbilt (34-0). The wins capped a 9-0 regular-season record and sealed Alabama's second straight SEC championship. Led by All-Americans Howell, Hutson and tackle Bill Lee, Alabama galloped west to Pasadena. Mel scraped together enough money from his teaching job to go with them. The trip took several days, the train stopping at appointed spots across the country so that the team could work out. The prac-tices were crisp, the hits hard. Alabama was ready.

For the first time in four trips to Pasadena, the Crimson Tide was not a big underdog. But Stanford, which featured three All-Americans itself in fullback Bobby Grayson, tackle Bob Reynolds and end Monk Moscrip, initially made the Tide look like one. With powerful tackle Bones Hamilton clearing the way, Grayson ate up large swaths of yards as Stanford lurched to a 7-0 lead. Then, under the blue, sunny California sky, lightning struck. Behind the pass-catch duo of Howell and Huston, the Tide scored 22 points in the second quarter to put the game away. Howell and Hutson were responsible for 24 points. Howell completed nine of 12 passes and punted six times for an average of almost 45 yards. After the splendid performance, Grantland Rice, the renowned sports-writer whose prose had given birth to Notre Dame's "Four Horsemen," dubbed Howell "the human howitzer." Hutson caught all six passes thrown to him for 164 yards and he scored two touchdowns, including one on a breathtaking 67-yard run.

Mel watched the Thomasmen execute the Notre Dame box offense, which Thomas adopted from his former coach, Knute Rockne, to perfection. Alabama's attack was swift, decisive and designed to score a touchdown on every play. Four players (Riley Smith, the quarterback; Howell, the left halfback; Jimmy Angelich, the right halfback; and Joe Demyanovich, the fullback) lined up in a T formation, but before the snap, they could shift into any number of sets, including a box behind the line. The four players hurried into new spots, going different distances while making the same number of steps. They chanted "Let's go now!" in unison to ensure they shifted with perfect cadence. Then, before Stanford could blink, the ball was snapped.

From the box, players sprung into a seemingly endless number of offensive maneuvers. Smith turned into a blocker, throwing a vicious flying hip into any opponent who got in the way, while Howell, the left halfback, became the star of the offense. Howell might try to hit Hutson on a deep route. Or he might fake to Demyanovich and run the ball himself. Or he might deliver a quick kick—a strategic move in this era of power punters—to pin the other team far back in its own territory. (Howell once booted a ball 89 yards against Tennessee.) Or he might give the ball to Hutson, who was fast enough to cover the outfield on Alabama's baseball team, or to Bryant on the end around. Or Howell might hand off to Angelich, who could run off the left side on the corkscrew play. Or Demyanovich might just catch a short snap and plow ahead.

With Alabama's players constantly moving behind the line, anyone could be practically anywhere before "Hut one!" "Hut two!" or "Hut three!" In the long-held Notre Dame tradition, no Crimson Tide player was bigger than the team. Only maximum effort on everyone's part made the box offense deadly. When Howell developed stomach pains against Stanford, Thomas sent in Joe Riley, who promptly hit Hutson for a 59-yard score just before halftime. Alabama's speed and efficiency mesmerized Stanford, and the Crimson Tide ran away with the game 29-13 to claim the national title before 84,474 fans in Pasadena.

"Howell to Hutson" became a national catchphrase as Alabama's golden boys posed for the cameras. After its taste of Hollywood, the Alabama juggernaut headed home to adoring fans in Tuscaloosa. Hank Crisp, the lines coach who also happened to coach Alabama's basketball team, reported back to his hoops squad. Crisp's team was the defending SEC champion and had a home-court winning streak that spanned six years. Yet he had paid his hoopsters little attention up to this point in the season in order to tend to King Football.

Skyrocket

Mel was still slender by his upperclassmen years at the University of Alabama, but he had grown to over six feet tall. He carried himself with confidence as he walked across the University's Quadrangle, the grassy area in the heart of campus surrounded by redbrick, white-pillared buildings. Mel's girlfriend, Miriam Rosenbloum, was often with him. Miriam, who was known as "Mimi," was a Jewish girl from Chattanooga, Tennessee. She was a campus beauty often pictured in the *Corolla's* annual photo spreads of student life. Mimi took Mel to her sorority functions, where other women fawned all over her boyfriend with brown hair that set off his hazel eyes.

Writing in a neat cursive handwriting in his blue examination books about unrest in Manchuria, Mahatma Gandhi seeking Indian independence and Adolph Hitler leading the Fascist movement in Germany, Mel breezed through his undergraduate classes.

"I wish to congratulate you upon the fine record that he has made, and to tell you how much we appreciate having a student of his ability and determination at our University," Alabama dean of men Dabney Lancaster wrote in a letter to Julius Israel concerning Mel in the spring of 1932. Mel had just finished his undergraduate studies at age 19, and he would enroll in Alabama's law school in the fall. Such precocity earned him the nickname "Skyrocket" among schoolmates.

During law school, Mel taught public speaking and debating courses to undergraduates, wrote sports articles for out-of-town Alabama newspapers and became well known on campus for his work with *The Crimson-White*. He was on the staff of the school paper for nearly his entire tenure at the University Alabama, which spanned over eight years as he worked his way through school. Mel wrote on talented *Crimson-White* staffs that included Hazel Brannon Smith, who later won a Pulitzer Prize for her sharp diction against racial outrages in rural Mississippi, and Carroll Kilpatrick, a *Washington Post* White House correspondent who covered Presidents Kennedy through Ford. Kilpatrick handled the Watergate scandal and President Nixon's resignation. Mel traveled around the Southeast as a member of the University's debate team and served as president of the Blackfriars, the University theatrical group. He portrayed numerous parts in Blackfriar plays. One role etched in his brother Larry's memory is that of a priest. It's a role that saintly Mel not only played, but embodied, even though he was Jewish.

James Permutt, a law school cohort and Kappu Nu fraternity brother of Mel's who went on to become a respected lawyer in Birmingham, remembers Mel as "very nice, courteous, even dignified." Bob Addie, a college classmate who later became a *Washington Times-Herald* and *Washington Post* sportswriter, once wrote that the college-aged Mel was "a gentle guy with a ready smile and an eagerness to help people." Mel, who showed enormous respect for his elders, had an angelic quality about him and seemed older and wiser than his years. Writing his "Around the Conference" column for *The Crimson-White*, Mel took his role as the University's sports bard extremely seriously, sometimes to the point of speaking in sermon-like tones. In a January 19, 1934, column, he scolded his Alabama brethren for "unsportsmanlike" outbursts:

> The University of Alabama has always had a fine reputation for Sportsmanship in the past, but it seems that a certain few individuals are attempting to destroy it by their conduct at recent basketball games. It's perfectly alright to ride a player in a good-natured sort of way, but it is an entirely different thing to 'tear the house down' when said player is in the act of shooting a foul shot. Such was the case in the L.S.U. series when Sparky Wade, diminutive Tiger guard, came in for considerable attention from the balconies, even during his free throws. The referee was forced to call time in order to silence the crowd. Conduct of that nature is absolutely unbecoming to an Alabama man, or any other individual, regardless of his affiliation. The least we can do, fellows, is to keep our mugs closed during foul shots. Of course we don't mean for you to remain Sphinxes throughout the contest. The spirit in the games has been excellent. But there is a wide gap between spirit and unsportsmanlike behavior. Let's show 'em we are fair winners and graceful losers; that we can take it as well as dish it out.

Mel's "Around the Conference" column, which presented Mel's smiling mug shot, became widely read on campus. Mel often wrote with a sarcastic, self-deprecating wit. "It's a great pleasure and a grand feeling to be able to return to dishing out copy without the thought of those dreaded final exams hovering menacingly around, disturbing one's equilibrium," he wrote on January 2, 1933. "Yowssuh! We is got one of them, too."

In "Around the Conference," Mel covered University sports, prognosticated regional and national football games—in that case referring to himself as "John Dopebucket"—and played campus bulletin board. "The Skeeters, independent basketball team composed of school boys, have worked up a rather good quintet, and would like, very much to schedule games with any one who cares to play them," he wrote on December 2, 1932. "Those interested should address their communications to the conductor of this column, general delivery."

Mel took every opportunity to defend the Capstone in his column, such as when Bucky Harris, who would later become Mel's good friend as manager of the Yankees in 1947 and 1948, brought his Boston Red Sox into Tuscaloosa in April 1934 for a barnstorming game against Alabama's baseball team:

> A clipping from a Boston newspaper of the Tide-Red Sox game reached this column the other day which stated that Bucky Harris' hirelings had very little competition from the collegians. The writer even went so far as to say that Boston failed to get a good workout. Permit the conductor of this column to answer that (although perhaps a bit biased) for seven innings the Crimson Tide had the Harrismen up the well-known creek with a one run lead over the big leaguers. Two important conference games following the Boston clash prompted Coach (J.B.) Whitworth to jerk his two star portsiders in favor of two less experienced chunkers in order that the former men might be in shape for those contests. Otherwise, Alabama might have maintained its lead for the remainder of the game, and emerged on the long end of a 3-2 score. The inability of the finishing pitchers to locate the plate resulted in the Red Sox scoring eight runs on one hit. At any rate the big leaguers had all the competition they wanted for seven innings—and they were certainly not fooling around. As to their failure to get a workout, permit us to say that the game was scheduled for 2:30, and they failed to arrive until approximately 2:45. As a result they were unable to obtain any hitting practice. But they got all the workout they could take in the game. Yessir!

Years later, reading Melvin Israel's "Around the Conference" would have embarrassed Mel Allen. The older, more polished Mel thought his college newspaper work was poor and immature. "Oh, hell," he would say. "I wouldn't want to see one of those columns now."

❋ ❋ ❋ ❋ ❋ ❋ ❋

The Depression hit Julius Israel's traveling sales work hard. By 1933, it even splintered his family. Anna and Larry went to live with her sister, Betty, and family in Toledo. Esther, who graduated from Tuscaloosa High School in 1932, went to work in Detroit, where she stayed with Anna's brother, Harry, and family.

Uncle Max, who lived and worked as a musician in Detroit, and two friends drove down in his swanky Auburn Roadster to take Esther north. Mel tagged along, too. Three of the kids sat in the Auburn's front, two in its rumble seat. As Mel and Esther rode with their hair blowing in the wind, they found much-needed refuge from the Depression's grim realities. When the Auburn reached a point where the Mississippi River touches Illinois, Max suggested they visit a girlfriend in Kansas City. The Auburn veered west. It eventually made its way back north and east, driving past the World's Fair in Chicago. No one could afford admission, but Max circled the grounds so his friends and cousins could get a taste of the extravaganza.

By 1934, Julius was financially able to reunite his family in Tuscaloosa. The Israels lived in a house on 13th Avenue. Bear Bryant and his wife, Mary Harmon, moved into an apartment across the street a couple of years later when Bryant worked as an assistant football coach under Frank Thomas. Julius occasionally babysat for the Bryants' baby, Mae Martin, as did Larry, who attended Tuscaloosa High School.

The Israel home would become a boarding house for Julius's relatives scattered throughout the state who wanted to go to the University. It was he and Anna's turn to reach out to family members in need. During the fall of 1936, the Israels rented two rooms to University of Alabama students while cousin Frank Sachs (the son of Julius's sister, Rosie) shared the house's sleeping porch with Mel and Larry, Esther slept in a cot in the breakfast room and another cousin, Elmo Israel (the son of Julius's brother, Sam), stayed in the attic. (Elmo Israel would become "Elmo Ellis" when he entered the radio business. He would rise to a vice president at Cox Communications.)

Esther attended the University of Alabama with Mel and soon realized that she would have to exist in her brother's shadow, which stretched over six feet but seemed even longer. Esther joined the Blackfriars, acting in a couple of plays and directing another. She appeared in line for the final available spot on its spirit committee, which rewarded special contributors to the dramatic group. The votes were nearly cast when Mel poked his head in the door.

"Hello there everybody," he said in a bit of eerie foreshadowing.

As an undergraduate, Mel had served as president of the Blackfriars and on the same spirit committee, but he was busy with other activities by the time he reached law school. On this day, Mel had just popped in to say "Hi." He had impeccable timing, a trait he would carry with him for most of his life. Mel, not Esther, got nominated for the final spot on the spirit committee. Even before the new spirit committee members were announced, Esther knew she was doomed. Her schoolmates were already hugging and kissing her in condolence. This would be the only time in Esther's life that Mel would stand in her way.

"I've often been asked, 'Weren't you jealous of your brother?'" she says. "I was not jealous of my brother Mel. I was proud of him."

Mel mostly stayed out of his sister's hair at the University. As a law student, Mel strove for a different kind of "A" than he had achieved in the classroom: A varsity letter. Mel joined the baseball team as a manager, carrying water buckets, raking leaves, cutting the grass and picking up wet jock straps and sweatshirts. But by doing so, he could proudly wear a big "A" on his button-down sweater. The letter would remain one of his most prized possessions, even years later after he had won dozens of awards as a nationally known sportscaster.

As a baseball manager, Mel would get to umpire intersquad games and sometimes work out with the team. The position also gave him the opportunity to serve as public-address announcer during baseball, basketball and football contests. Mel read off lineups, substitutions, tacklers and pitching changes to spectators. Frank Thomas, Mel's football coach and friend, didn't realize Mel's public-address chore was any different than broadcasting. When officials at Birmingham station WAPI, which carried Alabama and Auburn football home games, needed a new broadcaster in the fall of 1935, they sought out Thomas for recommendations. The guy who had broadcast the games the previous fall had left for another job right before the season was set to begin. Sportscasters weren't plentiful in the 1930s, and WAPI officials were frantic. Thomas immediately thought of Mel Israel, the sportswriter and "announcer" at University sporting events.

Mel's only broadcasting experience entailed listening to Ty Tyson call the Detroit Tigers and to sports broadcasting pioneers Graham McNamee and Ted Husing. Mel learned his audition would entail re-creating two minutes of a football game of his choice. He already knew Alabama's team "like a little brother," as he described years later, but he figured he had better do some other preparations. He thought about Husing, who had player stories and stats at his fingertips and was a stickler for accuracy. Mel researched the Crimson Tide's 7-7 Rose Bowl tie with Stanford in 1927, during which Alabama evened the score in the game's final minute. As he auditioned, he tried to think of himself as acting in a university play, sounding animated as he relayed the action in the present tense.

"Alabama's Clarke Pearce blocks a punt by Stanford's Frankie Wilton. The Crimson Tide recovers on the Stanford 14 yard line. Jimmy Johnson blasts into the end zone on a run. On the extra point attempt, Alabama breaks from the huddle, but halfback and captain Emile "Red" Barnes hesitates at the line, standing up to repeat signals. Stanford players relax, taking their eyes off Barnes and the ball. Alabama center Gordon "Sherlock" Holmes quickly snaps to Hoyt Winslett, who sets the ball on a perfect plane for Herschel "Rosy" Caldwell to split the uprights before Stanford can attempt a block."

Mel Israel wins an announcing job.

"I passed the audition," he recalled later. "'Course, from what I understand, I was the only one *to* audition."

Mel was offered $5 a game to broadcast over football flagship station WAPI and Birmingham's WBRC. When Mel walked into the booth at Denny Stadium on September 28, 1935, for Alabama's traditional opener with Howard College, he was alone with a roster, a microphone and an electrician. Mel just began talking, keeping a running account of the game on a notepad.

Later in his career, he worked with spotters who scoured the field with binoculars, identifying players who carried the ball and made catches and tackles. Mel had no such help for his first game. But he knew the Crimson Tide players by heart and loved talking about them. This wasn't so hard, he thought. Midway through the second quarter, Mel was overconfident.

"It's Alabama ball, second down, five yards to go on their 35-yard line," he told listeners.

Mel glanced at the scoreboard, which instead read third and five. While Alabama was still in the huddle, Mel hastily ran an imaginary running play into the line for no gain to even things up.

After the broadcast, Mel received some letters from listeners who caught the gaffe. He had learned his first broadcasting lesson. When you cover a game, you talk live for two to three hours straight. Mistakes aren't encouraged, but they're inevitable. After his first broadcasting experience, Mel told his audience when he made an error.

Mel's first game contained more valuable insight. Howard, which is now known as Samford University, traditionally played the part of Alabama's opening victim. The Tide had won 24-0 in 1934. But in 1935, Howard somehow managed a 7-7 tie with the defending national champions, who were mired in post Howell-to-Hutson hangover. No matter how much he loved his Crimson Tide, Mel somehow knew he had to be impartial on the air.

"Of course everybody was keenly disappointed, and the result of the game was difficult to believe," he wrote in his "Around the Conference" column following the game. "But it is true. Congratulations to Howard on their fine game. Football is an uncertain game. Anything might happen in a gridiron contest. It is this element of uncertainty that makes football the great sport it is today. Upsets make football thrilling."

❊ ❊ ❊ ❊ ❊ ❊

Alabama had a down year at 6-2-1 in 1935, but Mel didn't as his broadcasts drifted throughout Alabama.

"I enjoyed very much Melvin Israel's broadcast of the Alabama-Howard football game last Saturday and sincerely hope that he will broadcast other games, since he will evidently possess much talent along the line," Alabama comptroller Pete Jarman Jr. wrote in an October 4, 1935, letter to WAPI.

Mel's popularity grew as he called Alabama and Auburn home games live and re-created road games. Re-creations involved adding on-air excitement and color to telegraph play-by-play reports, which came to the studio from stadiums bare bones. Mel might only receive the words "Tennessee kicks off, Alabama receives the ball and returns it to its own 29-yard line." Through Mel's voice, the words would become, "We're all set to go. Tennessee kicks off. It's a nice, high kick going deep down to the five-yard line. Smith waiting for it, takes it on the five. He's racing back to the 10 ... the blockers form off the right. He's to the 15, to the 20, to the 25, he's hit at the 27 and downed on the 29-yard line."

Variety, a national publication based all the way in New York City, called one of Mel's re-creations between Auburn and Tulane "exceptional." The magazine further noted that "it was hard to detect that it wasn't the real McCoy. And, of course, there were no errors; the ticker doesn't get nervous."

In the spring of 1936, R.P. McDavid, who ran a Birmingham furniture business and sponsored Mel's football broadcasts, offered Mel a 500 percent raise (from $5 to $25 a game) for the following fall. Over the summer months, McDavid asked Mel to handle a WBRC news broadcast that the Birmingham businessman also sponsored. Mel became known as "Izzy" around the WBRC studios on Birmingham's First Avenue North, from which he broadcast his 15-minute *News of the World* program. Mel gathered and presented national and international news wire reports. Because WBRC was a CBS affiliate, Mel's broadcasts gained him network exposure. Referring to him as "Marvin Israel," *Variety* noted that "Israel's perfect diction is a source of strength" for *News of the World.* Mel's reports ran four times a day.

During his down time, he ran out to play semipro baseball. By this time, Mel had grown to his full height of 6-1$\frac{1}{2}$ and his frame had filled out. A right-handed hitter and solid all-around player, he held his own on the diamond among steel workers and coal miners.

After the summer of 1936, WBRC officials offered Mel a full-time job that combined his Alabama and Auburn football games with news and special feature broadcasts. They tempted Mel with $37.50 a week, the highest salary an announcer in Birmingham could make in these fledgling years of the radio business. But Mel had already accepted an offer from the University of Alabama. He had finished law school and become a member of the Alabama Bar Association, but had an opportunity to stay on at the University for another nine months to teach speech and coach the debate team.

The head of Alabama's speech department, T. Earle Johnson, had left Tuscaloosa that year to finish his doctorate at the University of Wisconsin. Johnson was probably the second most influential person in Mel's life at the University next to Frank Thomas. When Mel met him as a freshman, Johnson encouraged his debating skills. Johnson and Mel became friends and would play tennis together when they shared a spare moment.

When Johnson departed for Wisconsin, the University of Alabama offered Mel a teaching fellowship that would pay him $1,800 to temporarily take Johnson's spot in the speech department. Mel had never sniffed that amount of money before, which was hard to turn down in such difficult economic times. Mel also wasn't sure broadcasting was in his future, a sentiment he expressed in a portion of a letter to Johnson in the summer of 1936:

No, I am not asking you to release me from my work at school this year, although of course the station officials want me to do that. I told them that I had already accepted a job to teach at the University this year, but they were insistent on having me, so the only way out was for me to promise that I would write you and let you decide the entire matter.

Now, then, between you and me, I will [be] better off financially if I return to school, inasmuch as I am going to get $25.00 for every football game I call, and then, too, I shall be living at home, thus relieving me of about $15.00 a week living expenses in Birmingham.

If I had a chance of getting hooked up with a network then this job would be the means of finding that out. Incidentally, an NBC official from the Chicago studios was in Birmingham and took my name down after hearing one of my broadcasts.

I would like you to please write me a letter telling me that it will be impossible to release me from my job at school, so that I can show it to the station officials. They will understand, and it will serve to make my chances of getting a similar job with them for next year much better.

Though Mel didn't take the station's full-time offer, McDavid still allowed him to continue broadcasting Alabama and Auburn football games, which ran on WBRC in 1936. On September 25, 1936, Mel was pictured with a microphone at the top of page one of *The Crimson-White*. Underneath the photo, a headline read, "Broadcasts to feature Israel." Mel's reputation off campus had grown, too. Andrew W. Smith, radio editor of *The Birmingham News*, called Mel "the most accomplished football announcer developed in these parts in some time." Zipp Newman, *The Birmingham News'* sports editor who wielded a powerful pen in the South, went so far as to call Mel "one of the best football announcers in the country." Meanwhile, the *Southern Radio News*, published out of Birmingham, called Mel the sports find of the year.

While broadcasting an Alabama game in 1936, Mel got to meet one of his idols, Ted Husing, who was covering the contest nationally for CBS. In true Husing form, Mel had diligently prepared for the broadcast. He had made up some player charts and other material he thought Husing would want. Husing was thoroughly impressed. At halftime, the most recognized sportscaster in America put Mel on the national airwaves for a few minutes of color.

In addition to broadcasting games in the fall of 1936, Mel emceed football pep rallies on the steps of the Union Building and ghostwrote Frank Thomas's weekly column for the All-America Football Board, with Thomas's input. Mel and "Tommy" also did a weekly, half-hour coach's show on WAPI. Mel and Tommy talked football as they drove to and from Birmingham together. Their show began at 9 p.m. and the 58-mile trip home to Tuscaloosa on two-lane U.S. 11 could take an hour and a half.

Mel's father didn't rest until his son had made it home safely. Julius would pace the house, thinking about the crime and murder stories he had read in the newspaper until Mel walked through the door.

"Hi Dad, what are you doing up?" Mel would say.

"Oh, I'm just looking for something in the icebox," was the response.

"No, you were waiting up to make sure I got home all right."

"Naw, I was just up … going to get something to eat … "

"Oh, come on, Dad … you know you were waiting up to see me."

Julius would have much more of a chance to worry come Christmastime. Mel had worked solidly since his freshman year began in 1928 and felt he needed a vacation over semester break. There would be no Pasadena trip to ponder. Even after Alabama went 8-0-1 in 1936, college football's bowl committee snubbed the Crimson Tide. Mel suggested to some schoolmates from the Northeast that he give them a ride home and back to Tuscaloosa. In the meantime, he could take his vacation. The going rate on campus for a ride home to the Northeast was $20 a head, which five of Mel's friends agreed to pay him. Mel also arranged to stay with some of these friends when he reached the New York area.

Mel packed his pals and their belongings into Julius's car and headed north on a lark vacation. The six encountered snow about halfway to New York, but they pressed on for 36 hours straight before stopping in Newark, New Jersey, to drop off Irving Berlin Kahn at his home. Kahn was the nephew of the great composer, Irving Berlin. Kahn the younger had made a name for himself at the University of Alabama by twirling two sharp sabers as a member of the marching band. He would go on to become a cable television pioneer as president of BroadBand Communications Inc., developing an innovative electronic cue card used in the television and film industries known as the teleprompter.

Another stop for Mel and company along their drive was New Haven, Connecticut, where the family of fraternity brother Burt Levy lived. Mel visited the snow-covered Yale Bowl, walking out to the middle of the field in the empty stadium, which sat more than 70,000 fans. He had no idea, of course, that he would be back there someday to broadcast a game.

When Mel ventured into New York City, he was in awe. Walking along the bustling Midtown streets made him feel like he was at the center of the universe. Mel eventually found his way to CBS's Fifth Avenue studios. Mel didn't have enough money to do most anything in New York and hoped his connections with Birmingham's WBRC, a CBS affiliate, could get him free tickets to some radio shows. Mel especially wanted to sit in on *Gangbusters*, a cops-and-robbers precursor to *America's Most Wanted* that dramatized closed FBI cases. The show featured such amazing sound effects—machine-gun fire, explosions, gun battles and car crashes—that it spawned the phrase, "coming on like Gangbusters."

Mel had obtained a CBS station relations card from WBRC that got him into the New York studios and entitled him to a tour. Jack Stapp, a CBS evening network manager, showed him around. Stapp was originally from Nashville and knew that Mel had done football broadcasts in the South.

"Are you up here for the audition?" Stapp asked.

"What audition?" Mel said.

"We're having an announcer's audition this week. Would you like to take it?"

"No, I've got about four months of teaching and then I'm gonna practice law," Mel said.

Mel didn't think he had enough experience to be a CBS announcer. Besides, he had heard horror stories that CBS made candidates sit in a small, dark, windowless room, where they were asked to re-create a scene out of nothing and then improvise for an hour or so.

"I'm not ready for a New York job," Mel said.

"Mel," Stapp replied, "let me give you some advice. If you take this audition and fail, they won't hold it against you and you'll get the butterflies out of your stomach so that any time in future if you wanted to audition, you can come back and you will have that experience under your belt."

If Mel took the audition, he thought, he could also go home to Alabama and tell his fellow WBRC announcers whether those tales about network tryouts were true. He decided to go for it, and he found the audition much easier than he had been led to believe. CBS officials asked Mel to read a commercial and a symphony program to see if he could pronounce European composers' names correctly. No improvisation was necessary.

About 60 applicants auditioned for the same staff announcing job. CBS production manager John S. Carlile requested Mel leave his contact information in the New York area before he left. Mel didn't think anything of the request. A few days later, he was at Irving Berlin Kahn's house on Harding Terrace in Newark preparing to go out on New Year's Eve when a telegram arrived for him:

> Will you defer your return South until Monday night or Tuesday so that second audition can be arranged Monday morning. Think there is a good chance.
>
> J.S. Carlile

Mel returned to CBS's Midtown Manhattan offices. He was the only person the network had brought back in for a second audition. He went through some more tryout exercises, after which he was asked, "When can you go to work?" Mel was floored.

"It was like a bombshell," he said later.

Mel was due back in Alabama to grade midterm examination papers and teach the second semester, but the CBS people were persistent. They would hold their job open for a few weeks, enough time for Mel to wrap up his semester in Tuscaloosa. Mel said he would get back to them and drove home to Alabama with a $45-a-week offer in his back pocket. The more he thought about the opportunity, the more he wanted to try and get out of his spring obligation in Alabama. He could spend those four and a half months in New York. "I figured I'd get a little of the hayseed out of me," he said later.

His father didn't share that sentiment.

Julius was a self-made man who hardly underestimated the value of a bachelor's and advanced degree in 1937. He and Anna considered radio announcing acting, in their minds a fickle occupation next to the law. "It's just plain foolishness for you to go all the way through college and law school for eight years, and work as hard you've worked, just to throw it away talking on the radio," Julius said. Anna, this time less outspoken than her husband, had a bit softer take on the situation. "Let the boy have a few months in New York to have some fun and rest up before he starts with the lawyer's office," she said to Julius.

Mel's father relented, but had a prophetic prediction for his son: "If you go to New York, you'll never come back."

Mel would only return to Alabama as a visitor, although at the time, he didn't intend on staying in New York permanently. He expected to come home and practice law, as he had been trained to do. But Mel would soon realize that his true training came from dramatics, the debate team and covering sports, activities he once thought were mere diversions from studying.

"My avocation became my vocation," he liked to say. "I grew up under writers and coaches and accidentally prepared myself for a career."

PART II

GOTHAM
(1937–1945)

CHAPTER 5

Truth or Consequences

Mel turned in his midterm grades in Tuscaloosa, packed his clothes and headed north. He found accommodations at a New York City YMCA and eagerly reported to CBS as a staff announcer on Monday morning, January 18, 1937, only to be stunned by the network's first request. CBS asked Mel, albeit politely, if he would change his last name.

"Not that we have any objection to the name Israel," he was told, "but we just think it's a little too all-inclusive."

In a society stricken with prejudice, the radio industry, like the movie business, preferred anglicized names.

A few years back when Abraham Leibowitz had died, Mel took his grandfather's Hebrew name, "Avrom," for his own middle name as a tribute. Mel tried to honor his father in the same way by submitting Julius's middle name of "Allen" to CBS for consideration.

"I think your choice of Melvin Allen as a name is a very good one and it will be entirely satisfactory to us," production manager John S. Carlile told Mel in a letter.

"Mel Allen" rolled off the tongue as smoothly as the kid's Southern voice sounded. Mel enunciated the long "L" in his first name with his accent, which was subtle on the air. He said the "A" in Allen with the same hint of a Southern drawl and euphoniously strung the first and last names together as if they were one: "Melallen." It was a natural. Just not at first. Several days after changing his name for CBS, "Mel Allen" was paged in a hotel lobby. Mel continued to sit, thinking nothing of what he had just heard. He finally realized he was "Mel Allen."

Mel Allen's first days were spent opening CBS's morning programming at 6 a.m. and announcing organ pieces on the mighty Wurlitzer. Before coming to CBS, Mel had never even done a station break, so his New York work was a little shaky at first. At 6 a.m., CBS required Mel to strike a gong with a hammer, which hung on a nearby rope, and say, "Good morning, this is Melvin Allen with CBS News."

On one of Mel's first days at CBS, the hammer slipped out of his hand and repeatedly clanged against the gong as Mel frantically tried to quell the clatter. "There goes my brief network career," he thought.

Mel had nothing to worry about, though. Colleagues and listeners heard a voice that was forceful yet flavored with just the right amount of Alabama honey. They called him "The Colonel," a nickname that played off his uniquely Southern sound.

Within three months of starting at CBS, Mel auditioned for and won an announcing role on the popular *Pick and Pat* nighttime minstrel show. The 30-minute program featured comedians Pick Malone and Pat Padgett (who were also known as "Molasses 'n' January") doing a black-faced *Amos 'n' Andy* routine. Their standup comedy and skits, which poked fun at themselves and each other, were interspersed with orchestra music and singing. Mel made an extra $50 a week for announcing *Pick and Pat*, which U.S. Tobacco sponsored, bumping his weekly salary up to close to $100. That was more than enough for a young man to live on in 1937, even in New York. Back in Birmingham, he would have made one-tenth of that clerking in a law office.

Mel learned that working at CBS gave him opportunities that were once unimaginable to him. When 27-year-old William Paley assumed control of the network in 1928, radio was thought to be a fad. But Paley built CBS into a media empire that set the standard for the radio and later the television industry with a full spectrum of programs. CBS kept America smiling and dancing in the Depression era with the music of Benny Goodman and the Dorsey brothers. It told of the harsh realities of besieged London through Edward R. Murrow's World War II accounts. It shaped and reflected American society with cutting-edge broadcasts on racism, feminism, McCarthyism, Vietnam and Watergate. And it let the country exhale with *I Love Lucy* and *All in the Family*.

From the studio, Mel spoke to CBS reporters around the world like Murrow, the network's most memorable war correspondent. "This is London calling," Murrow would reply after Mel introduced him. Mel ran over to Carnegie Hall at 57th Street and 7th Avenue to announce New York Philharmonic performances. On May 6, 1937, he interrupted the *Kate Smith Hour* to read a bulletin that the Hindenburg passenger zeppelin had crashed and burned in Lakehurst, New Jersey. ("Dame Luck dumped one of the biggest assignments of the year right in my lap," he said at the time.) In December 1937, Mel interviewed John C. Evans, chief engineer of the new Lincoln Tunnel, as their car sped through the underground structure that connected New York City and Weehawken, N.J.

Mel's favorite part of his new job was traveling around greater New York announcing the big bands of Goodman, Tommy and Jimmy Dorsey (and their young singer Frank Sinatra), Glenn Miller, Perry Como, Count Basie, Duke Ellington, Sammy Kaye, Fred Waring, Harry James and other musicians.

Dressed formally with his hair slicked back, Mel introduced the same musicians that he had heard on the radio before bed in Tuscaloosa to late-night dancers and Americans around the country. Mel particularly "went off into outer space," when he was assigned to announce the sweet swing music of Miller, Goodman or Tommy Dorsey.

Mel took taxis to different Manhattan hotels, such as the Pennsylvania at Seventh Avenue and 33rd Street and the Commodore at Lexington Avenue and 42nd Street, where the bands played over CBS's airwaves from 11 p.m. from 1 a.m.

"How do you do, everyone?" Mel would begin in a soft voice that was as silky smooth as the music. "For the late dancers, CBS offers Benny Goodman and his orchestra, coming to you from the Manhattan Room in the Hotel Pennsylvania in New York City. Melvin Allen speaking; this is the Columbia Broadcasting System." Mel would then introduce each selection: "Presenting the Goodman trio: Teddy Wilson at the piano; Gene Krupa, drums; Benny Goodman, clarinet; and they're gonna send you their arrangement of *I Can't Help Loving That Man* ... "

Mel eased back into a chair as the music drifted through the room and into hotel lobbies.

"Sometimes I forgot what was going on because I fell in love with the sound I was listening to," he remembered later.

He once memorably lapsed while Kaye's band played at the Commodore. "Good evening, ladies and gentlemen," Mel said. "CBS takes great pleasure in presenting for your dancing pleasure the music of Sammy Kaye and his orchestra, coming to you from the Pool Room—I mean the Palm Room!—in New York City."

Feeling belittled, Kaye glared at the youthful announcer. That didn't matter to Mel. He was schmoozing with the biggest celebrities in music, and he frequently wrote home to Tuscaloosa to tell his family of his fortune.

"I just felt like I was up in the sky somewhere looking down at myself," he said some 50 years later. "I felt like I was a having an ice cream with double dip."

Mel was especially smitten when he announced the *Saturday Night Swing Club*. The country's hottest jazz performers congregated at CBS headquarters at 485 Madison Avenue, at the corner of Madison and 52nd Street in Midtown, for the weekly jam session. "The *Saturday Night Swing Club* is now in session!" Mel told his audience at the beginning of the show.

The *Swing Club* featured friendly competition among musicians who vied for their screeching audience's attention with freestyle solos.

"And so we herald the opening of the first anniversary session of the *Saturday Night Swing Club*, marking a full year of a series of programs devoted by the Columbia Network to that thing called swing," Mel said to begin the

Swing Club's first anniversary broadcast on June 12, 1937. "In celebration, we have an hour and a half international roundup of the world's greatest swing artists. And here's your old, old swing commentator, Paul Douglas—and what I'm talkin' about from way back, ever since the program got started … old Paul Douglas, set to open our gala session. Swing it, Mr. Douglas. … "

Over his first few years in New York, Mel quickly developed a knack for introducing *Swing Club* host Paul Douglas and other on-air associates. He also learned to become an expert huckster for his program's sponsors such as Crisco cooking oil, which supported *This Day Is Ours*, a daytime serial he announced: "Yes'm, as our baking tests show, new sure-mix Crisco will give you higher cakes, lighter cakes and tenderer cakes you ever made before with any other household shortening we know of, and Mmm-mmm! What good-eating cakes they'll be too."

✿ ✿ ✿ ✿ ✿ ✿ ✿

Ted Husing, the most glamorous sportscaster in America, usually gobbled up CBS's top sports assignments. But on July 3, 1937, when Husing was on assignment, CBS needed a savvy replacement. The week before, when CBS had exclusive rights to the Poughkeepsie Regatta, a collegiate rowing showcase on the Hudson River, Graham McNamee of NBC had pirated the event by describing it from an airplane. CBS wanted revenge against the other major radio network.

Right after the Poughkeepsie fiasco, John Fitzgerald, the top assistant to CBS network news director Paul White, called Mel into his office.

"This week we're going to try to blast them with two barrels," he told Mel.

NBC had exclusive rights to two of the upcoming weekend's big sporting events, and CBS intended to swipe them both. The network planned on sending Husing out to Des Moines, Iowa, to cop track & field's Drake Relays from a telephone pole. CBS also wanted to nab the Vanderbilt Cup, an automobile race at Roosevelt Raceway in Westbury, Long Island. Fitzgerald offered the Vanderbilt Cup job to Mel. It would be Mel's first network sports assignment.

"We're going to go up in an airplane," Fitzgerald told him.

Mel dreaded flying, He had gained a grave fear of it as a boy when he saw a man killed in a plane's propeller at a Bessemer, Alabama airfield. But Mel knew he had to accept CBS's request. "It was my big chance," he later recalled.

Mel stayed up until midnight the night before the Vanderbilt Cup researching the race, then tossed and turned in bed thinking about what would be his first flying experience. He arrived at the airport the next day and heard the five-year-old daughter of one of his engineers gleefully gabbing about how she was going to get to fly for the first time. If this little girl was brave enough to go up in a plane, Mel thought, so was he.

Mel stepped into the twin-engine Douglas liner that Eastern Airlines had donated for free publicity. He closed his eyes as the plane rolled onto the runway and opened them as it lifted into the sky. The ride was smoother than a car's. Feeling loose, Mel began to broadcast: "Good afternoon, ladies and gentlemen … this is Mel Allen speaking to you on behalf of the Columbia Network."

The plane circled over Roosevelt Raceway. Mel told his listeners that 33 cars had lined up 11 rows deep and sat three to a line. He pointed out how qualifying speeds determined the lineup. The cars below were not moving. Mel had clipped the race's lineup from *The New York Times*, and he used it to go over each driver, his position, his car and his qualifying time. Still no movement below. Because there was a good chance of rain that day, Mel talked about the dangers of hairpin turns in slick conditions. The cars remained still.

"I must really be up in the air," Mel thought.

Finally, CBS's John Fitzgerald, who was also aboard the plane, slipped Mel a note.

"Better sign off," it read. "Let's go down and see what's happening."

Mel glanced at the window and saw raindrops. He told listeners that it was starting to rain and that officials might postpone the race from Saturday until Monday, then signed off. When the CBS crew landed, they learned that the race had indeed been postponed, as had Mel's first sports assignment. But a CBS vice president had heard Mel, who filled 52 minutes of broadcast time with straight ad lib. The VP wanted to know more about this guy who had artfully occupied otherwise dead air.

Mel was always at his best during rain delays. His descriptions of cars, drivers and qualifying times lacked the detail of the colorful baseball yarns he spun years later when the tarpaulin covered the Yankee Stadium infield. But the 1937 Vanderbilt Cup made Mel's most memorable rainy days possible. Before the auto race, Mel still wasn't sure he wanted to stick with broadcasting. He was having a ball in New York, but he figured he was just scratching a Big Apple itch. He thought he would go back to Alabama. But Mel's blithe performance on an otherwise bleak day at the races earned him more and more sports assignments from CBS and elsewhere, sending his sports casting career soaring. With each new sports gig, Mel's thoughts about returning home grew more and more faint.

Sportscasting quickly became a passion for Mel, a method of curbing a ravenous urge to play and watch sporting events that he had felt as long as he could remember. Mel attacked his new sports endeavors. When CBS sent him to Hanover, New Hampshire, to cover the Dartmouth Winter Carnival in February 1938, Mel spent a week in the library reading up on skiing. When he arrived at his inn in New Hampshire, he cornered a former Olympic skiing champion and talked to him for almost four hours, learning technical terms he could use during his broadcast. Skiing didn't exist back home in Alabama, and Mel had to be prepared.

In the spring of 1939, CBS sent Mel along with Husing to the Kentucky Derby. Mel handled winner's circle interviews and hustled to find famous spectators.

"I wish I had time to tell you about the celebrities down here," Mel told his Derby audience. "Almost everybody who is anybody can be found here at Churchill Downs."

Mel came across Al Jolson, known as the "World's Greatest Entertainer" for his versatility as a singer and actor on the screen and stage.

"Hi'ya boy!" Jolson said.

"Well, of all people … Al Jolson!" Mel replied. "Al, I just heard you flew in from Hollywood."

"Flew in? Flew isn't the word for it. I came in on that new Douglas airliner, 268 miles an hour … left Los Angeles last night, arrived this morning … my stomach'll be in Tuesday."

"Man, that's traveling," Mel said.

A 30-year-old actor named Don Ameche joined the discussion.

"Hey Mel, why dontcha ask if he can pick the winner?" Jolson said.

"Oh, I got a winner," Ameche said.

"Who is it?" Jolson said.

"I'm not talking," Ameche said.

"What am I, an enemy?" Jolson asked. "Can't you let a friend in on it?"

"I promised I wouldn't even tell my own mother," Ameche replied.

Covering sports, Mel also got to know one of his favorite celebrities: idol-turned-co-worker Ted Husing. Mel observed how Husing used perfect diction and pronunciation, even during the vigorous pace of sporting events, and called games exactly as he saw them. "Back in the days when radio was full of fakers straining dramatic license to the breaking point because they knew the audience couldn't see what was happening, Ted was reporting on the facts accurately, expertly with a cool detachment that underscored, instead of detracting from, the color and drama and excitement of the medium," the great sportswriter Red Smith once said about Husing.

Following Husing's example, Mel learned and grew as a sportscaster in the late 1930s as his list of assignments swelled. He covered college basketball's prestigious National Invitation Tournament at the old Madison Square Garden, located at 50th Street and 8th Avenue in Manhattan, and tennis's National Singles Championship at the West Side Tennis Club in Forest Hills, Queens. Mel handled an in-studio basketball roundup show, called polo matches between Great Britain and the United States and got a taste of golf, track & field and boxing. Over his career, Mel would cover virtually every sport imaginable, except hockey, although he interviewed hockey players like the Boston Bruins' Eddie Shore on *Sports Review*, a 15-minute CBS sports show he hosted. *Sports Review* ran three evenings a week in the late 1930s and early 1940s. Mel's guests included Ty Cobb, Eleanor Gehrig (Lou's widow), heavyweight boxing champion Max Baer, New York Giants football coach Steve Owen, Fordham University publicity director and future *Look* magazine sports editor Tim Cohane, *New York Daily*

Mirror columnist Bob Considine and Bear Bryant, then still an assistant football coach at Alabama.

Mel knew all about Bryant and Southern football, but in New York, he sat at the center of the college football world. Fordham, Columbia and New York University had powerful programs that attracted the best teams in the country and enormous crowds to the Polo Grounds and Yankee Stadium. Because CBS only covered one college football game a week, which Husing handled, the network allowed Mel to broadcast area football games for local stations. Mel covered Fordham at the Polo Grounds, nestled on the Harlem River in upper Manhattan, in 1937 and 1938 and Columbia contests at Baker Field, located at 218th Street and Broadway, in 1939 and 1940. Mel also covered the National Football League's New York Giants at the Polo Grounds and Brooklyn Dodgers at Ebbets Field, Flatbush's home to football and baseball, in 1939.

On September 30, 1939, Mel and Bill Stern, one of Husing's top sportscasting rivals, called college football's first televised game, from Triborough Stadium on Randall's Island. Mel and Stern followed Fordham's 34-7 drubbing of Waynesburg (Pennsylvania) College for New York's W2XBS, which became WNBC-TV. The station used two cameras on portable dollies and its signal traveled about 50 miles. The broadcast entertained attendees at the nearby World's Fair at Flushing Meadows, Queens. Because no television networks and few TV sets existed in America, the game didn't even reach Waynesburg, located about 400 miles away.

After hearing Mel do college football play-by-play, noted *Daily News* radio critic Ben Gross called him "one of the most promising of the young announcers in New York" and commended Mel's pace on a 1939 Dartmouth-Princeton football broadcast.

"Mel, who hasn't been at this sort of thing as long as some of the others, showed signs of hopping into the front rank in another season or two," Gross wrote.

❉❉❉❉❉❉❉

Mel fed off New York's frenetic pace. There was an insatiable energy in the ambitious faces that passed him on the sidewalk. If he walked too slowly, he knew he would be trampled. So Mel moved at the speed of New Yorkers. When a co-worker was sick, Mel announced two radio shows back-to-back, broadcasting Fred Waring's music program from 7 to 7:15 p.m. and then Harry James's spot from 7:15 to 7:30 in a different Manhattan studio six blocks away. Mel arranged to do the last commercial for Waring's show two and a half minutes before the program ended, giving him just enough time to scurry to a cab he had waiting outside. A police friend led the cab through traffic and red lights. When Mel reached the second studio, he dashed through its rear entrance, which brought him right out on stage. His producer held out a script, which Mel snatched as he ran by.

Mel outhustled his competition when CBS sent him to cover Howard Hughes's return from an around-the-world flight on July 14, 1938. Twenty-five thousand people awaited Hughes's arrival at Floyd Bennett Field, New York City's first municipal airport, located in southern Brooklyn between Flatbush Avenue and Jamaica Bay. Police roped off an area of the runway to keep the crowd away from the pilot. As Mel saw Hughes's Lockheed 14N Super Electra making its final approach, he pushed to the rope and pleaded with a policeman to let him through. The officer repeatedly rejected Mel's request, then got distracted amid the chaos surrounding Hughes's completion of a three-day, 19-hour, 17-minute journey. Mel ducked under the rope and rushed from the pack to become the first reporter to interview the pilot.

By 1941, Mel had signed a CBS contract promoting him to coverage of sports and special events exclusively, and Mel was reportedly making a whopping $30,000 a year. CBS also permitted him to announce NBC programs if sponsors, the lifeblood of the radio networks, requested him to do so. Only Husing and ace newsman Bob Trout had such favorable CBS contracts.

As with Husing, Mel worked as an understudy to Trout, the nation's top special events reporter. Mel and Trout covered Franklin Delano Roosevelt's third inauguration together in January 1941. CBS perched Mel high in the U.S. Capitol's dome, where he commented on Roosevelt's motorcade as it made its way down Pennsylvania Avenue. Mel handed the air back to Trout when the procession reached the Capitol's steps and the swearing-in ceremonies began. It was frigid outside, and Mel had borrowed someone's hulking, cinnamon-colored fur coat to keep warm. As Mel felt the wind whip through the dome, he pulled the coat, which had a large, awkward, collar, over his head and huddled between two columns. Suddenly, someone yanked Mel by the shoulder. He turned around and saw about a dozen secret servicemen pointing revolvers at him.

"It seemed that I looked like a brown bear sitting up on top of the dome looking down," Mel recalled later. "They scared the devil out of me."

✻ ✻ ✻ ✻ ✻ ✻ ✻

As his voice spread across the CBS and NBC airwaves, Mel narrated a series of 15-minute daytime dramas that were the precursors of today's soap operas. Mel's shows included *This Day Is Ours*; *Vic and Sade*; *Her Honor, Nancy James*; *Our Gal Sunday*; and *Kitty Foyle*. *This Day Is Ours* told the heart-wrenching story of Eleanor MacDonald, a missionary who worked in war-stricken China. Misfortune didn't spare MacDonald, or anyone around her. Her child was kidnapped, one of her parents died, she lost her memory, she nursed her husband back to health after a bad accident and she helped a friend find a dangerous killer. Mel spoke in hushed tones to capture her daily struggles.

"Poor Myrtle Simpson, bewildered, disillusioned, unable to find happiness with the man she married," Mel said softly as organ music played in the background at the end of a 1939 episode. "Will her pathetic story influence Eleanor and Curt, even though they're now determined to marry?"

Vic and Sade was the polar opposite of *This Day Is Ours*. It was a whimsical, warmhearted and often-humorous look at the life and times Vic and Sade Gook, who lived in "a small house halfway up the next block" in Cooper, Illinois. The program captured the toils and triumphs of middle-class America.

"Well sir, it's a delightfully mild mid-afternoon for a day in mid-November as we stroll along pleasant Virginia Avenue now," Mel said to begin one episode. "And as we approach the small house halfway up on the next block, we discern young Russell. He's partaking of an after-school slice of buttered bread with sugar on it, and he lounges negligently on the top step a while. And at this moment a second friend of ours appears. Listen … "

The episode drifted into dialogue between Russell, the nephew of the show's title characters, and his Uncle Vic. Actors read these roles. Making up names as they went along, Russell and Vic tried to fool Sade by showing her photos of people they didn't know. Their intent was to give her "a shot of her own medicine" for boring them with pictures of people who meant nothing to them. Sade, a notorious gossip, ended up knowing the names of the people in the planted pictures anyway.

Mel took a 180-degree turn from daytime dramas to play a prominent role in a first of its kind stunt show, *Truth or Consequences*, which clanged its audience over the head with 30 minutes of humor and intrigue. Ralph Edwards, the creator and host of the show, adopted it from an old parlor game. In this radio forerunner to reality television, Edwards required contestants to perform outrageous acts for incorrectly answering trivia questions. About three minutes before airtime, Edwards gave suitcases to two men from the audience—usually sailors or other servicemen. He told the men that the first one of them to get dressed with his case's contents would win a prize. The cases were filled with bras, girdles, slips and other women's clothes, which the men stretched and pulled as they tried to put them on. The studio audience erupted into laughter. Mel began speaking at the height of the noise.

"Hello, there. We've been waiting for you," Mel said. "It's time to play Truth … "

An organ glissando sounded.

" … or Consequences!"

A razzing buzzer, affectionately known as Beulah, groaned.

Allen and Edwards, two babes with boundless futures in the radio business, became fast friends. On the air, they were a natural tandem. Their exchanges drew loud laughs from the audience.

"Say, are you the life of the party?" Mel said in cheery voice at the beginning of one show. "Can you roll peanuts across the floor with one ear and carry a tune with the other? Can you step out of character and dress at the same time? Then meet that prize-winning pixilater of front-parlor pastimes, that *Truth or Consequences* man, Ralph Edwards!"

Stagehands held up signs for the audience that read "Applause" and "Or else."

"Good evening, party players," Edwards said. "'Can you step out of character and dress and the same time' ... Where'd you get that one, Mel Allen?"

"It's just exactly like you wrote it, Ralph," Mel said.

"Yeah, yeah, well," Edwards stammered, " ... all contestants have been chosen right out of audience, only a moment before you folks out there joined up with us ... "

"And then, remember, you wanted me to say, real loud, 'Ralph Edwards, the darling of the dipsy dialers!' " Mel interjected, cutting off his friend.

"Look, Mel," Edwards replied, "do me a favor, will you? Bring the first contestant up to the microphone."

The contestants were more like victims. The questions Edwards fired at them ranged from difficult ("What's the most abundant metal found on earth?") to impossible ("How many men does it take to plant a tree?"). If the contestants answered the questions correctly, an infrequent occurrence, an organ glissando sounded and they won $15. If they failed, Beulah, the fastest buzzer in radio, loudly rang and Edwards said, "You did not tell the truth, so you must pay the consequences."

The consequences were the centerpiece of the show, and contestants dreaded them. The $5 the players received for enduring tasks bordering on torture was a bargain for CBS.

"These good sports haven't any more idea what's going to happen to them than the man in the moon," Edwards would say. He called a consequence "a funny little parlor stunt that shouldn't bring anyone harm, as long as his insurance is paid up."

In one episode, Edwards made a man who incorrectly answered a question eat an apple with his hands tied behind his back. Mel dangled the piece of fruit in front of him with a stick and Edwards made the guy recite the children's nursery rhyme about Little Bo Peep as he chewed.

"Now Mel, hold it just so it's even with his mouth," Edwards said as the audience's hysterics hit a fever pitch.

The man willingly took his medicine.

"Little Bo Peep has lost her sheep and doesn't know where to find them," he shouted with a mouthful of apple. "Leave 'em alone and they'll come home ... "

An organ glissando and applause interrupted him. Edwards had seen enough.

"The apple's all over the studio now," he said.

For a second consequence, Edwards made a stenographer from Birmingham get down on her knees and propose to a complete stranger.

"Will you marry me?" she said in a distinctly Southern drawl.

"I'll meet ya outside, honey," the man replied.

Edward saved the most brutal consequence for the episode's third contestant.

"Can you imagine anything more impossible than standing up here in front of a radio audience of some 15 million people and making love to a seal?" he said.

"Uh-huhhh … " the male contestant said sheepishly.

Edwards asked him to lie down on the floor.

"You're Mr. Seal calling to his mate," he said.

The man wailed off key as the audience roared again. The crowd noise nearly blew the roof off the studio when Edwards pushed the envelope even further.

"Well, what do you know, here comes a real live seal on the stage," he said as the animal was brought out.

Edwards asked the man to serenade "Sarah the seal." Laughing throughout, the contestant sang the lyrics to *Let Me Call You Sweetheart* as Sarah gleefully barked back to him. The man won the grand prize for the show, earning $20 in addition to his $5 for being victimized.

Working with Edwards, Mel learned perhaps his most important broadcasting lesson. His friend taught him how to stay loose on the air by envisioning that he was having a conversation with one person, a blank face just a few feet away, instead of a large audience. With this loosey-goosey approach, Edwards launched *Truth or Consequences* into a nationwide phenomenon. The radio program spawned a TV version that Bob Barker hosted and the name of a town in New Mexico.

Edwards and Mel were part of a talented CBS staff that also included Bert Parks, Paul Douglas and André Baruch. Parks would later become CBS's familiar emcee of "Miss America" pageant telecasts. Douglas moved on to acting while Baruch became a versatile disc jockey and accomplished radio and television announcer.

The CBS staff of the late 1930s was extremely close-knit. Announcers, engineers and producers bonded on a retreat at a New Jersey lake and played together on a softball team that Mel organized. Mel, Ralph and another announcer pooled their funds together to go in on a Midtown Manhattan apartment at 100 West 55th Street, just below Central Park and a couple of blocks from glittering new Radio City Music Hall.

Before the trio could move in, though, CBS fired the third roommate, leaving Mel and Ralph without enough money to pay the rent. Baruch saved them by stepping in. Baruch, who was born in Paris and spoke seven languages, was a great foil for the two front-parlor pranksters. Edwards and Baruch also loved to dupe innocent, angelic Mel. When Mel was getting ready for bed, his roommates would tell him someone was at the front door and ask him to answer it. When Mel, decked out in his red pajamas, opened the door and peeked outside, his roommates locked him out.

"He fell for it for weeks," Baruch said later.

❄❄❄❄❄❄❄

As Mel was rising to fame in New York, his father was sinking into ill health in Alabama. Wellness issues such as heart trouble and high blood pressure dogged Julius for much of his life. By 1939, the year Julius turned 50 years old, Mel was pleading with his parents to come to New York and make a home for him. Julius and Anna moved north to an apartment in Jackson Heights, Queens, where Esther and Larry eventually joined them. The Israels later moved to an apartment in the Riverdale section of the Bronx.

Mel felt responsible for his family and took over its caretaking duties once illness hindered his father's ability to work. Mel paid for the rest of Larry's schooling at the University of Alabama and, covered Esther's bill for an appendicitis operation. When Esther married Daniel Kaufman, a Brooklyn boy who became a Long Island urologist, in 1944, Mel also paid for their wedding.

Before Esther moved the New York, she would sometimes visit Mel and his roommates. Edwards and Baruch just loved Mel's sister. When Esther visited, they left flowers and notes for her saying, "Hurry up, we're waiting for you for dinner." Baruch got Esther tickets to the shows he announced, including the wildly popular *Kate Smith Hour*. Esther eventually worked for Edwards once she moved to New York. At that time, he was just getting *Truth or Consequences* off the ground. In fact, Esther typed up the script for the very first episode, which debuted on March 23, 1940. Esther also got to meet several hopeful actors whom Edwards employed in various gopher roles. "Give the boys 10 spots," Edwards would tell her after they worked hard on a Saturday night.

❄❄❄❄❄❄❄

Mel's New York success made him a hero back in Tuscaloosa. When Alabama was selected to play California in the 1938 Rose Bowl, students compiled a 5,000-name petition demanding that he call the contest for NBC. They sent the document to the Associated Press and United Press International.

"We, the undersigned, realizing the color and interest that Melvin (Israel) Allen, one of Alabama's native sons and a University graduate, can add to the Rose Bowl game, January 1, 1938, join the campaign launched by *The Crimson-White* to have NBC feature him on the broadcast of Alabama-California game," read the petition.

Mel didn't make it to Pasadena that year, but in some ways, his Alabama brethren had already won. Like Wallace Wade, Frank Thomas and later Bear Bryant, Mel was another hometown boy who conquered the Yankees. Alabama hadn't seen anything yet.

CHAPTER 6

Play Ball!

Mel had a special retreat during his first few years in New York City. It was a five-cent subway ride away from his Midtown apartment and office. On his days off from work, Mel journeyed far uptown, past Columbia University, across the Harlem River and into the Bronx, to the corner of East 161st Street and River Avenue. There sat Yankee Stadium. Babe Ruth had christened it in 1923 with an Opening Day home run and baseball legends had played there ever since. Mel couldn't keep away.

There were always plenty of places for him to sit in the cavernous 70,000-seat ballpark. With a towering, steep-sloped upper deck and grand façade, the place had the air of a castle or cathedral. Mel liked to settle in the back row behind first base, far enough from the other fans to be alone but still close enough to survey the field. He watched manager Joe McCarthy bark instructions from the dugout, Lou Gehrig swing for right field's short porch and Joe DiMaggio gallop after balls headed for the depths of center. Talking to himself, Mel described the crowd, called pitches and learned the rhythms of the game. If he wanted a moment's break, he admired the façade that hovered above the massive triple-decked stands.

"God," he thought to himself, "I'd give up just about anything to broadcast in a place like this."

That was virtually impossible when Mel came to New York. The owners of the Yankees, Brooklyn Dodgers and New York Giants—the city's three major league baseball teams—had signed a five-year deal to keep their games off the air through the 1938 season. Before that, major league games had only been on the air sporadically in New York. Yankees, Dodgers and Giants owners believed that daily radio coverage in a three-team market would kill their attendance. New York was the radio anomaly of baseball.

In Chicago, the Midwest metropolis where the White Sox and Cubs played, Hal Totten broadcast both teams' home games, and the two clubs welcomed the free publicity. But in the Big Apple, where Ruth, Gehrig and DiMaggio were creating dynasties, baseball was only on the air on Opening Day and during the World Series.

CBS covered the Series every year, however, and in October 1938, when the Yankees took on the Cubs, the network picked Mel to do color commentary for Bill Dyer, who broadcast Philadelphia Athletics and Phillies games, and France Laux, an announcer of the St. Louis Cardinals and Browns. Mel had gone to see the Dodgers play the Reds on June 15 of that year in the first night game ever held at Ebbets Field. (He got an added bonus when Cincinnati's Johnny Vander Meer tossed his second straight no-hitter.) But Mel hadn't covered any baseball in 1938. In fact, the 1938 World Series marked the first baseball broadcasting assignment of his career. At a mere 25 years old, Mel turned in impressive work and returned to do the Series from 1940 through 1942 before serving in World War II.

Four different networks handled the 1938 Series. A team for NBC included Paul Douglas, Mel's *Swing Club* buddy on Saturday nights, and Red Barber, a brash, young Cincinnati Reds announcer. On a cold, raw autumn afternoon in Chicago, Mel watched a dazzling Game 2 duel between two future Hall of Famers: New York's Lefty Gomez and the Cubs' Dizzy Dean. A sore arm had reduced Dean's once-blazing fastball to a series of changeups, but Dean shrewdly took a 3-2 lead into the eighth inning.

"He was a man holding off lions with a fly swatter," Mel wrote in his 1959 book, *It Takes Heart.*

In the eighth, light-hitting Yankees shortstop Frank Crosetti parked a Dean pitch in the left-field stands, putting the Yankees ahead 4-3 and hushing the crowd of 42,000 at Wrigley Field. The aging Dean was done, though DiMaggio officially knocked him from the game with a two-run homer in the ninth. The Yankees won 6-3 and went on to sweep the Cubs.

After the 1938 season, New York's baseball radio freeze began to thaw. Bill Slocum Sr., a former sportswriter for the *New York Journal-American*, was working on the three New York teams in an effort to uncork the city's baseball radio market. Slocum supervised radio sports activities for General Mills, a big player in the baseball sponsorship game. Slocum had a major ally in Brooklyn's Larry MacPhail, a maverick who had enraged league owners and baseball purists by installing lights at Cincinnati's Crosley Field when he ran the Reds and at Ebbets Field after he assumed control of the Dodgers. On December 6, 1938, MacPhail announced that he would broadcast Brooklyn's games during the upcoming season. MacPhail hired Barber away from Cincinnati to call them.

Though the anti-radio pact among New York clubs expired after the 1938 season, Ed Barrow, the Yankees' bottom-line team president, and Giants owner Horace Stoneham still were leery of putting their games on the radio. But MacPhail forced their hands. For the 1939 season, the Yankees and Giants partnered for joint broadcasts of home games, which ran on CBS's flagship station,

New York's WABC. To accommodate the arrangement, the teams ensured that while one of them was home, the other played on the road. Like Brooklyn, the Yankees and Giants would sometimes re-create their road games over the air from New York.

General Mills, Procter & Gamble and Mobiloil/Mobilgas sponsored a 1939 Yankees-Giants broadcast team of Arch McDonald, a Washington Senators announcer, and Garnett Marks, who had covered major league baseball in St. Louis. Mel had tried out for a Yankees-Giants spot, but was edged out. But CBS asked if he wanted to take McDonald's place as the Senators' play-by-play voice in Washington.

Mel's plans to go to Washington changed drastically when Walter Johnson walked into Senators owner Clark Griffith's office, giving Griffith an idea: The Hall of Fame pitcher and Washington icon could broadcast his games. For the first time, but not the last time, an ex-athlete had taken Mel's spot in the booth.

"It's kind of a thrill to think I was nudged out of something by Walter Johnson," Mel said later.

Mel thought about returning home to Alabama to practice law, but the kind of coincidence that had brought him to New York interfered again during a game about six weeks into the season.

"Ladies, before we go to the last of the third," Marks told his baseball listeners, "gather 'round your sets because I want to talk to you for a moment about *Ovary* Soap."

When Marks realized his gaffe, he laughed but tried to correct himself. He said "Ovary Soap" two more times as he giggled. McDonald was practically on the floor of the booth he was laughing so hard.

Procter & Gamble, which didn't find Marks's mock of its product nearly as hilarious, asked CBS to fire him. CBS sought out Mel, not knowing that his only baseball broadcasting experience entailed four games of the 1938 World Series.

"I told the only lie I ever told," Mel said later with a grin. "Professionally, I mean."

Mel was in. For the rest of the 1939 season, he watched DiMaggio, Charlie "King Kong" Keller, Red Ruffing, Lefty Gomez and the rest of the star-studded Yankees win their fourth pennant in a row. Across the Harlem River at the Polo Grounds, he followed stars Mel Ott and Carl Hubbell. And most importantly, he said "Ivory Soap" correctly.

Mel also pitched General Mills's new product, a breakfast cereal called Wheaties. When a Yankee or Giant hit a home run, Mel would say, "Boy, Babe Dahlgren must have had a heaping dish of Wheaties this morning," or "Jo-Jo Moore gets a case of Wheaties," or even "that ball was hit into Wheatieville." As the players rounded the bases, Mel said, "Wheaties do wonderful things for you. And you, too, ought to eat Wheaties."

✸✸✸✸✸✸✸

From the beginning of his baseball-broadcasting career, Mel had close contact with dugouts full of legendary baseball names. Before games, the Yankees and Giants would let him put on a uniform and work out with their players. Off the field, the great Joe McCarthy openly chatted with him. McCarthy was known among his players as a rigid disciplinarian, but Mel found him as accessible as any baseball man he encountered during his career.

"Remember one thing," McCarthy said to the young broadcaster. "We don't win a World Series on a Murderers Row. It's nice to have one on your side, but you win with defense. In a World Series, the really good pitcher will always have an edge over the hitter."

As Mel eagerly listened, McCarthy told him the secret to the Yankees' success: stellar pitching, defense and hitters who put pressure on the other team. The Yankees won when the opponent cracked.

Yankees president Ed Barrow, who could be a taskmaster like McCarthy, also took time to counsel young Mel Allen. When Mel learned he would have to miss covering the 1943 World Series on account of World War II service, Barrow wrote to him in a letter dated December 3 of that year, "I can understand your disappointment about not being able to broadcast the World Series and hope that war conditions will adjust themselves so that you can come back and do our broadcasting next year. Keep your chin up and be a good soldier no matter what happens."

Nearly five years later, after Mel covered the world middleweight title fight between Tony Zale and Rocky Graziano, Barrow sent him the following message via telegram: "Congratulations. You and Zale both became champions last night."

When Barrow died in 1953, Mel hailed "Mr. Barrow" on his NBC radio show, *Sports Daily*, as "the builder of the Yankee dynasty" (the Yankees won 14 pennants and 10 World Series under Barrow's watch) and "one of the greatest friends I ever had."

Mel's Yankees career began as another man's long, storied tenure with the team was ending. In 1938, Lou Gehrig had hit .295 with 114 RBIs, a down year by his standards, and then managed a meager four singles in the World Series. Fans assumed that he was just in a slump. But in 1939, everyone knew there was something seriously wrong with the Iron Horse.

During spring training in St. Petersburg, Florida, Gehrig dragged his feet as he walked and fell off his clubhouse stool while trying to tie his shoes. On Opening Day at Yankee Stadium, where he started his 2,124th consecutive game at first base, Gehrig went hitless as the Yankees beat the Boston Red Sox 2-0. During the game, Gehrig bounced into two double plays and made an error when he couldn't clasp his mitt tightly enough around a routine throw. After eight games, he had hit .144 and committed two errors. On May 2, Gehrig and Joe McCarthy decided the Iron Horse should sit out of a game for the first time in 14 years. Less than a month later, Gehrig was diagnosed with amyotrophic lateral sclerosis (ALS), a neurological disorder that now bears his name. The disease was a death sentence.

On July 4, 1939, an otherwise pleasant Independence Day of blue skies and comfortable temperatures, nearly 62,000 fans showed up at Yankee Stadium for Lou Gehrig Day. A box seat went for just $2.20, but the stadium wasn't full, fueling speculation that the public didn't know Gehrig was a dying man. After the Yankees lost Game 1, a doubleheader with the Senators, New York's players lined up on the third-base side of the field, Washington's on the first-base side. From a box alongside the Yankees dugout, members of the 1927 "Murderers' Row" team, the first Yankees club to sweep a World Series, walked onto the field. During a 40-minute ceremony, the Yankees retired Gehrig's No. 4, a first in baseball history, and showered him with gifts. Mayor Fiorello LaGuardia, Babe Ruth and other dignitaries spoke. Then Gehrig, once a strong, sturdy man who now walked on extremely wobbly legs, made his way to a bank of microphones at home plate. He had tears in his eyes and appeared too broken up to talk before composing himself. "Catch him if he goes down," McCarthy said to Babe Dahlgren, the man who replaced Gehrig at first base. Gehrig stood tall, forced a smile and began his famous speech:

"Fans, for the past two weeks you have been reading about a bad break I got. Yet today I consider myself the luckiest man on the face of the earth … "

As he went on, practically everyone present started crying, including Mel Allen. When Gehrig finished, Ruth, with whom he had feuded for nearly five years over a comment Gehrig's mother made about the Babe's wife, embraced his old teammate. The image of that embrace would find a prominent place in baseball history and on the wall of Mel's home. Mel was not an active participant on Lou Gehrig Day, but he observed everything: the tears, the smiles, and the majesty of a baseball tribute only the Yankees could duplicate. The day also marked the beginning of the Yankees' annual ritual of honoring its stars of the past on Old Timers' Day, an occasion that would soon conjure up thoughts of Mel Allen in fans' minds.

❋ ❋ ❋ ❋ ❋ ❋ ❋

Eight days after Gehrig's tear-jerking Yankee Stadium farewell, Mel and booth partner Arch McDonald journeyed to an out of the way village on a lake in central New York. There, they covered the coast-to-coast broadcast of the formal dedication of the Baseball Hall of Fame in Cooperstown. A virtual Mount Rushmore of baseball's early stars attended the festivities, including Babe Ruth, Ty Cobb, Eddie Collins, Tris Speaker, Cy Young, Grover Cleveland Alexander, Connie Mack, Nap Lajoie and George Sisler. Mel's heart pounded as he interviewed Ruth, Mel Ott, Hank Greenberg, Dizzy Dean, Charlie Gehringer, Lefty Grove and others.

Baseball had taken a one-day hiatus so that two stars from each team could travel by train to Cooperstown for an exhibition game. Honorary managers

Wagner and Collins, two of the first 26 men elected to the Hall between 1936 and 1939, threw a bat in the air and chose up sides hand over hand, as America's youth used to do in these days before Little League. The Philadelphia Athletics' Frankie Hayes doubled in Pittsburgh's Arky Vaughan with the winning run in the bottom of the sixth inning as "The Wagners" beat the "The Collins" 4-2 in the seven-inning affair, which began the annual tradition of the Hall of Fame Game. Mel would often journey to the same Doubleday Field to call the contest, which now pits two major league teams against one another in an exhibition.

After the 1939 season, McDonald decided to return to the Senators' booth in Washington. Walter Johnson hadn't proven to be a skillful broadcaster while McDonald, a good ol' boy born in Arkansas, wasn't the right fit for New York, either. McDonald's bucolic style was more tailored to fans in a smaller, Southern city like Washington than the city slickers of New York. McDonald was nick-named "The Old Pine Tree" because he often quoted the hillbilly ballad, "They Cut Down the Old Pine Tree." If his team pulled off a double play to stunt an opponent's rally, McDonald would drawl, "Well—they cut down the old pine tree." When a hitter smashed a ball, he "laid the wood to it." Base runners were "ducks on the pond." The most famous phrase McDonald brought into baseball lingo, though, was "the Yankee Clipper," his nickname for DiMaggio.

Mel, who had a brisk, lively on-air pace to match th speed of New York, seemed a natural to replace McDonald as the No. 1 broadcaster for Yankees and Giants games.

"Why should there be any doubt about who'll take Arch McDonald's place as broadcaster for the Yanks and Giants, when his fine young assistant of the last year, Mel Allen, is around and spitting on his hands—ready to see an irrevoca-ble affinity between Joe DiMaggio's batting swing and that fragrant, long-burn-ing, success-provoking cigarette," New York columnist Bob Considine wrote in *The Sporting News* on February 8, 1940.

CBS gave Mel the job for the 1940 season, and J.C. Flippen, who later became an actor, broadcast the Yankees' games with him. Joe Bolton, who had done Jersey City Giants minor league baseball games in 1938, assisted Mel with the major league Giants. R.J. Reynolds Tobacco Company sponsored the broad-casts, and Mel and his partners pitched Camel cigarettes on the air.

Mel watched both his new teams work out in Florida, then ambled north on a barnstorming tour with the Giants. During this railroad era, major league teams made circuitous voyages home from spring training, stopping to play in Southern spots in front of fans who didn't otherwise have the chance to see major league baseball. Barnstorming gate receipts helped teams pay for their travel expenses. Barnstorming was often unscripted and unpredictable. During one stop in Atlanta, Giants manager Bill Terry decided he wanted to take a day to drive to his home in Memphis. Before he left, Terry approached Mel.

"You're from Alabama," Terry said. "You want a ride?"

Terry drove the 150 miles of curvy, two-lane roads at about 75 to 80 miles per hour.

"It was the wildest ride of my life," Mel recalled later.

On another of Mel's barnstorming trips to Greenville, Texas, a game ended on close play at the plate. Before the cloud of dust at home had settled, catcher Bill Dickey, Mel and the rest of the Yankees were racing to catch their train.

"I don't know to this day if that runner was called safe or out," Mel said in 1981.

On April 16, 1940, Mel found himself in the booth high above home plate at the Polo Grounds, staring at the 50-foot wall in dead center that was 483 feet from home plate as he broadcast the Giants' opener with the Philadelphia Phillies. On April 19, Mel handled the Yankees' home opener—against the Senators—at Yankee Stadium. During the thousands of times he would walk into the park as a broadcaster, Mel thought of the words, "the House that Ruth built," which gave him goosebumps.

"Every time I stepped inside of it, I had to pinch myself," he once said.

Before one game that 1940 season, Mel was on the Yankees bench when a player appeared from the runway that led to the dugout. "Lou's here," he said. Mayor LaGuardia had given Gehrig a job in New York, and city employees would sometimes take him to Yankee Stadium in a limousine. Mel heard Gehrig slowly shuffle with his cane down the tunnel from the dressing rooms. A Yankee then helped the once-Iron Horse up the dugout stairs. As Gehrig inched around, Mel could see that ALS was squeezing the life out of him. Players greeted Gehrig as if nothing was wrong. They yelled "Hi Cap!" and "Hiyah Lou!" and patted him on the back as they ran out to take infield, but Mel could read the sorrow on their faces. McCarthy was so broken up that he made up an excuse and left the dugout, too, leaving Mel alone with Gehrig. The two sat next to one another on the bench. Gehrig broke the uncomfortable silence by tapping Mel on the thigh.

"Mel," he said, "I never got a chance to listen to your broadcasts before because I was playing every day. But I want you to know that they're the only thing that keeps me going."

"Thanks a lot, Lou … " Mel said.

It was the greatest compliment Mel ever received, yet he couldn't even look Gehrig in the face when he thanked him for it.

"Lou, excuse me. … I gotta go upstairs and get things ready," he said.

Mel hopped off the bench and ran down the dugout steps and up the tunnel. He put his head against a wall and cried. When the Iron Horse died the next year, Mel was moved to write a note of sympathy to Gehrig's mother, Christina, and forward her similar letters the Yankees had received from fans. Mel got a response on May 10, 1942:

> Dear Mr. Allen:
> Thank you sincerely for your kind sentiments, and for the telegrams forwarded which were sent to me in your care. You might be interested to know that I have received over nine hundred of such messages from young men all over this country and Canada. Such tribute

paid my boy has filled my heart with pride. The thought of so many youths in America receiving inspiration from Lou Gehrig has made me a very happy mother of this Mother's Day. Please convey my thanks to them.

Sincerely,
Mom Gehrig

✿ ✿ ✿ ✿ ✿ ✿ ✿

Mel was an established CBS broadcaster before he ever covered baseball, but getting the Yankees-Giants beat sent his career on an upward gust. His youthful face was plastered all over New York newspapers in stories and advertisements. An item about him landing the Yankees-Giants gig ran in the same entertainment column that led with Katharine Hepburn's plan to do the movie *Keeper of the Flame.* When Mel walked into Toots Shor's, the famous restaurant and watering hole at 51 West 51st Street, he was on a "hello" basis with the celebrities who frequented it. On a random day in 1941, as Mel lunched at Toots' with *Birmingham News* radio editor Turner Jordan, he was greeted by Everett Crosby, Bing's brother and agent, and Bill Corum, the well-known *New York Journal American* columnist. When Mel sat down and ordered something to eat, Shor, a husky six-foot-two, 250-pound ex-underwear salesman turned caterer to the stars, came over to his table and asked him if everything was all right. As Mel was about to begin broadcasting the 1942 baseball season, a telegram from Toots Shor arrived for him at the Polo Grounds: "Good luck, Mel. I know you will be the best. Just be yourself."

Not to be outdone, when Al Schacht, a former major league pitcher later famous for his on-field comedy routine (Schacht was known as "The Clown Prince of Baseball") opened a rival sports celebrity joint at 137 East 52nd Street in 1942, he sent Mel a telegram inviting him to a press preview. "Hope you can make it to help toss out the first highball," Schacht said.

In 1939, the New York Advertising Club chose Mel to its "Order of the Rake," an honorary society of America's 13 most successful young men 30 years old and younger. According to the club, these men "scratched their own opportunities rather than waiting for them to occur." This isn't the way Mel saw himself landing perhaps the most coveted announcing job in the major leagues at age 27.

"Thinking back, I still sometimes don't believe it," he said later. "A guy [Garnett Marks] made a mistake and is let go, Arch doesn't like his new city and goes back to the old, for some reason they pick me to succeed him. Everything worked out—everything *had* to work out—for me to get the chance I did."

Once Mel landed the "New York plum" of a job, as one publication called Mel's Yankees-Giants role, and many New Yorkers got a long glimpse of him, they liked what they saw. Mel smiled and waved to everyone from elevator operator to cab driver. He answered all of the fan letters he received. He devoted his time to charitable causes. He tried to attend every speaking engagement to which he was invited. People at these lunches and dinners saw a tall, handsome, engaging man with a personality as charming as the one they heard on the air.

"Our nomination for the post of All-American swell guy is Mel Allen, the young rising star among the nation's sports commentators," wrote a columnist from Port Chester, New York, when Mel attended a dinner in the suburban Westchester County town. The writer found Mel "modest" and "unassuming" as he spoke to a group that ate him up like the heaping dishes of spaghetti before them. "Mel took the section by storm as the principal speaker at the Thunderball dinner the other evening," the columnist continued. He wrote that Mel gave a "neat, concise resume of the major league baseball picture."

Mel's broadcasting work was gaining recognition, too. On May 25, 1940, after Mel covered the first night game played at the Polo Grounds, the *Daily News'* Ben Gross wrote, "Mel turned in a first-rate job." Meanwhile, *Radio Daily* called Mel "baseball's best announcer for our coin." Mel earned spots on the broadcasting teams for five straight major league All-Star Games between 1939 and 1943. He covered the game with France Laux for CBS from 1939 to 1941 and worked with Boston Red Sox and Braves announcer Jim Britt and "voice of Chicago sports" Bob Elson in 1942 and Barber and Corum in 1943 over the Mutual Broadcasting System.

Radio Daily called Mel and Laux "two of the best announcers in the business" when reviewing their coverage of the 1940 All-Star Game at St. Louis's Sportsman's Park. The game was a snoozer that the National League won 4-0 after scoring three times in the first inning. Still, when Laux, a fine nuts-and-bolts announcer, handed Mel the air, the action accelerated. While Laux merely described relevant details, Mel somehow made listeners feel the "scorching Missouri sun" on their backs and the cool breeze "roaring from right toward left" across their cheeks. Mel's diction wasn't always perfect, but he was constantly chattering, painting a picture while masterfully setting his voice to the pulse of the game. He liked to think of himself as a boat out at sea. Nautical waves pushed the boat up and down just like sound waves ruled Mel's tone on the air. His voice rose and sped up with the screams and cheers of fans, then quieted and slowed as the crowd settled down.

That voice was rich, deep, nasal and resonant. It could yell above the crowd when necessary. And Mel's zippy tones spoke of action and movement—Ott adjusting his sunglasses as he ran onto the field, Luke Appling wiping the dirt out of his eye as he stepped out of the batter's box, Hank Greenberg looking up into the bright sun from left field—that injected the stagnant game with life. Meanwhile, the shouts of fans at Sportsman's Park drowned out Laux's voice after the National League's Billy Herman legged out an infield single.

Mel saw himself as the narrator. The athletes were his actors: "Terry Moore bats 'em right-handed … hitting .265 on the season … outfield over toward left for him. Ruffing blows on his pitching hand and starts the windup, sidearm pitch swung on, fouled off to the right of the plate up into the upper deck for strike one."

In between pitches, Mel's eyes constantly scanned the field, using his 20-20 vision as he looked for further ways to tell his story. They settled on a familiar figure: "Casey Stengel, manager of the Boston Bees, coaching at first, rubbing his hands, creating a little fuss as he always does out on the coaching line. One of the most colorful characters in baseball. … "

The Ol' Perfessor, who managed the Yankees into another dynasty period beginning in the late 1940s, would become one of Mel's favorite baseball figures. So would Ted Williams and Joe DiMaggio. In 1941, Williams hit .406 and stroked a ninth-inning blast into the second deck of Detroit's Briggs Stadium to beat the National League 7-5 in the All-Star Game as Mel watched from the CBS booth. As Williams ran to first base, he clapped his hands, endearing himself to Mel forever. Over the years, Mel reflected on his job with the same jubilation.

"I guess I'm a fan, not a broadcaster," he once said.

Mel wouldn't have the same bird's-eye view of the on-field action on July 17, 1941, as the Indians snapped DiMaggio's 56-game hitting streak at Cleveland's Municipal Stadium. No station or sponsor picked up Yankees and Giants broadcasts after CBS's two-year deal with General Mills expired, though Barber and Al Helfer broadcast Dodgers games over New York station WOR from Brooklyn.

With the Yankees off the air in 1941, Mel followed the feats of Williams and DiMaggio closely while tending to his non-baseball announcing duties. Mel thought Williams was the best hitter he ever saw, while DiMaggio was his top all-around player. Williams and DiMaggio also played the game hard and respectfully. In the heat of the action, they carried themselves in the same work-manlike manner in which Mel operated. On the field, Mel carefully gathered color. In the booth, he painstakingly ensured he and his statistician, Jack Slocum, the son of Bill Sr., had their figures correct.

✿ ✿ ✿ ✿ ✿ ✿ ✿

On April 20, 1941, a day Mel would ordinarily be broadcasting baseball, he reported to Long Island's Mitchell Field for a special CBS assignment. Adolph Hitler's Nazis were stampeding through Europe and the United States was draft-ing men into service. Meanwhile, Mel was readying his listeners for World War II.

"Two days ago, general George C. Marshall, United States Army chief of staff, announced that this country had completed plans which were another step in its preparation for any emergency," he said over the air. "The very heart of this plan is the everyday American citizen, the civilian who must act as the eyes of the defending air force and who must transmit to the Army Air Defense headquarters the vital information that he has cited airplanes. ... If they are enemy aircraft, the army will have enough warning to intercept the bombers before they can complete their missions of carnage and death."

Mel was describing the Aircraft Warning Service, which the U.S. military employed from 1942-1944. Several hundred thousand patriotic volunteers from across the nation served as watchdogs for suspicious planes. Upon spotting them, they knew to contact the Army Air Defense headquarters. Plotters could then quickly chart the planes' positions and the military could dispatch interceptor aircraft. During a 15-minute CBS program, Mel detailed a demonstration of how the warning service could swiftly stunt bombers hovering perilously close to New York over the Long Island Sound.

The airwaves flashed to a call from a scratchy male voice ("nine bombers ... seen ... north ... four miles ... heading west") then to a lieutenant at Mitchell Field trumpeting orders ("your engines are hot ... guns are totally serviced ... use actions above 12,000 feet"). CBS correspondent John Charles Daly reported from the air with imaginary enemy bombers. "If we're successful, we hope to leave New York short of necessary power, the East River at least temporarily blocked and Brooklyn Navy Yard docks and ships in shambles," he said. But the Air Force came to the rescue. The ripple of machine-gun fire and whirr of diving planes raged over the CBS airwaves. "The planes have driven the bombers down into the range of artillery fire," Mel told his listeners.

Though the military succeeded in its fantasy demonstration, Americans faced the realities of war. Young, strong and unmarried, Mel was an ideal draft candidate. He had plenty of reminders of his inevitable orders from Uncle Sam in the early 1940s. He hosted an NBC radio show called *News from Home,* on which he relayed sports scores to the boys overseas embroiled in "the most important of all contests." Mel and Barber also reconstructed a radio roundup of the 1943 All-Star Game from Philadelphia's Shibe Park for American troops.

"Hello fellas," Mel said in an uncharacteristically mellow tone, "it's really swell to be able to talk to you."

****

General Mills was back as the main sponsor of Yankees and Giants games in 1942, and the broadcasts ran on radio station WOR. (Brooklyn's games moved over to WHN.) Mel partnered with Connie Desmond, a WOR staff announcer with that station who later gained notoriety with the Dodgers. Mel thoroughly enjoyed working with Desmond, a gentle-tempered Midwesterner. The feeling was mutual. Desmond always felt he made a mistake in 1943 when he moved over to Brooklyn to join Barber, who could be abrasive.

Mel didn't travel with the Yankees and Giants in 1942, but he occasionally re-created road games from Western Union telegraph reports sent from ballparks to the studio. Re-creations blanketed baseball's landscape before World War II.

Traveling was expensive and teams were still experimenting with radio. Some announcers chose to embellish their re-creations by making phony sound effects like knocking two blocks of wood together to mimic the crack of the bat. A 1930s minor league broadcaster in Des Moines named Dutch Reagan once dreamed up an endless string of foul balls and a fight between two boys in the stands over one of them after he learned his wire had gone dead. After becoming president, Ronald Reagan joked about the incident decades later with the press.

If Mel had a wire failure while doing a re-creation, he chose to tell his listeners.

"I might tell a white lie to a friend of mine, but when it comes to a mass of people, you have an obligation to them, you have an obligation to the people you work for, you have an obligation to yourself," he once said regarding re-creations.

Mel felt that if he told tales during re-creations, he risked losing his listeners' faith in believing him as he called live games. So he would have Joe Gordon at second base and Crosetti at short crouch into fielding position and Red Rolfe, the third baseman, creep in for the bunt. He would also make Yankees infielders and outfielders shift to the right to play Ted Williams to pull.

From a telegraph message that read, "Ball one, low outside," Mel would say something like: "Spud Chandler looks in, gets the sign from Bill Dickey, shakes him off and steps off the rubber. Now he goes into the windup, around comes the right arm, in comes the pitch and it's low and outside for a ball." By adding in only baseball idiosyncrasies—and not false action—he was giving listeners a picture of the game without altering any of its events.

❊ ❊ ❊ ❊ ❊ ❊

The Yankees wrapped up their sixth American League pennant in seven years in 1942 and returned to the World Series, as did Mel. The Gillette Safety Razor Company, the Series sponsor, and commissioner Kenesaw Mountain Landis picked him and Barber to do play-by-play of the Yankees-Cardinals clash for Mutual. Corum, the husky-voiced *Journal-American* columnist, did pre- and postgame color.

Before the Series began, *Time* magazine ran a short preview story entitled "50,000,000 Ears." Under a picture of a smiling, Barber, Corum and Mel, the cutline read:

Barber, Corum & Allen
They will bend 50,000,000 ears.

The first paragraph of the story began:

In U.S. drugstores, barbershops, lunch wagons, parlors and pool halls, over 25,000,000 radio listeners will cock their ears next week to listen to three men—the sportscasting trio that broadcasts the World

Series. Their play-by-play highlight of baseball's Big Hour will be short-waved to U.S. fighting men overseas and will be revamped into Spanish for Latin Americans.

The *Time* story also said Mel "wears clothes like a fashion plate from *Esquire* and "like Red Barber ... seldom gets ruffled."

As advertised, Mel seemed composed as he readied for Game 1 at Sportsman's Park. He went over his notes as his producer counted down until airtime. "Five minutes!" "Three minutes!" "One minute!" "30 seconds!" This was all routine stuff. Mel had broadcast the World Series before. But suddenly, Mel, who had picked up a 15-cent copy of *Time* before the Series, thought of those 50 million ears. He momentarily forgot Ralph Edwards's advice about thinking of his audience as one person.

Mel began to tremble. Then he started to hyperventilate. The man who could talk nonstop for a two-and-a-half-hour ballgame was breathless. Mel's voice was paralyzed for a full minute before he managed to spit out a few words. Slowly, he got back to his sprightly sounds, just in time to do his Gillette commercials.

"To make shaving thoroughly pleasant and refreshing, there are just three things to remember; you might call them the ABC's of shaving comfort: A, use the Gillette Blue Blade in B, your Gillette razor, and C, prepare your beard with Gillette shaving cream, either lather or brushless. Both are super. Ask your dealer for Gillette shaving cream, only 25 cents, and you see how much faster and easier you shave this all-Gillette way," he read.

As Mel broadcast the game, he watched the Yankees' Ruffing take a no-hitter deep into the eighth inning. As Ruffing's teammates avoided talking about his feat in the dugout, Mel did the same in the booth: "Harry Walker coming in to bat for Harry Gumbert. ... Five to nothing the score in favor of the Yankees. ... On deck is Jimmy Brown, then will come Terry Moore. Fans are settling back, wondering ... a lot of wondering going on right now. ... "

Throughout his career, Mel bowed to the player superstition by not saying "no hitter" on the air as a pitcher worked on one.

"I like to respect the traditions of the field," he would say. "I know, some people say this is being sophomoric and silly. But to me it's part of the romance and flavor of the game. It's one of the great things that separates it from other sports, like the seventh-inning stretch or *Take Me Out to the Ball Game.*"

Mel would drop in plenty of on-air hints that players were working on no-hitters, as he did while Ruffing pitched to Harry Walker: "Ruffing bobs that ball around in his pitching glove, all eyes are certainly on the Yankee right-hander. ..."

After Ruffing struck out Walker, Mel continued to walk the tightrope: "And with that putout, Red Ruffing tied a World Series record, which we will give to you in a little while. We're gonna hold it for the moment ... for a reason which we'll tell you later."

Brown hit a short pop up into left filed. The ball threatened to drop between Yankees shortstop Phil Rizzuto and left fielder Charlie Keller. Mel's voice accelerated with the ball as it sped toward the ground: "Rizzuto racing out, Keller coming in, Phil's under it and makes the catch for the out. … And with that out, Ruffing sets a new World Series record. And again, we're respecting an age-old tradition … won't tell you just what it is at the moment but in due time, we will tell ya. … So don't go away."

The next batter, Moore, singled to right field to end Ruffing's no-hit bid. Mel could stop sounding wishy-washy.

"So there it is," he said. "The time has come now when we can tell you. That's the first hit off Red Ruffing, who went seven and two-thirds innings without allowing a base hit."

Gillette didn't seem to mind Mel's superstitious approach. Advertising manager A. Craig Smith wrote him to say that "all hands agree that your work on the Series was brilliant and I certainly put in 100 percent."

Behind Ruffing, the Yankees took Game 1 7-4, but the Cardinals won four in a row to wrest the World Series title from the Bronx. The Yankees played without first baseman Johnny Sturm and outfielder Tommy Henrich, whom they lost to the rapidly expanding war effort. World War II would gut baseball of its top players, and of the top announcer for the Yankees and Giants.

CHAPTER 7

Army Hour

As Hitler's Nazis conquered most of Europe and the Japanese pummeled Pearl Harbor, Uncle Sam hurriedly enlisted virtually every able-bodied American male between the ages of 18 and 38 in the United States military. The U.S. plunged into World War II, its best athletes leaving the country's serene fields of sport for the bombed-out pastures of battle.

The war nearly brought the sports world to a halt. Alabama and Stanford, whom Mel had watched in that glorious Rose Bowl game on New Year's Day 1935, gave up on fielding football teams until the fighting was over. Baseball, the national pastime, went on by mandate of President Franklin Delano Roosevelt. Roosevelt was trying to salvage America's morale, even as the game's stars— DiMaggio, Williams, Greenberg and Bob Feller just to name a few—entered the war. Five hundred major leaguers were GIs when World War II ended.

The Yankees and Giants disappeared completely from the airwaves in 1943. The Dodgers, under the guidance of the opportunistic Larry MacPhail, remained on, though the team's talent level didn't justify it. The big leagues were barely the bush leagues. A collection of guys who couldn't pass the military's physical examinations played in America's major league parks. They used a ball with a core comprised of cork and tree sap. It was as lifeless as the play on the field.

Mel's draft orders finally came through in the fall of 1943. Around the same time, Gillette and Mutual picked him for the World Series broadcast team. Mel's announcing career was on a meteoric rise. He attributed much of his success to being in the right place at the right time and working hard to make the most of his opportunities. The 1943 World Series was one of those opportunities. After he enlisted in the Army, Mel wrote to Yankees president Ed Barrow and James A. Farley, an influential American who had served as Democratic Party chairman and U.S. Postmaster General, in hopes of obtaining permission to cover the Series. Farley told Mel in a September 29, 1943, letter that Mel's commanding officer at Fort Benning, Georgia, wouldn't grant him such permission:

> I am terribly sorry, Mel, but it is just one of those breaks we have to take with a smile. Don't worry about it. This war will soon be over and you will be able to take up your old location again. Your reputation is such that you won't have any difficulty taking up where you left off. I am sure of this. Just go on and do your job in the Army and do it as well and as successfully as I know you can. As we go through life we run into a great many disappointments, and if we worry about them it just hinders us as we go along. Just treat this as one of them and forget all about it.

But Mel couldn't forget. Missing the 1943 World Series, which he followed on a radio at Camp Croft in Spartanburg, South Carolina, was a major disappointment in his life. Just before his departure for military service, Mel said to Frank Slocum, another son in Bill Sr.'s baseball family, "I hope they remember me when I get back."

A second concern also tormented Mel before he joined the war. His college sweetheart, Miriam Rosenbloum, was still a part of his life. Miriam lived down South, but she and Mel kept in close contact. Miriam had visited Mel in New York, staying with the Israels. Julius and Anna were very fond of her. What was not to like? She was beautiful, nice and, of course, Jewish. Mel and Miriam had had a long romance, and Mel faced a decision. Here was a girl whom he could marry. In 1957, Mel told the *New York Post*'s Leonard Shecter that he was even engaged when he entered the war.

"With all my income cut off I let my head rule my heart," Mel said. "She got tired of waiting I suppose."

Miriam ended up marrying a New York doctor. Esther and Larry never heard about Mel getting engaged, and Mel was closer to them than to any of his friends. Their brother kept his personal relationships to himself. Throughout his life, he told his family only tidbits about girlfriends and dates.

❊ ❊ ❊ ❊ ❊ ❊ ❊

Mel enlisted in the army in September 1943, but he planned to move over to the air force, which intended on sending Glenn Miller and his band around Europe to entertain U.S. troops. Miller wanted Mel to join him as sort of a traveling disc jockey who introduced the music to soldiers. The air force would make Mel a captain for doing so. Mel waited anxiously at Camp Upton, a holding ground on Long Island for draftees until the military decided where to send them.

But an army general thought Mel Allen the broadcaster was trying to maneuver his way into the air force. Enraged, the general burst into Mel's barrack at 3 a.m. and woke him up.

"Pack your duffel bag!" he yelled. He rustled Mel out of bed and pushed him on a train that had its shades drawn. Mel rode all night and wound up at Camp Croft. The general had put Mel in the infantry and also likely saved his life. In December 1944, Miller's plane disappeared over the English Channel after it set off from England for France. Miller's fate remains unknown.

"It is entirely conceivable that I could have been on that plane with him," Mel said somberly during a 1980s interview. "I've always thought about that."

Mel endured basic training at Camp Croft and was prepared to fight in Europe when his profession again threatened to influence his military assignment. This time, army officials saw Mel's broadcasting ability as an asset. They assigned him to Fort Benning to work in a new public relations division. The army sought to improve the image of the infantrymen, whom Americans saw as the dirt-eaters and mud-sloggers, the guys at the bottom of the military's pecking order. But these men were crucial to Allied success in the war.

Mel broadcast over the Armed Forces Radio Service, which reached millions of U.S. troops around the world. He handled a five-minute segment on NBC's the *Army Hour*. The weekly program was designed to boost infantry enlistment before and after D-Day (when the Allies invaded Western Europe on June 6, 1944) and morale among troops and their families.

The *Army Hour* gave listeners an opportunity "to meet some of the men and women who have been doing the bombing," in the words of Ed Herlihy, the show's narrator. Herlihy reported on war happenings around the world, checking in with correspondents from Hawaii to New Zealand to China to Iran to England to France to "somewhere in Scotland." The words "Japs" and "Nazis" flew around like bullets as Herlihy drove home a consistently patriotic theme. "Hitler's air force has lost its sting!" he boldly declared. The program began with blaring trumpets and beating drums and episodes were interspersed with triumphant military verses. *Day and night, march and fight, we're the infantry! Never stop, 'til we drop, smash the enemy!*

Reporting from the infantry's officer candidate school at Fort Benning, Mel profiled a different weapon in each *Army Hour* segment. He told of how the 50-caliber machine gun could be put on a jeep and "the little rascal'll hold its own against a big plane." He proved it with an action-packed dramatization. These re-enactments of combat situations were set to loud bursts of gunfire (albeit blanks), vrooms of diving fighter planes and the thunder of rolling tanks. During one episode, Mel took off in a plane full of paratroopers, hanging on for his life with one arm and holding a microphone with the other as he described their jumps. Mel didn't jump, though. The episode wasn't about him, but the men in the field of battle.

"This is Sergeant Mel Allen on Hook Range at The Infantry School," he said to begin his June 25, 1944, segment. "Wherever the war is being fought, from the smallest island in the Pacific to the roads and lanes leading to Paris and Berlin, the sounds of battle are the same: the zoom of a bomber, the thud of artillery, the blast of a mortar shell, the whine of a rifle bullet—ugly, harsh, angry sounds. Added to them is the sound of one of the infantry's most versatile and destructive weapons. Listen … "

Loud, shuddering gunfire sounded.

"That's the anti-tank rifle grenade, a grenade with a sheet-metal body, a round nose, weighing about a pound and a half," Mel said rapidly. "It's fired by a rifle-grenade cartridge from a launcher which fits under the muzzle end of the rifle. Striking with the velocity of about 150 feet per second, it'll blow a hole in the armor of all enemy tanks, except the heaviest. Launchers have been devised to fit any of our rifles. Today, the doughboy can shoot the grenade eight times the distance he can throw it by hand. When it hits a tank, it punctures and destroys, spraying the inside with slivers of white-hot steel and flame …"

Mel asked an Army captain what he thought of the weapon. "Well, the battleground is a real proving ground," the captain said in a drawl dripping with the sounds of Oklahoma, "and I'll tell you, the rifle grenade is a honey."

This man had seen the weapon in action in the Americans' Sicily campaign prior to D-day. Mel's *Army Hour* segment re-enacted his experience with it.

"Yes, the doughboys were on the move, taking ground, when they walked into a German tank park," Mel energetically began. "The Americans were first to act. Quickly, a bazooka team went into action and fired."

As a mock battle erupted, Mel spoke at the rapid-fire pace of a machine gun to keep up with the action.

"The anti-tank rocket smashed through the armor of the front tank and knocked it out, and immediately the other tank then backed off. … All became quiet suddenly. Several hours later, the doughboys were awaiting orders when the growling of enemy tanks again reached their ears. Five German tanks came rambling into attack, spearheaded by a light tank out front. An infantryman armed with a Browning automatic rifle cut loose. The hail of bullets splattered against the tank, flattened out but did no harm. The tank kept coming."

The boys were lucky they had their anti-tank rifle grenade. "All ready, a rifle grenadier was set," Mel said. "The grenadier waited, eager to fire but holding himself in check until the tank got close enough. And now the tank was within 15 yards of the doughboys and the grenadier fired his anti-tank grenade. The grenade hit the upper part of one of the tank treads, kept going, sliced through the soft underside of the tank body and set it afire. … Nazis began to pour out of the top to escape the licking flames, only to be mowed down by a barrage of rifle and machine-gun fire. … Other anti-tank grenadiers or anti-tank rocket teams, meantime, smashed away at other tanks, halted them. The tank attack was stopped."

Of course, the Americans always defeated a hostile enemy on the *Army Hour*.

"It turned out to be an important assignment," Mel said decades later. "I don't mean to imply that that made the difference in winning the war … but it was something that the top brass, the chiefs of staff, evidently had decided was important to do and we did it." Mel wrote and produced his segments, and he rehearsed and performed them with an actual platoon. He had a first lieutenant urge him which weapons to promote and ensure the accuracy of his writing.

Mel earned respect for his *Army Hour* work and rose to a rank of staff sergeant. The army also let Mel bring his car down from New York to Fort Benning, where he drove Larry around while his younger brother went through training before heading to Europe. The two brothers were a team. On his vacations home to New York from the University of Alabama prior to the war, Larry had sometimes filled in for Jack Slocum as Mel's baseball statistician. When Larry entered the Army, the brothers bonded in name.

Due to Mel's success, people often identified his immediate family members as "Allens." Julius, Anna, Esther and Larry repeatedly had to explain that their last name was Israel. To avoid confusion, Julius and Anna began to answer to "Mr. and Mrs. Allen" and Esther used "Esther Allen" in the *Truth or Consequences* credits. But Julius and Anna kept Israel as their official last name, while Esther's became Kaufman when she got married. When the army required Mel to enlist under a legalized name, Julius and Anna told him to change his to "Melvin Allen," with one request: That Larry also becomes an Allen. They wanted their boys to stick together.

❄ ❄ ❄ ❄ ❄ ❄

"Hello there everybody, this is Sergeant Mel Allen," Mel said as he signed on to do many of his Army broadcasts. Over the rest of his life, Mel would charm millions with his "Hello there everybody" introduction. The phrase was simple yet catchy. Mel said it with his smooth, Southern voice in such a folksy way that he sounded like he knew every one of his listeners. They certainly felt like they knew him.

"I want to thank you for helping me through a very lonely period when I was away from home," a man from the Bronx wrote in a letter to Mel in 1964. "Your voice came through on my small transistor one night in Germany through the facilities of the Armed Forces Radio Service. Mel, it was like a long awaited letter from home. I will never forget it. It meant a great deal to me then and it still does."

Mel's voice was a comfort to troops around the world. In addition to broadcasting the *Army Hour,* Mel re-created sports contest with real-time intensity, allowing soldiers to relax with a diversion from home. Mel and Joe Hasel, known for broadcasting West Point sporting events before the war, re-created the all-St. Louis World Series of 1944 (the Cardinals defeated the Browns in six games) for troops via the British Broadcasting Company. Mel also handled NBC's hour long *Football Roundup,* during which he reconstructed top college football games. The bounce in Mel's voice gave these artificial broadcasts life. Listeners could practically see Alabama's box offense shift with precision into its innumerable formations as they sensed abrupt changes in the action with the rapid lifts of Mel's voice.

Mel also hosted NBC's *Sports Quiz*, a lively trivia show that mirrored a prewar radio program he did called *Choose Up Sides*. Servicemen stationed around the world were urged to write in questions that would stump two teams of sports celebrities, which competed against one another. The prize offered to the winning team struck a patriotic chord. "It's just that good, old-fashioned pride in winning," Mel said.

The Allies were winning. They made it official when the Germans surrendered on May 7, 1945, and the Japanese, gasping for air after atomic bombs decimated two of their major cities, followed suit that summer. Mel remained in the service, letting many of the boys triumphantly stream home before he did. Finally, Mel's job with the Armed Forces Radio Service became obsolete. The army discharged him on January 20, 1946.

❊ ❊ ❊ ❊ ❊ ❊ ❊

As he served, Mel often wondered what he would do when World War II was over. James Farley's letter reassuring Mel that he would have no trouble reestablishing himself in his field was little consolation to him. Mel didn't realize that Americans who served in World War II were guaranteed to get their former jobs back. Instead he thought about the burgeoning field of broadcasting and how so many guys coveted major league jobs like the one he had before the war. The Yankees and Giants had used new announcers in 1944 and 1945 over New York's WINS under Gillette's sponsorship. Don Dunphy, who would become famous for his boxing work, and Bill Slater, a track and football guru, did the games in 1944. Slater and Al Helfer picked them up in 1945.

Dunphy, Slater and Helfer were mere fill-ins in these baseball roles. Mel found that out while in New York on furlough from Fort Benning in late 1945, when he ran into Giants owner Horace Stoneham at Toots Shor's.

"When are you getting out?" Stoneham asked Mel.

"I don't know," Mel said. "Depends on how soon, I guess, they start releasing the troops."

"If you want your job back when you get out, you got it with the Giants," Stoneham said. "We're going to split up."

"We" meant the Giants and Yankees. The Yankees were under new ownership. The inimitable Larry MacPhail had decided he wanted to dump the Dodgers and buy into the Yankees, baseball's dominant franchise. Jacob Ruppert had died in 1939, and his heirs wanted to sell New York's American League franchise. MacPhail assembled two high rollers—New York jet setter and professional football owner Dan Topping and Arizona developer Del Webb—and in January 1945, the trio had bought the Yankees for $2.8 million. MacPhail, who took over Yankees operations, told Stoneham that his team was breaking free from their prewar broadcasting partnership. And there would be no more Western Union-aided re-creations of Yankees road games. Once World War II was over, MacPhail would broadcast every home and away game, giving him a competitive edge over the Giants and Dodgers. New York's two National League teams wouldn't send their broadcasters on the road until 1948.

After Stoneham told him about the Yankees' new ownership group, Mel was sure MacPhail would hire Barber to do games in the Bronx. After all, Barber had been MacPhail's broadcaster when the owner ran the Reds and Dodgers. Therefore, Mel was extremely grateful that Stoneham had offered him the Giants job.

"I 'bout jumped 20 feet in the air," he said later.

MacPhail did go after Barber, but Barber decided to remain in Brooklyn. He was the first radio voice of Ebbets Field and had what he felt was an unbreakable bond with Dodgers fans. Brooklyn's blue-collar residents took pride in their own borough and were exceeding loyal to two of its institutions: Their baseball team ('dem Bums) and its broadcaster (the Ol' Redhead). During World War II, Barber had used the Ebbets Field booth to solicit blood donors for the American Red Cross. (Barber, who was married with a child, wasn't drafted.) The Red Cross work brought him even closer to the Brooklyn faithful.

"The blood of Brooklyn, in this broadcasting booth, washed over me when I sat down," Barber would write in his 1970 book, *The Broadcasters*.

When Barber turned MacPhail down, the new Yankees owner moved his attention to Mel. MacPhail, a colonel on the staff of General George C. Marshall stationed in Washington during the war, had kept tabs on when Mel would be discharged. When Mel finally got out in early 1946, MacPhail called him. Mel knew instantly what he wanted. But Mel didn't think he could accept the Yankees job. He had made a verbal agreement with Stoneham, one of the owners who put him on the air during for first big-league baseball gig.

Mel decided to see MacPhail only out of respect to the Yankees' new owner. MacPhail, who had lined up radio station WINS for Yankees games, offered Mel the job as their chief announcer. Mel told him about the offer Stoneham had extended to him.

"I feel sort of a moral obligation to Mr. Stoneham," Mel told MacPhail.

Mel went back to see Stoneham again, telling him of MacPhail's offer.

"Then you may not *have* a problem, Mel, and the reason is because I *do* have a problem," Stoneham said.

"What do you mean?" Mel said.

"I don't have a station," Stoneham said. "I've been reduced to either WNYC or WMCA."

Neither one appealed to Stoneham. WNYC was city-owned, while WMCA's owners weren't sports people. To them, games were a necessary evil, a way to make money.

"WMCA knows that they've got me over a barrel and they're really charging me an excessive amount, so it may be that we don't even get on the air,"

Stoneham said. "So if the job with the Yankees is still open, I release you from your moral obligation."

To complete a frantic 24-hour period since MacPhail first called him, Mel went back to see the Yankees' owner and accepted his offer. Circumstance, Mel thought, had landed him a coveted job once again.

Had Mel taken the Giants' microphone and Barber settled into the Yankees' booth, who knows how they would have altered the future. Where Allen and Barber remained, however, they jump-started a glorious era for radio and baseball.

PART III

GLORY
(1946–1964)

CHAPTER 8

The Voice

A s the boys returned home from World War II, baseball assumed a spot atop the sports world. The return of DiMaggio, Williams and the rest of the game's elite players, who replaced the major league's wartime scabs, signified normalcy in America. The war was truly over.

Baseball attendance soared as Americans flocked to ballparks to see their heroes. The working man identified with these players who didn't make the exorbitant salaries of today. Major leaguers competed vigorously for World Series checks that would give their families better lives, and players often held non-baseball jobs during the off season. Announcers transformed these otherwise ordinary Americans into legends.

If a person walked down New York City neighborhood streets on summer afternoons in the late 1940s through the early 1950s, he met Mel Allen and Red Barber. Air conditioning and television weren't commonplace yet, but radios were on and the baseball voices drifted out of open store and apartment windows. Sometimes one could go for blocks without missing a pitch. As Allen and Barber's passionate calls blended with cracks of bats, thumps of balls into gloves, hearty yells of umpires and peanut vendors and claps and cheers of fans, masterpieces were painted. And because baseball broadcasters gave fans sight and sound, their calls were coated with a divine-like sheen. Five words that Russ Hodges repeatedly yelled—"The Giants win the pennant!"—did as much to make Bobby Thomson famous as his National League-winning 1951 homer off Brooklyn's Ralph Branca. Fans remember the call as much as the homer. Most of the biggest names in baseball broadcasting history—Allen, Barber, Hodges, Harry Caray, Curt Gowdy, Ernie Harwell, Vin Scully, Bob Wolff, Jack Buck and more—did games during this glorious era for their profession.

Six years before Hodges made his earth-shattering 1951 call at the Polo Grounds, he was an assistant broadcaster for Arch McDonald with the Washington Senators. Mel first heard Hodges while introducing big-league broadcasts to soldiers overseas during his final days of military service. Hodges's voice wasn't overly strong, but it was warm and pleasant. It also bled emotion during the biggest moments of games. When Mel needed to hire an assistant for his Yankees broadcasts in 1946, he called McDonald, who said Hodges was a loyal, unassuming partner whom players loved.

Over lunch at Toots Shor's with Hodges, Mel realized those qualities and noticed a wonderful chemistry with McDonald's assistant. Like Mel, Hodges was a lawyer-turned-sportscaster from the South (he was born in Dayton, Tennessee) who had stumbled upon his profession. Playing football at the University of Kentucky, he broke an ankle and lost his scholarship. He became a spotter for the team's radio broadcasts and a new career was born. Of course, none of this happened according to his mother's plan. She wanted her son to become a musician. Yes, Mel Allen and Russ Hodges had a lot in common.

Mel and Hodges made baseball history in 1946 by doing the first live broadcasts of major league road games. As the Yankees' No. 1 announcer, Mel allotted Hodges's play-by-play innings. In these days, the No. 2 man served as a relief pitcher of sorts, giving the top guy a breather when he needed it. Mel usually let Hodges do the third and seventh innings of Yankees games. That pattern changed two weeks into the season when Cleveland's Bob Feller no-hit the Yankees at Yankee Stadium. That afternoon, Hodges finished the third inning and handed the air back to Mel. Mel followed Feller's fireballs as they breezed past the Yankees' vaunted hitters, his voice rising with each of the pitcher's 11 strikeouts as the crowd of 37,000 became Indians fans for a day. Mel watched people rise and sway each time the right-hander began his windup and delivered his pitches. Mel, who liked to picture himself as a player on the field or at the plate as he called a game, became completely absorbed in the action. He sailed through the seventh inning without giving Hodges the air. When Mel realized what he had done, he introduced his partner to do the eighth. Hodges, who knew Mel had never called a no-hitter, tapped him on the sleeve.

"Never mind, Mel," he said, "I've worked a couple of these myself."

Mel turned back toward the field and called the game's final drama. In the top of the ninth, Cleveland's Frankie Hayes hit a solo home run off the Yankees' Bill Bevens, who was valiantly dueling Feller. In the bottom half of the inning, the Yankees' George Stirnweiss bunted, eliciting boos from fans, and reached base safely on first baseman Les Fleming's error. As Fleming booted the ball, the crowd groaned. Feller now had to face the Yankees' three most feared hitters—Tommy Henrich, DiMaggio and Keller—in succession. Henrich laid down a sacrifice bunt, which moved Stirnweiss to second. DiMaggio worked Feller to a full count, the crowd thundering through each pitch, before the right-hander coaxed the Yankee Clipper to ground out to shortstop Lou Boudreau. Feller then got Keller to hit a grounder to second baseman Ray Mack. Mack fielded the ball and threw to Fleming, who couldn't find first base with his foot. He finally did, a split-second before Keller got to the bag. Cleveland won 1-0 and Feller had his no-hitter.

In reflecting upon his career, Mel identified the game as one of the most exciting he ever called. He also liked to talk about how Hodges, who had worked with him for just a brief time, handed him back the eighth inning. That story made its way to Bill Corum, who wrote it up in his *Journal-American* sports column: "If Russ hasn't been officially welcome to New York before this, I hope he knows now that he belongs."

Mel quickly grew to like and trust his partner more than just about anyone he knew.

"Russ Hodges was, from all standpoints, the most workable assistant that Mel had, from being friendly, for pitching in, for covering it, for knowing when to say something and when not to say something," says Mel's brother Larry, who served as statistician for Mel and Hodges. "He was a sweetheart."

During Hodges's three seasons with the Yankees, when efficient WINS engineer Al Werner also worked in the booth, Mel found the broadcasts more smooth and enjoyable than at any other moment in his Bronx tenure.

"It got to the point where we could almost read each other's minds," Mel once said about Hodges.

"Allen?" Hodges said in 1948. "As grand a man to work with, to be associated with, to know, as you will find from one Portland to the other!"

Yankees sponsors—Pabst Blue Ribbon and Ballantine Beers and White Owl Cigars—played off Mel and Russ's fun-loving relationship by having them do two-way commercials. The two announcers read from scripts, Mel asking questions and Hodges answering them. For laughs, Mel sometimes subbed in his own questions. This made Hodges giggle so much that he often ran out of the booth so he could compose himself.

Hodges took a low-key approach to broadcasting, making him a great foil for Mel, who was easily consumed by his work. Once the game was over, Russ's mind was elsewhere.

"Do you think Stirnweiss should have swung at that three-and-one pitch?" Mel might ask Russ after a tough Yankees loss.

Hodges would give Mel a hard time about being too wrapped up in his job, and the two would soon be in stitches.

"After the last man is out, Hodges is off and running at Pimlico," Mel once joked about his partner.

Before a game, Mel was the one running around. He answered fan mail and spent time on the field or in the locker rooms gathering color. As he made his way up to the broadcast booth, which was located in Yankee Stadium's third tier behind home plate, he greeted hordes of hot dog vendors, guards and other Yankees officials. Always before the first pitch, Mel flew through the doorway of the broadcast booth, sometimes just in time to say, "Hello there everybody, this is Mel Allen ... "

Mel was never late, even if that meant traveling from the Bronx to Brooklyn to get to the microphone. That happened once when the baseball Yankees played a doubleheader at Yankee Stadium, and the professional football Yankees, a team that Dan Topping ran, took on football's Brooklyn Dodgers at Ebbets Field on the same day. The football clubs were in the All-America Football Conference, an NFL competitor that arose in the mid-1940s. Mel stayed behind at Yankee Stadium to finish the baseball doubleheader while Russ and Larry left for Ebbets Field to set up for the football game. It was a sweltering day and Mel's shirt was drenched as he wrapped up the second baseball game and zipped over to Ebbets Field. Just before kickoff, Russ and Larry heard the patter of his feet outside the broadcast booth.

"And now, here's Mel … " Hodges began. Mel slid into his chair and took over.

Perhaps the most classic Mel Allen moment Hodges experienced came during a 1946 game as DiMaggio and Henrich chased a deep drive toward the right-field wall. Mel could see pitchers standing in the bullpen and fans scrambling to get in position to catch the ball, so he began to say, "It's going … going … " Then he noticed that the Yankees outfielders were still playing the ball and thought for a second that it might stay in the park. When Henrich and DiMaggio finally dropped their gloves, Mel safely said, "gone!"

He turned to Hodges.

"Jiminy Cricket!" he said. "I sounded like an auctioneer trying to call that one."

Fan letters flooded into Yankee Stadium about Mel's new call. He had stumbled upon one of his signature phrases. Cincinnati Reds broadcaster Harry Hartman is credited with first using the call during a game in 1929, but Mel made the words famous by uttering them with rapidity and effect: "There's a fly ball out to right field—that ball is going, going, it is gone!"

Even while describing batted balls he wasn't sure would turn into home runs, Mel could blend his call into a broadcast as naturally as DiMaggio handled a bat: "Outfield swung around toward left, infield shaded well around toward third. Joe with that classic stance of his, bat cocked up off his right shoulder. The next pitch, he swings and sends a long drive. If it stays fair, it will go all the way. It is going … it is going … it is gone!"

❊ ❊ ❊ ❊ ❊ ❊

The Yankees finished third in 1946, a season in which they had three managers: McCarthy, Bill Dickey and Johnny Neun. Joe McCarthy and Larry MacPhail, two tough-minded, controlling baseball men, almost instantly clashed. Thirty-five games into the 1946 season, McCarthy quit, leaving the Yankees without the cohesiveness Mel and Hodges shared in the broadcast booth.

Mel did the 1946 All-Star Game for Mutual from Fenway Park with Boston announcer Jim Britt and Corum and, after the season, won *The Sporting News'* esteemed award naming the American League's top play-by-play broadcaster. A boy-faced 29-year-old Cardinals announcer named Harry Caray won *The Sporting News'* National League honors.

"Mel Allen selected Best Baseball Announcer of American League Games," read the back cover of the March 19, 1947, issue of *The Sporting News*, then considered the bible of baseball coverage. Three separate black and white photos showed Mel sitting at a microphone while clutching Chesterfield cigarettes between his fingers. *The Sporting News'* presentation to Mel with this award would become an annual event. On the field at Yankee Stadium or before a gathering of colleagues a Toots Shor's, he would receive a three-and-a-half-foot trophy from a dignitary such as baseball commissioner Happy Chandler, New York governor Thomas Dewey or *New York World-Telegram* sportswriting dean Dan Daniel. *The Sporting News* presented Mel with the honor six consecutive times. When AL teams began to gripe to publisher J.G. Taylor Spink, he discontinued the award.

※ ※ ※ ※ ※ ※ ※

When the Yankees needed a new statistician for the 1947 season, Mel approached Larry about the job. Back from serving in the war, Larry was pondering law school. Mel saw the statistician's job as an opportunity for the brothers to look out for one another. Mel would be fulfilling his role as family caretaker by helping Larry to find work, and in return, Larry could watch his brother's back in the cutthroat broadcasting business.

"I can't recommend you," Mel told Larry. "I'm gonna have to recommend someone else, but I would rather have you, and you can apply and see what happens."

Larry was a rabid sports fan. As a boy in Tuscaloosa, he would run over to the University of Alabama's campus after school to watch Frank Thomas's teams practice. On game days, Larry went over to Denny Stadium before it opened and hopped a fence crowned with iron points. The pain Larry sustained getting over the sharp tips eased as he watched his Crimson Tide play. Larry would also try to get into Alabama basketball games by saying, "I'm Mel Israel's brother."

On one such occasion, Hank Crisp, who was then Alabama's athletic director, stood behind Larry in line. "Don't ever do things on your brother's name," Crisp told him. "Do them on your own." Years later, when Larry ran into Crisp, he reminded him of that meeting and said, "That's one of the best pieces of advice anyone ever gave me."

The Yankees hired Larry, who became well respected among the team's broadcasters for thorough research and diligent stat keeping in his pristine print handwriting. From 1947 through 1964, Larry kept statistics for Mel's Yankees home and road games and spotted for his brother on college and pro football broadcasts. (Spotting entailed helping Mel and other broadcasters identify key players on the field.) Larry was the brains behind many Yankees announcers' comments, handing them nuggets of background information or statistical gems on slips of paper. During football broadcasts, he was "the best spotter in the world," according to his brother.

This distinction was accurate whether they were working or not. Larry tirelessly helped Mel keep up with his correspondence and appearance requests. Friends as well as brothers, Larry and Mel lived with their parents in an apartment on Netherland Avenue in Riverdale, a sleepy section of the Bronx beyond the northern tip of Manhattan. The close-knit family would dine together there or on Long Island with Esther and her husband Danny.

Mel was lucky to spend one or two nights a week with the family. As his fame increased, so did his career opportunities. The Yankees allowed Mel to freelance as a sportscaster. His voice had become so synonymous with them that anywhere he used it only brought more notoriety to the empire.

In 1946, Mel began working for Fox Movietone News, which occupied two nights of his week for the next 17 years. Mel wrote, edited and narrated sports newsreels that fans saw nationwide in movie theaters. Mel dove headfirst into other assignments, too, covering college and pro football, college basketball, boxing, track & field and even dog shows from Madison Square Garden. He also served as a disc jockey on WINS, hosting *The Mel Allen Show* ("three hours of your favorite melodies—new songs and old—with everybody's favorite emcee") and handled a weekly college football highlights show for Mutual.

❈ ❈ ❈ ❈ ❈ ❈ ❈

One of Mel's assignments in 1946 and 1947 involved hopping into Babe Ruth's Cadillac and driving the Bambino to schools, boys clubs or other venues, where Mel would introduce Ruth to adoring fans. Even long into retirement, Ruth was the biggest star in sports.

"I still felt seven years old," Mel said about working with Ruth. "I was sitting next to Babe Ruth! That was like sitting next to God for me."

Mel and Ruth also worked on an NBC radio show together called *On the Ball*. Like those in the audience, Mel got Ruth's autograph.

"To My Pal Mel Allen," Ruth wrote neatly on the cover of some sheet music a New York music company dedicated to the Babe. "From Babe Ruth."

When he and Ruth attended functions together, Mel observed closely how the Babe interacted with kids. There was a genuine joy on everyone's face, including Ruth's.

"Hello boys and girls!" Ruth blared.

"Hi, Mr. Babe!" They screamed back.

"Just Babe, not Mr. Babe."

Mel noticed how Babe spent time with individual children, especially if they were confined to a hospital bed.

"What's your name, sonny?" Ruth would say. "You got a favorite team?"

"The Yankees," was often the reply.

"The Yankees! Good for you!"

Ruth remembered these children when the Yankees hosted Babe Ruth Day at the stadium on April 27, 1947. By this late stage of his life, Ruth was in and out of the hospital and spoke with a hoarse whisper, a reminder of the throat cancer that would kill him. When Mel, the day's master of ceremonies, called Ruth from the Yankees' dugout, the crowd gave the Bambino a thunderous ovation, which *The New York Times'* Louis Effrat called "the greatest in the history of the national pastime."

Mel himself would never hear a louder sustained roar of a crowd. Ruth trudged out toward a bank of microphones at home plate wearing his familiar tan camel's hair coat and cap. Ruth had had a massive coughing spell before the proceedings but was determined to talk to the crowd. Bronzed from a recent stay in Florida, the Babe carefully surveyed the crowd. He was hunched over and looked wrinkled and gray at age 52 thanks to decades of hard living. As Ruth spoke, the microphones magnified his shaky, frog-like voice:

> Thank you very much, ladies and gentlemen. You know how bad my voice sounds. Well, it feels just as bad. You know this baseball game of ours comes up from the youth. That means the boys. And after you've been a boy, and grow up to know how to play ball, then you come to the boys you see representing themselves today in our national pastime.
>
> The only real game in the world, I think, is baseball. As a rule, some people think if you give them a football or a basketball or something like that, naturally, they're athletes right away. But you can't do that in baseball. You've gotta start from way down at the bottom, when you're 6 or 7 years old. You can't wait until you're 15 or 16. You've let it grow up with you, and if you're successful and you try hard enough, you're bound to come out on top, just like these boys have come to the top now.
>
> There's been so many lovely things said about me, I'm glad I had the opportunity to thank everybody. Thank you.

Listening to Ruth suffer through his speech, the more than 58,000 fans on hand and millions of others tuned in on radios around the world could feel his illness. As Ruth spoke, Mel's mind drifted back to his encounter with the sickly Gehrig in the Yankees dugout seven years before. The Babe was also a dying man. As Mel's eyes got misty, he swallowed hard to try to compose himself. As Ruth finished, Mel nodded and smiled. Along with those encircling the Babe— Cardinal Francis Spellman (the Archbishop of New York), Baseball commissioner Happy Chandler, American League president Will Harridge, National League president Ford Frick and Larry Cutler, a teenager representing American Legion baseball teams—and everyone in Yankee Stadium, Mel broke into wild applause.

Ruth would receive one last ovation upon the celebration of the silver anniversary of Yankee Stadium on June 13, 1948. Mel introduced members of the 1923 club who inaugurated "the House that Ruth Built," including the Babe himself as the Yankees retired his uniform No. 3. The pinstriped flannel that once hugged Ruth's massive frame now draped over his frail torso like it was on a hanger. Ruth propped himself up with a bat. But the crowd of 49,641 remembered a man of cherubic vitality and cheered him. As the applause went on and on, Mel yelled through the din, "Babe, do you want to try to say something?" Ruth put his lips to Mel's ear. Tears were streaming down his face.

"I must," he replied in his husky voice. Ruth again croaked into the microphone. He said he was privileged to have hit the first homer at Yankee Stadium and glad to be back with his old pals. Like many others on hand, Mel wept as he watched this sickly representation of Ruth. To conclude his speech, Ruth said, "Whatever you do, folks, never, never forget the kids." About two months later, the Babe died.

For the rest of his life, Mel tried to keep Babe's words alive. He devoted much of his free time to youth organizations such as the Boy Scouts and Boys Clubs of America, the Boys Athletic League and Little League Baseball. He always took time to step out of the broadcast booth to wave to swarms of young admirers in the upper deck. When they ran to him outside Yankee Stadium, Mel signed as many autographs as he could.

"On Monday, July 29th, you were standing outside the Yankee Stadium and I approached you and asked you if my grandson Tommy could have your autograph," a man from Binghamton, New York, wrote to Mel in 1963. "You graciously consented and autographed his book and thanked him for stopping and asking. Mel, you don't know what you have done to that boy. He is going around telling all his neighborhood pals that he met Mel Allen and got his signature. I guess you must like kids as well as I do."

Letters from fathers and grandfathers who thanked him for being kind to their boys inspired Mel to do more. "I was just a poor little kid from Alabama who came a long way," he once said.

Mel handed out sports equipment for the Boys Athletic League at Christmastime. Another year, he made a New Year's resolution to further "give my time to youngsters whose parents are not in a position to afford the simple luxuries." Mel also found ways to reach children who weren't able to meet him in person, such as the boy from Manchester, Connecticut, he touched in 1957.

"This is just a short note to let you know how happy you made a little boy before he died," a man from nearby Willimantic, Connecticut, wrote to Mel in a letter. "You heard about his illness, and during one of your broadcasts, you mentioned him over the air. He was listening to the Yankee game, his favorite team, while in the oxygen tent. Before he died on Sunday, all he talked about was how you talked about him. For bringing a smile and a few days of happiness to Bobby, you deserve the blessings of the Almighty."

❖ ❖ ❖ ❖ ❖ ❖ ❖

Behind Bucky Harris, a veteran who had previously managed the Senators, Tigers, Red Sox and Phillies, the Yankees won the 1947 American League pennant by 12 games over Detroit. In the National League, Jackie Robinson broke the majors' color barrier and starred as a first baseman for the Brooklyn Dodgers, who outlasted the St. Louis Cardinals to set up the first of seven Subway Series that would captivate New York over the next 10 seasons. Mel broadcast the 1947 All-Star Game at Chicago's Comiskey Park with Britt for Mutual and found himself back behind Mutual's World Series microphone with Barber in October.

The Sporting News named Allen and Barber as its top baseball play-by-play men of 1947. The World Series, heard over 400-plus Mutual stations by more than 70 million people, cast them before the nation not only as America's pre-eminent baseball broadcasters but as natural rivals. They were the distinct voices of the two teams that clawed through a seven-game war in 1947 and became archenemies over the next decade. And like the public images of those clubs—the cold-hearted, aloof, upper-crust Yankees and the lovable, blue-collar Dodgers—the on-air personalities of Allen and Barber clashed sharply.

"Mel had a lot better voice than Barber—Barber had a weak voice," says Ernie Harwell, the Hall of Fame voice of the Detroit Tigers who assisted Barber on Brooklyn broadcasts in the late 1940s. "He didn't have Mel's enthusiasm. Mel didn't make use of his intellectual background as much as Red did. Red approached everything as a reporting assignment. I think Mel approached everything as sort of a Yankee rooter and a guy who would enjoy himself. In basic broadcasting, they were both very good."

Mel, loud and loquacious, yelled and screamed like a fan.

"Here I was living the life of every guy that was playing sports," he once said.

Barber, who became a licensed lay preacher of the Episcopal Church in 1951, was more reserved and thought of himself as an instructor of baseball.

"The satisfaction I got was in doing my work, not in watching the game," he said after he retired.

The New York Times referred to Allen and Barber, respectively, as fire and ice. Jim Woods, a broadcaster who spent time in the booth with both men, labeled them as a machine gun and a violin.

"Barber was white wine, crepes suzette and bluegrass music," says Curt Smith, author of the definitive history of baseball broadcasting, *Voices of the Game.* "Mel Allen, hot dogs, beer—Ballantine naturally—and the United States Marine band."

The broadcasters even differed on trivial matters. Mel, who had 20-20 vision, used a small scorecard during games, while Barber, who wore glasses, scribbled on large notebook that contained score sheets. As they worked, both broadcasters gave the score to listeners frequently, but Mel just mentioned it when he thought to do so, while Barber used a three-minute egg timer as a reminder.

Yankees and Dodgers fans disputed the merits of Allen and Barber with the same fervor they debated shortstops Phil Rizutto vs. Pee Wee Reese. Ire especially resounded from the Dodgers' side. Brooklyn had a tight-knit, almost small-town feel to it that Barber reflected with the touch of provincialism he gave his broadcasts. The Dodgers were "sittin' in the catbird seat" with a six-run lead. Duke Snider was "tearin' up the pea patch" during a long hitting streak. Managers and umpires got into "rhubarbs" over close calls. The bases weren't loaded, they were "FOB" or "full of Brooklyns." While using such phraseology, Barber, who was born in Mississippi and raised in Florida, spoke with an accent that somehow brought out both the South and Brooklyn. Allie Reynolds got Carl Furillo out on a "slidah." Game 7 of the World Series was "for the mah-bles."

Mel sounded Southern on the air, too, but to Brooklynites, his booming, easily excitable voice emanated the arrogance they felt the Yankees represented.

"Rooting for the Yankees is like rooting for U.S. Steel," movie actor Jimmy Little once told Dodgers announcer Vin Scully after a 1950s World Series game. Scully fed his friend's line to *The New York Times*' Arthur Daley, the *Journal-American*'s Frank Graham and other elite New York columnists. The comparison became commonplace. To those who didn't root for them, the Yankees were a cold corporation, run with machine-like efficiency from executive offices on Fifth Avenue. As suits operated the team from the Squibb Building, located across the street from Tiffany's and near the Plaza Hotel, the team won relentlessly in the most palatial park in baseball.

If they felt they needed another player to win the pennant, the Yankees simply bought Johnny Mize or traded for Enos Slaughter, both Hall of Famers. The Yankees just as easily discarded whomever they thought was disruptive or wasn't useful anymore: Vic Raschi (who held out for a better contract), Billy Martin (who was linked to a brawl at New York's Copacabana nightclub), Casey Stengel (who turned 70), Roger Maris (who had a sub-par season after playing with a broken hand). Even George Weiss, the general manager who orchestrated scores of ice-cold transactions over the years was eventually swallowed up by the system when Topping and Webb deemed him old and expendable. Names were replaceable as long as the team kept winning.

Brooklynites' hatred of this outwardly cold, calculating Yankees franchise grew each time Mel yelled, "Going, going, gone!" during a DiMaggio home run. Though Mel screamed loudly after every great Dodger play when Brooklyn faced the Yankees in the World Series, Brooklynites felt he praised his own team more.

There were more opportunities for Mel to do so. The Yankees won five of six Subway Series from the Dodgers between 1947 and 1956.

As the Yankees and Dodgers tussled in Game 4 of the 1947 World Series at Ebbets Field, so did the broadcasting approaches of Allen and Barber. Mel called the first half of the game, during which Bill Bevens, an otherwise-pedestrian right-hander, no-hit the Dodgers. As was his custom, Mel avoided saying that Bevens was pitching a no-hitter. Barber shunned such superstition.

"I am a broadcaster, a reporter. I deal in facts," he wrote in his 1968 book, *Rhubarb in the Catbird Seat.* "If the big fact of the game is the number of hits a pitcher has allowed, I broadcast it."

Upon taking the microphone from Mel, Barber immediately told listeners that Bevens had given up no hits.

"The breath gurgled in Allen's throat like a country boy trying to swallow a chinaberry seed," Barber wrote in *The Broadcasters.*

Bevens lost his no-hit bid with two outs in the ninth inning when Brooklyn pinch-hitter Cookie Lavagetto drove in two runs with a shot off the right field wall. With the same swing, Lavagetto also won the game for Brooklyn, 3-2, in front of the hysterical Flatbush faithful.

Fans praised Mel for his 1947 World Series performance. Yankees supporters and a couple of local radio announcers panned Barber, however, for mentioning Bevens's no-hit bid on the air. This was an era when superstition seeped from dugouts into broadcast booths and press boxes. Barber felt guilty before Game 5, so he told Bucky Harris and Bevens about revealing the no-hit bid on the air.

"It wasn't anything you said," Bevens told him. "It was those bases on balls that killed me."

Bevens had walked 10 batters in the game. Barber was fully exonerated when the Yankees won the World Series in seven games.

＊＊＊＊＊＊＊

Just before the 1948 season began, the Yankees took a train from their spring training home in St. Petersburg, Florida, to Birmingham for a barnstorming game with the minor-league Barons. As Mel stepped back onto the grounds of Rickwood Field, where he saw his first baseball game at age two, Birmingham adopted him as its "favorite son in the radio world," as *Birmingham News* sportswriter Alf Van Hoose wrote.

A day of festivities celebrated Mel's return home. As always upon his trips back to Alabama, Mel received royal treatment. Birmingham's Chamber of Commerce presented him with a gold key to the city. WBRC gave him a silver cigarette lighter. WAPI, the other radio station on which Mel's first sports broadcasts aired, lavished him with a silver tray. Mel's old buddy Coach Tommy, now serving as Alabama's athletic director, presented him with a combination record player and radio on behalf of some folks back in Tuscaloosa. Tommy assured everyone on hand that Mel "still wears the same size hat that he did when he left Birmingham 11 years ago." *The Birmingham News'* Harry Vance verified that sentiment in a column:

> I followed Mel Allen's features pretty closely throughout Monday and there was never a trace of boredom coming into his countenance. … He was back with the home folk and they were having a downright good time in honoring him. But it was pretty well evident that the fellow who had the best time in a day-long party arranged for him was Mel Allen. There was a very real buoyancy in his very being. He was glad that the home folks loved him. And there was no question about his loving the home folks. I knew as I watched Mel Monday that no matter how altitudinous the pinnacle he might climb in the future, he would always love the home folks, and he'd get a kick out of being with them.

Much like Alabama's newspapers praised him throughout his life, Mel always embraced the state of Alabama. He kept in touch with his Southern friends like Coach Tommy and speech professor T. Earle Johnson. Amid the bustle of the Yankees' season, Mel voluntarily came home to serve as master of ceremonies or in other capacities for charity sporting events. These included the East-West game, which pitted the top high school baseball players from the east and west sides of the city against one another, and University of Alabama functions.

Mel got more nervous talking to people who knew him as a youngster than he did emceeing Old Timers' Day in front of 60,000 fans at Yankee Stadium.

"What can I tell them about me that they don't already know?" he would say about Alabamians.

Mel's old collegemate, Irving Berlin Kahn, remarked in 1987 how Mel's diction could sound at times as if he didn't have a Southern accent. That is, until he came home.

"Put him in with a group of southerners," Kahn said, "and in a minute or two he goes right back to it, even now."

When Mel was inducted into the Alabama Sports Hall of Fame in 1974, he said: "Of all the great thrills that I have experienced in my long career, none can compare with the thrill of being inducted into the Alabama Sports Hall of Fame. This honor coming to me from my home people, the people I love, and those who were helpful to me along the way, makes this experience my greatest thrill of all."

After the Yankees smoked the Barons 12-1 on Mel's day in Birmingham, the party drifted to the farm of Barons vice president Al DeMent, which was located on the Cahaba River. A feast of barbecue, hush puppies, corn on the cob, sweet potatoes, buttermilk and cake awaited Mel and the visiting Yankees players and writers. As Mel cut the dessert, he thought about Julius and Anna, who had traveled to Birmingham to be with him for the occasion.

"I don't know to whom I should present the first slice of the cake," Mel said, "but I believe I'll ask Pop to come up and get it. After all, Pop is responsible for my being here."

Next to Julius, Anna also beamed. In a 1950 article for *Radio and Television Mirror* magazine, she called this day in Birmingham "among the proudest of my life, to see my boy honored by the dignitaries of cities where he grew up with only the average opportunities and advantages that every American boy has." She wrote further: "If I had never known before what a wonderful land of opportunity America is, I did then."

❖ ❖ ❖ ❖ ❖ ❖ ❖

In June 1948, Mel had an opportunity to announce the world middleweight title fight between Tony Zale and Rocky Graziano for Mutual. Mel often stayed away from boxing. Once in a while, he would drive up to The Grossinger Hotel & Country Club, a Catskill Mountain resort where boxers often trained, to cover a fighter's camp for one of his sports shows. That was usually the extent of Mel's boxing coverage. Ted Husing once advised Mel not to pick up boxing assignments unless he did them regularly, otherwise he would have trouble getting a feel for the sport.

"You can't always tell who's leading," Mel once said about boxing. "And punches which look damaging at home can be ineffectual seen at ringside. You have to interpret."

There was little to interpret with Zale-Graziano, because one of the boxers always ended up flat on the canvas. Mel couldn't resist covering the third installment of the rivalry. Zale, a rugged puncher from working-class Gary, Indiana, and Graziano, a street fighter from New York, brawled more than boxed. In their first fight at Yankee Stadium in 1946, each knocked the other down before a battered-looking Zale floored Graziano for good in the sixth with a left hook to retain the title. In their rematch less than a year later at Chicago Stadium, Graziano won the middleweight crown by shaking off a third-round knockdown and pounding Zale into the ropes for a technical knockdown in the sixth.

Mel announced the rubber match, held June 10, 1948, at Roosevelt Stadium in Newark, New Jersey. Zale, a 12-5 underdog, jumped all over Graziano from the start. Landing hard jabs as Graziano flailed and missed, Zale waited for his opening, then dropped his opponent with a left hook and right cross. In the spirit of past Zale-Graziano bloodbaths, Graziano sprung up and attacked his opponent. Both men viciously pounded on each other through the first-round bell until they were pried apart. The fighters continued to slug it out in Round 2, and in Round 3 Zale drove Graziano to the canvas with two hard lefts. After Graziano got up on a count of seven, his legs wobbling, he missed Zale with two wild rights. Zale blasted Graziano to the head with a series of savage punches, knocking him out with 1:08 left in the round.

Mel would call the fight one of the most enthralling sporting events he ever covered. The evening's drama hadn't just included a boxing match, either. Before the fighters even squared off, Mel heard a loud outburst of noise in the distance. When the sound reached a continuous roar, Mel knew a celebrity was arriving. Then Joe DiMaggio appeared.

❄ ❄ ❄ ❄ ❄ ❄ ❄

A 1948 baseball season that began for the Yankees with celebration in Birmingham ended with a disappointing third-place finish. The Yanks were the first to falter in a down-to-the-wire, three-team race with the Indians and Red Sox and finished two and a half games behind first-place Cleveland. That season, the Mutual team of Allen and Britt did both the All-Star Game at Sportsman's Park in St. Louis and the World Series between the Indians and Boston Braves.

Before the Series, Mel covered the Yankees-Red Sox season finale from Fenway Park for New York's WINS and WOR. He watched DiMaggio play that day despite a right heel injury that felt like an ice pick was stabbing him and a charley horse in his left thigh. DiMaggio couldn't even lift the left leg when he got into a cab. DiMaggio could have crippled himself in this meaningless ball-game. (The Yankees had already been eliminated from the American League pennant race.) But to DiMaggio, the game was full of purpose. His brother Dom was a member of the Red Sox, who had a shot at tying Cleveland atop the AL.

"If I stayed out of the lineup some people might interpret that as trying to help his team win," DiMaggio said.

Running on his toes and dragging his left leg, DiMaggio got four hits in the game, which Boston won 10-5.

The Yankee Clipper's heroic performance highlighted a day Mel would never forget. After the game, Mel felt a mounting fever. He saw a doctor, who put him to bed at the Massachusetts Eye and Ear Infirmary. Mel's temperature rose to 103 degrees as he nursed a heavy cold and sore throat. Like DiMaggio, he pulled himself out of bed Monday to broadcast a one-game playoff for the AL pennant between the Red Sox and Indians. After the final out, Mel returned to the hospital. The World Series was set to begin Tuesday at Boston's Braves Field. Mel had missed his next-to-last opportunity to cover the Series under circumstances he couldn't control while he was in the Army. As long as he could speak, he damn sure wasn't going to miss the 1948 Series. Mel bundled a towel around his throat and slipped on a Red Sox windbreaker and camel's hair coat. He donned a Braves cap for added warmth and headed to Braves Field in a limousine. As he worked Game 1, Mel sipped from four glasses of milk in an attempt to soothe his throat. Afterwards, the limousine returned him to his hospital bed and back and forth again for Game 2.

When the Series shifted to Cleveland, so did Mel. He coughed throughout the long train ride as he sat next to Barber, who was working on the still-experimental television side of the Series broadcast. In Cleveland, where Mel worked three more Series games, a doctor gave him penicillin shots. Mel returned to Boston for Game 6, which the Indians won behind right-hander Bob Lemon's seven and one-third strong innings to give Cleveland its first World Series title in 28 years. Still feeling ill, Mel traveled back to New York, where he was diagnosed with viral pneumonia.

"I couldn't have worked that seventh game," he wrote in a letter to a doctor who had cared for him in Boston. The pneumonia stayed with Mel for more than a month.

Gillette president J.P. Spang Jr. called Mel's Series performance "heroic." Gillette advertising manager Craig Smith told him, "Your work was superb." Wrote Mutual president Edgar Kobak in a note to Mel: "It worried me a great deal when I saw you in Boston to have you take the risk of injuring your health to do the Series. I realize how important the Series was to you, but your health comes first. You're a great trouper and you did a wonderful job and we were proud to have you on the network for the Series. But now, Mel, take good care of your health. We need you for future series and future work."

Mel wouldn't heed Kobak's advice in the future. His DiMaggio-like performance during the 1948 World Series despite a case of pneumonia was indicative of his career. Wherever he was, whatever the circumstances, he did whatever necessary to make it to his next assignment.

In 1951, while taking a train to Detroit, where he was set to do the major league All-Star Game with Al Helfer for Mutual, Mel cut up his hand opening a bottle of soda when it exploded on his lap. The train stopped at the nearest station, where a doctor was summoned. He recommended Mel check into a hospital. But Mel was determined to make his broadcast the following day, and he had the doctor apply stitches to him on the train so that he could press on.

Unlike Mel's 1948 fight with the flu, however, this incident did prompt a change in Mel's habits: after it, he preferred drinking water to soda.

CHAPTER 9

Yankee Doodle Dandy

When Horace Stoneham needed a new lead Giants broadcaster for the 1949 baseball season, he asked Mel for recommendations. "Russ Hodges," Mel said. Mel didn't want to lose his faithful partner, but he thought Hodges deserved a shot at a No. 1 job. Stoneham and Liggett & Myers tobacco scooped up Hodges, who, along with Mel and Barber, serenaded the city of New York with a trio of Southern baseball voices.

The Yankees conducted a national search for Hodges's replacement, sending out 300 letters to potential candidates. One of them reached Curt Gowdy, a kid announcer for station KOMA in Oklahoma City. Mel listened to a record of Gowdy's voice, which rolled over the airwaves steadily and harmonically, much like the wind whipped through Gowdy's home state of Wyoming. Allen and Gowdy met in person at the Yankees' Fifth Avenue offices in December 1948. "Curt," Mel said over lunch at Al Schacht's, "I'd like to have you with me and I'm pretty sure it will work out that way."

Later that day, general manager George Weiss offered Gowdy the job of assisting Mel with Yankees baseball and All-America Conference football. About as quickly as he accepted the position, Gowdy realized how far he was from Oklahoma. As KOMA's top announcer for University of Oklahoma football and Texas League baseball, he had broadcast alone. He wasn't used to bantering back and forth on the air, something Mel liked to do with Hodges. When Gowdy first started working games with Mel, he uncomfortably shook and nodded his head in response to his partner's questions. "Nobody can see you," Mel said.

When Gowdy read commercials for Ballantine beer and White Owl cigars, the Yankees' joint principal sponsors from 1947 through 1955, he sounded stiff and awkward. Meanwhile, Mel was as crisp as that first sip of Ballantine after hard day at the office: "Well, while the fans are out here takin' that stretch, it's a mighty good time for you to take a quick trip to the refrigerator for a bottle of Ballantine beer. If you're listening at your favorite tavern, don't just say, 'One up,' but be sure to ask the man for Ballantine. Enjoy the two B's, baseball and Ballantine. As you linger over that sparkling glass of Ballantine beer, as you feel it trickling down your throat, you'll say, 'Ah, man, this is the life.' Baseball and Ballantine beer. And while we're on this pleasant subject, folks, I'd like to remind you that it's a smart idea to keep plenty of Ballantine on ice at home at all times, to serve at mealtimes, to enjoy during leisure hours, so at your dealer's be sure to look for the three rings. Ask him for Ballantine beer."

Mel described a Yankees home run as a "Ballantine blast" or a "White Owl wallop." He could even work both sponsors into one call: "Folks, that ball was foul by no more than a bottle of Bal- … No, that ball was foul by the ash on a White Owl cigar!"

Between innings, Mel moved swiftly from game to commercial without changing his tone of voice: "Boy, that sure was close—a tough decision for the umpire. But you don't have a tough decision when it comes to White Owl cigars."

Though corny, Mel's plugs were extremely effective. For millions of fans, the mere sound of his voice conjured up as many images of the three interlocking rings on the label of a bottle of a Ballantine beer and thoughts of the mild flavor of a White Owl cigar as of baseball and the Yankees.

Mel coached Gowdy on how to deliver commercials with more punch. When his assistant didn't improve over a couple of months, Mel got testy. He was a perfectionist in the booth. He felt the Yankees and their legions of listeners demanded a sharp broadcast. Mel was known to throw pencils or papers when an assistant broadcaster or statistician made a mistake or wasn't paying attention.

"If I snap at you, it's just the intensity of the moment," he would say before a broadcast. "After it's over, we'll go and get a beer or a soda and forget about it."

Mel's prodding frightened and frustrated Gowdy. He had been a big fish in Oklahoma City, but in New York, he felt like a guppy. After the first game of a day-night doubleheader with the Senators in Washington, Gowdy told Yankees publicity director Red Patterson he wanted to quit. He stormed out of Griffith Stadium and went to the Shoreham Hotel to fetch his wife, Jerre.

"We're going back to Oklahoma," Gowdy told her.

"No we're not," Jerre replied. "I love it in New York."

Jerre was an Oklahoma girl who had just recently joined her husband in the Big Apple.

"What's the matter?" she said. "Mel get on you?"

"Yeah," Gowdy replied.

"Did you ever stop to think that if he didn't care for you, he wouldn't be trying to make you better?"

"You think so?"

"I know so," Jerre said. "He's very fond of you. He's told me so. Now go and apologize."

Gowdy went back to Griffith Stadium and told Mel he was sorry for his outburst. Mel grabbed his partner and bear-hugged him. The two never exchanged harsh words again.

Gowdy rededicated himself to commercials. He practiced reading them at home, at the ballpark or wherever else he had a spare moment. He eventually developed a casual style like Mel's. Mel schooled Gowdy on much more than just commercials. He taught his assistant to look for details that would help paint a robust picture of the game's atmosphere. Before he worked in New York, Gowdy thought a foul ball was just another strike. Mel had him follow the ball into the stands and describe where it landed. He made Gowdy tell listeners about the enormous shadows and blinding late-afternoon sun that tortured fielders at Yankee Stadium.

"Curt, the whole stadium is your field," Mel said, "not just the diamond."

Gowdy learned to constantly scan Yankee Stadium for broadcast color, moving his eyes from the big "Ballantine Ale and Beer" sign and Longines scoreboard beyond the right field wall to the "No Betting" sign in center to the billboard ads for Philip Morris cigarettes and Gem razor blades in left and through the triple-decked stands surrounding the rest of the field.

As he gained a keen eye for his surroundings, Gowdy saw a complimentary side of Mel. After Gowdy called a triple play as perfectly as the Yankees executed it in the field, Mel leaned over and said, "That was a great call you made. One of the best I ever heard."

As he did with Hodges, Mel recommended Gowdy for a No. 1 announcing job, pitching his partner to Red Sox owner Tom Yawkey. After two seasons with the Yankees, Gowdy left for Boston, where he spent the next 14 years before moving to NBC, for whom he would cover the network's showcase events like the World Series, the Super Bowl, the NCAA Final Four and the Rose Bowl.

More than a quarter-century after Mel served as the best man at Gowdy's wedding in 1949, the two were catching up in a Yankee Stadium dugout. A television reporter sat between them.

"He was my mentor," Gowdy told the man.

Mel poked his head into the conversation.

"Tor-mentor!" he cracked.

Gowdy smiled and said, "It was the greatest break I ever got in my life. I worked under the master."

❀ ❀ ❀ ❀ ❀ ❀ ❀

A debilitating heel injury sidelined DiMaggio for the Yankees' first 65 games of the 1949 season. In mid-June, he gingerly stepped out of bed and felt no pain. DiMaggio took batting practice until his hands bled to ready himself for a three-game series with the Red Sox. Even without their star, the Yankees had torn through April with a 10-2 record under the guidance of Casey Stengel, a lightly regarded manager who replaced Bucky Harris after Harris's team finished third in 1948. By June 28, when New York headed to Fenway Park, it led the second-place Philadelphia Athletics by four and a half games and was five games ahead of third-place Boston and Detroit.

Fenway's fans greeted DiMaggio with a standing ovation as he walked to the plate for his first at-bat of the series. DiMaggio lined a fastball from Mickey McDermott for a clean single. Up in the booth, Mel watched the ball travel over shortstop Junior Stephens's head and land safely in the outfield grass.

"Back in the lineup after 65 games, the incomparable Joe DiMaggio hits a single," he told his Yankees radio listeners. "How about that?"

In his next at-bat, DiMaggio clubbed a home run over Boston's Green Monster in left field.

"How about that! How about that! How about that!" Mel shouted in disbelief.

Over the three-game series, which the Yankees swept, DiMaggio blasted four homers and collected nine RBIs. Mel set the performance to a symphony of "How about thats!"

Several days later, Mel was broadcasting in the open-air booth at Yankee Stadium when he heard fans collectively yelling something. When Phil Rizzuto made a spectacular play at shortstop, he figured out the chant: "How about that!"

Mel had said "How about that" throughout his childhood and even uttered it several times on the air during the 1942 World Series. But while calling DiMaggio's Boston breakout, Mel had attached himself to these three simple words. "How about that," which neatly bundled wonder with excitement, became his signature call and identifying phrase to describe something extraordinary in the field, such as a colossal Mickey Mantle home run or lumbering Larry Doby's ill-fated attempt at stealing home. "How about that" banners popped up in Yankee Stadium crowds. Organizations put the expression on billboards and fliers promoting Mel's speaking engagements. A letter even made it to Mel addressed simply: "How About That! New York City."

"Performers are always looking for some sort of tag line, some identifying label," Mel said in 1956. "Many never come up with one. Here I have one and I can't honestly say how I ever started using it. It's something you can't develop by trying. It just happens."

✻ ✻ ✻ ✻ ✻ ✻ ✻

In the late 1940s, the Yankees experimented with a handful of telecasts over the pioneering DuMont Network. Television wasn't a national craze yet, but there were 1.7 million sets in the greater New York City area alone by 1950. Mel's radio broadcasts served as the audio for some of DuMont's televised Yankees games. The colorful Dizzy Dean, who made butchering the English language an art form, helped out with the other telecasts. (To Dean, a country boy from Arkansas, runners "slud" into second and were "throwed" out at third.) Mel would climb down a small ladder from his radio booth and help out Dean for a couple of innings.

Baseball was still a pre-modern game in the late 1940s and early 1950s. Fans relied on radio broadcasts and teams traveled by rail. Mel stayed at the Yankees' road hotels—such as Philadelphia's Warwick, Cleveland's Statler, Boston's Kenmore and Detroit's Book Cadillac—and hustled to make team trains on getaway days. Once aboard, he and the Yankees ate together and played cards on rides that could take 30 hours if the team was traveling to St. Louis to play the Browns.

"There was a great togetherness that you don't have now," Mel said in 1981.

During the 1946 season, Mel's first covering road games for the Yankees, DiMaggio stopped him in the lobby of Chicago's Del Prado Hotel.

"What are you doing?" DiMaggio asked.

"Uh—nothing," Mel said.

"Come on," DiMaggio said, leading him to a hotel coffee shop.

For the rest of the afternoon, DiMaggio poured out his troubles with his estranged wife, actress Dorothy Arnold, to the wide-eyed broadcaster. DiMaggio was a staunchly private man, and Mel was one of the few people he trusted with his confidence. Mel would rather die than violate it. Talking to Mel, who had that priestly, angelic air about him, could be like going to confession.

The Yankees' Dan Topping and Red Sox owner Tom Yawkey once brought him into their discussion about swinging the biggest blockbuster in baseball history: DiMaggio for Ted Williams. But Topping and Yawkey feared a fan revolt, and they nixed the proposed trade, knowing that Mel would keep it confidential.

Mel and DiMaggio shared a pinstriped kinship. They ascended to fame in New York around the same time and approached their Yankees duties with similarly unflappable earnestness. DiMaggio's famous words on his tribute day at Yankee Stadium in 1949—"I want to thank the Good Lord for making me a Yankee"—could also have come out of Mel's mouth.

During a 1951 train ride, as Mel passed DiMaggio's cabin and noticed the door was open, he popped in to say "Hello."

"Joe, when did you change your stance?" Mel said.

"I haven't changed my stance," said DiMaggio, who was mired in a slump.

From his vantage point during games, Mel could usually see the entire "5" on the back of DiMaggio's jersey as the Yankee Clipper batted. But during DiMaggio's hitting drought, Mel only noticed half of the "5."

"Well, I could be wrong because of the perspective from the press box," he said, "but I thought you moved your right foot back."

DiMaggio grumbled a response and Mel excused himself.

During the Yankees' next game, DiMaggio moved his right foot forward so Mel could see the full No. 5 again and clocked three homers.

"I got a great boot out of being able to help such a great guy," Mel said later.

Mel aided many other Yankees, too. He told Whitey Ford where to find quality suits at a great price in New York and gave rookies Yogi Berra and Spec Shea rides from Yankee Stadium to their hotel in Manhattan. Mel owned a metallic-gray Buick convertible that had red-rimmed wheels and red seats. The engine purred so softly that the young players barely knew the car was running as it made its way through Harlem and Central Park.

"We wished we could get a ride all the time," Berra says.

Mel also gave the Yankees' manager a lift. After a game in Washington, Mel noticed a frown on Stengel's face in the lobby of the Shoreham Hotel.

"What's the matter, Skipper?" Mel asked.

"They didn't tell me this was a 'blue' town," Stengel said.

Stengel had hoped to have a few belts before bed, but it was after midnight on Sunday morning and D.C.'s bars had closed.

"Skipper, don't worry about it," Mel said. "I happen to carry a fifth of scotch with me in my bag. I use it in emergencies, and this is the first emergency I've ever run into."

Mel invited the Yankees' manager to his room for a drink.

"Boy, I never saw him move that fast," Mel said later.

When the two got upstairs, Mel called for soda and ice.

"We don't have to wait on ice, do we?" Stengel asked.

The Yankees' manager downed nearly two glasses of scotch before the ice arrived as Mel sipped from his drink.

After a while, Mel looked at his watch. It was 2:30 a.m.

"We have a doubleheader this afternoon, don't we, Skipper?" he said.

"Yep," Stengel replied, pouring another drink.

Sometime after 3 a.m., Stengel polished off the last drop of the bottle and got up to leave. He spent another 15 minutes at the door jabbering to Mel in his circuitous, ambiguous, adjective-laden double talk that was affectionately known in baseball circles as "Stengelese." Stengelese was rampant with dangling participles and it lacked proper names.

"These men, if their arms are good, I think they'll give a good account of themselves because they're not what you call frightened or anything because it is a World Series," he would say. "They've already been in a World Series and have a good record. Why should you be frightened if you did go into a World Series? The only thing is, it's a question of your arm. If their arms are good, I think they'll help our club hold our own in the Series."

Stengel relied more on psychology than diction. If a Yankee was sick or injured, the manager still wanted him to suit up and sit in the dugout to give the opposition the impression he could be used as a pinch-hitter. Or Stengel might chew out Andy Carey about how he handled a play in the field with the intention of sending a message to fellow infielder Gil McDougald, who was sitting next to Carey on the bench. Mel became an expert on Stengel's mind games, and he even used one of his own on the Yankees' skipper in 1953. As Yankees players raucously played 20 Questions on their train's dining car after a 12-4 loss at Washington, Mel turned to Stengel, who was sitting across the aisle.

"To hear all this chatter, you would have thought they won today," Mel said.

The manager, already steamed over the jovial atmosphere, exploded.

"I've got some questions to ask," Stengel growled to his players. "Where are you going to be playing next year?"

The manager fumed about how the Yankees couldn't afford to get soft after winning four straight World Series titles. After the tirade, the Yankees won 20 of their next 21 games and a record fifth consecutive Series championship. And they never played 20 Questions again.

✵✵✵✵✵✵✵

Mel liked to throw parties for Stengel, Yankees players and their wives at his house in Bedford Village, New York, a Westchester County hamlet about 40 miles northeast of Yankee Stadium. Mel set up a bar and fired up a grill, which cooked steaks and corn on the cob. Anna never had these affairs catered. She made her own hors d'oeuvres and fresh tossed green salad, which she served with Italian bread. Players sang and danced to the sounds of a band as they ate and drank.

During a 1952 party, Yankees Mickey Mantle, Billy Martin and Bill Miller took out a rowboat on one of the two lakes on Mel's property and tipped it over.

"We're going to lose tomorrow, and they'll blame it on the party," Mel said.

Sure enough, Detroit's Virgil Trucks pitched a no-hitter against the Yankees the next day.

Trucks's feat against New York was an aberration. During the 19 consecutive seasons Mel was the club's broadcast voice (1946-1964), the Yankees won 15 American League pennants and 10 World Series titles. Mel's voice, which called each championship season, was considered a major part of the team, both among fans and players.

"He died with us," says Tommy Henrich, a gritty Yankees outfielder and first baseman from 1937 through 1950. "When we'd lose a ballgame, he was just as mad and downcast as the rest of us."

Henrich was one of Mel's closest friends on the Yankees. "We had an open communication," Henrich says. "Anything he wanted to say to me, he said. I did it too. If I was with him, whatever he was gonna do, I'd do it with him."

Like DiMaggio, the hard-nosed Henrich was Mel's kind of player. After he broke a toe during the 1949 season and doctors told him he would be out of action for at least a week, Henrich played the next day. Henrich always seemed to come through with decisive hits in the late innings of games. He was a .282 career hitter, but pitchers dreaded facing him as much as anyone in the AL.

Mel dubbed Henrich "Old Reliable" for his clutch hitting, playing off the name of an old Louisville & Nashville train that rolled through Birmingham. Henrich says the nickname originated when he got the game-winning hit on a getaway day in Philadelphia.

"Old Reliable Tommy Henrich," Mel said a the time. "Looks like we'll catch the train after all."

Mel invented a lineup of other nicknames for Yankees players. "Joltin' Joe" DiMaggio was always a threat to profoundly influence a game. "Man of the Hour" Hank Bauer was also dependable with his bat and glove. The "Springfield Rifle," Vic Raschi, was a hard thrower from Springfield, Massachusetts. The "Naugatuck Nugget," pitcher Spec Shea, was from Naugatuck, Connecticut. "Chief" Allie Reynolds was part Creek Indian. (After he tossed two no-hitters in 1951, Reynolds became the "Superchief.") Junkballer "Steady Eddie" Lopat wasn't a hard-thrower like Reynolds and Raschi, but he was a dependable starting pitcher nonetheless.

Players might hear Mel use his monikers while listening to his broadcasts from Yankee Stadium clubhouse before or after a game or if they took a cigarette break in the middle of one. The voice always took hold of the room, whether Mel was piped in on the radio or walking around with a microphone and calling casually to Yankees he wanted to interview.

"Hey Yogi, come here!" he shouted after the Yankees clinched the 1949 AL pennant by beating the Red Sox. "Yogi commere," he said more pointedly when Berra didn't immediately respond. Berra bashfully accepted Mel's invitation to chat.

"How'd ya feel catching Vic today?" Mel said.

"If he had to win one-nothin' he woulda done it Mel," Berra responded. "He had great stuff today."

"He really did?" Mel asked.

"Oh boy."

"You're really swingin' that bat pretty well."

"Well I'm tryin'."

"Elston Howard, come here right quick," Mel yelled to another Yankees catcher after New York beat Brooklyn in Game 7 of the 1956 World Series. "You got your second World Series homer off Don Newcombe. What'd he throw you?" he asked Howard.

"He threw me a straight changeup, Mel," Howard said.

Just like the questions Mel soft-tossed to Yankees players, whether he was covering the game locally or nationally.

"He didn't bother you, unlike some guys who go in there looking for something," Berra says. "If you played lousy or something, he never would say that. He was a good guy. Everybody like him. A hell of an announcer, too."

Instead of second-guessing Yankees players, Mel was a master of positive reinforcement.

"Yogi, I don't believe you ever had a greater World Series," Mel said to Berra in his lead-in statement to an interview after Game 7 of the 1956 World Series.

"We had a lot of respect for him," says Moose Skowron, a Yankees first baseman from 1954-62.

By the early 1960s, when the American League had expanded to the West Coast and teams traveled through the air, leaving baseball's intimate railroad era in its jet stream, Mel wasn't as close with Yankees players as he used to be. He often flew and met the team on his own from other assignments. But Yankees players still saw Mel as one of them.

"He was a true Yankee," says Johnny Blanchard, a reserve outfielder and catcher for the team from 1955 through 1965.

Says Luis Arroyo, a Yankees reliever from 1960 through 1963: "He was in the family."

This man who liked to wear a fedora and wield a microphone was a cheery, chattering constant in players' lives.

"I never socialized with Mel, I don't think any of the players did," Tony Kubek, a Yankees infielder and outfielder from 1957 through 1965, told the *Daily News* when Mel died. "But we knew he was a giant."

Says Bobby Richardson, a Yankees infielder from 1955 through 1966: "It was just like he was part of the locker room, he was part of the airplane, he was just part of the Yankees in every capacity. He was such a great broadcaster that his reputation preceded him, so that he had a celebrity about him."

✳✳✳✳✳✳✳

Millions of fans identified Mel with the Yankees' dominance.

"He's never won a ball game for the club, but you'd never know it from the number of scorecards he signs between innings," a writer from *Cue* magazine wrote in 1950.

Mel was fans' main connection to the Yankees' dynasty teams of the late 1940s through mid-1960s. That could be on 1010 WINS in New York or the dozens of other stations comprising the club's "Home of Champions" radio network, which stretched across northern and western Pennsylvania, upstate New York and New England and down into New Jersey. Or it could be at Yankee Stadium, where Mel was always the master of ceremonies for Old Timers' Day and manned the mike for the celebration day for a Yankees star like DiMaggio, Berra, Henrich or Ford.

"Since 1939 you have exemplified everything I have loved about baseball— quality, integrity and loyalty," wrote a fan from Kennebunkport, Maine, in a letter to Mel in 1964. "You have never been an announcer to me—you have been the game itself."

Wrote another man from Baldwin, New York, in a note to Mel that same year: "As long as I can remember, Mel Allen has represented not only the Yankees but a good way of life and has been sort of a public therapist at the same time. For instance, I recall driving down from Westchester on an early may afternoon some years ago and feeling out of sorts. ... I turned on the car radio and caught your broadcast of a Yankee ballgame. Suddenly, everything assumed its proper perspective. Mel Allen was doing the play-by-play and all was right with the world."

Mel thought of himself as one Yankees fan telling others about happenings with their team. Some Dodgers and Red Sox supporters claimed that they could switch on a radio and immediately tell if the Yankees were leading or trailing by Mel's sanguine or somber tones. To the objective ear, though, Mel remained rosy in describing the achievements both sides. He always said he was partisan but not prejudiced toward the Yankees. He wrote numerous syndicated articles in an attempt to fend off accusations that he showed a bias toward the Yankees over the air.

"Partisanship, I think, is all right," he would write. "It gives color and excitement to a broadcast, and it makes the hometown fans happy. To be prejudiced means you can only see one side and dislike the other side. Partisanship means you appreciate both sides, but favor one."

Mel routinely made predictions that favored other teams besides the Yankees. When the son of Yankees publicity director Red Patterson graduated from Notre Dame in 1954, a radio interviewer asked him whom he thought would win the World Series. "The Dodgers," he said. When the young Patterson was asked if someone told him that, he replied, "Mel Allen." Mel never openly rooted for his team on the air like the Pirates' Bob Prince, the Cardinals' Harry Caray or other announcers in smaller baseball towns did. "We had 'em alllll the way!" Prince would exult after a Pittsburgh win. Mel didn't call the Yankees "we" during his broadcasts. He couldn't get away with being such a homer in New York, where thousands of transients rooted for teams other than the Yankees.

"I like the New York Yankees as a team and as individuals," Mel wrote in a 1958 column. "I have been broadcasting their games for 18 years. I am definitely a Yankees fan. But when I am in front of the microphone, I am a reporter. I try to broadcast the game from a reporter's viewpoint, impartially and factually. ... Naturally, I want the Yankees to win. But I'll never color my descriptions of a game for the sake of making my team look good. I try to give the other team and players their just and accurate due, but I save my extra emotions for the Yankee side."

Mel would roar for opposing players on local broadcasts like a 1960 Yankees-Senators game that Washington's Bob Allison won with a homer off the Yankees' Art Ditmar: "Ditmar delivers and Allison swings and lines it deep to center field, it is going, going, it is gone and the ballgame is over!"

Yankees general manager George Weiss occasionally even questioned Mel as to whether he supported the Yankees enough. Mel's on-air demeanor was directly proportional to the intensity of the contest and the noise level of the crowd. He didn't like to work lightly attended games.

"I sometimes feel like a damn fool getting excited all by myself," he once said.

The Yankees received a stack of critical fan mail about Mel after a 5-1 victory over the Indians in a mundane game on a cold, dank, drab night in front of a sparse Cleveland crowd. After each Yankees base hit, Cleveland Stadium was virtually silent. Sometime after the game, Weiss called Mel into his office. "You were rooting for Cleveland," he said. Some fans thought Mel's uncharacteristically quiet on-air demeanor revealed he was upset the Yankees had won.

"Most fans are strongly partisan for one club or another and, when listening to the broadcast of a game, hear only what they wish to hear," Mel would say.

Mel's praise for the Yankees' opponents sounded even stronger on national broadcasts like the 1952 World Series between the Yankees and Dodgers.

"There's a smash … Reese grabs it! How about that play! The great Pee Wee!" he exclaimed after Dodgers shortstop Pee Wee Reese snared a liner off the bat of the Yankees' Phil Rizzuto during Game 7.

When Brooklyn's Carl Furillo hit a two-run, ninth-inning homer off the Yankees' Reynolds to tie Game 6 of the 1953 Series, Mel screamed so loudly that Yankee Stadium's switchboard lit up with calls. Some Yankees fans temporarily thought Mel was a turncoat, as they did during Game 2 of the 1958 World Series when the Braves scored seven runs against the Yankees in the bottom of the first inning and Mel yelled right along with the delighted Milwaukee fans.

"I considered it complimentary, in a way, when some folks accused me of being anti-Yankee," Mel said later. "I felt such criticism by New Yorkers proved I wasn't letting my Yankee partisanship show through."

After the 1958 Series, in which the Yankees beat the Braves in seven games, one television critic wrote: "Although Allen is on the Yankees payroll in the regular season, he was eminently fair in his comments, as he always has been in his long turn at Series broadcasting."

Many fans also recognized Mel's even-handed approach to broadcasting.

"I can't see how anyone can accuse you of favoring Yankee players on great catches, or ability at the plate, when you, more than any other announcer, is the one to give credit where credit is due," wrote one fan from Manhattan in 1955.

Wrote another man, from Derby, Connecticut, in 1961: "I'm a Red Sox fan but I want to say I think you've always given the Red Sox credit, even though from my point of view the Red Sox have made me sick year after year."

Doing network broadcasts that extended beyond the Yankees, Mel was extremely careful to be unbiased. When asked to predict the winner of the Michigan State-UCLA Rose Bowl he was set to call in 1954, Mel said, grinning: "I'm not making any predictions. I can't. But people often accuse broadcasters of being prejudiced. It just sounds that way. The team that's winning gives a man more to talk about and more to praise. But you can bet I'll be playing it straight down the middle today as always."

Even in the waning minutes of Duke's 52-0 football blowout of Pennsylvania in 1954, which Mel covered for NBC, he managed to sneak in a compliment for the beleaguered Quakers: "And the Duke Blue Devils have over-powered an inspired red-and-blue team here in the second half."

Such a level approach got Mel in trouble with a contingent of irate University of Washington fans as they watched his telecast of the Huskies' 17-7 Rose Bowl win over Minnesota in 1961. Minnesota shut out the Huskies 7-0 in the second half, and Washington fans turned off their television sets with the memory of Mel calling Minnesota highlights. Several of them signed a letter from an Everett, Washington, dentist to NBC suggesting Mel was biased toward Minnesota:

> Dear Sir:
>
> I would like to express my dissatisfaction with Mel Allen et al, regarding the coverage of the Rose Bowl Game. It was difficult to believe that the U. of Minn. was not at least five touchdowns ahead from the continuous and elaborate praise given them. It is a good thing we knew beforehand that the U. of Wash. was also playing because we may never have found out unless we had been listening very carefully.
>
> Most of us in this area watched the game in groups of 10 to 20, and speaking for our group and individuals from other groups repre-senting about 200 people, the opinion was unanimous—Mel Allen has to go! The situation was summed up nicely by one member of our group at half time when the camera was on the Minn. drum major just as he dropped his baton and the comment was, 'Did you see the sig-nificant manner in which he picked up that baton?'

A fan from Portland, Oregon, voiced similar sentiments in a letter to Gillette, the Rose Bowl's sponsor: "Minnesota didn't win; Washington did. Why continually praise the losers as though they are winners?" Wrote a male Washington rooter from Seattle: "The poorest loser seemed to be Mel Allen, and not Minnesota."

Mel explained himself in this excerpt of a letter responding to irate Washington fans:

> In the broadcasting of any sports event the atmosphere is charged with emotion, and it is only natural that people react accordingly. We never have an interest in the outcome of the game but hope only for a good game. We always respect peoples' feelings and can readily under-stand how they might place interpretations on voice inflections and innocent comment that lead to conclusions never intended. We con-stantly strive toward a neutral report, hoping to balance comments for

either side but it naturally follows that the winning team will give you more, as a rule, to talk about. On occasions, as in the Rose Bowl, the losing team provided us with the most verbal ammunition in the second half. Our statements are meant to be declarative rather than comparative. If we say something good about a team or player, we don't mean to imply that the opposite group or individual is bad. ... When emotions prevail, logic is lost.

Mel couldn't win. He often got hate mail from fans of both teams he covered. After doing a network broadcast of a Notre Dame-Oklahoma college football game in 1952, Mel received about 1,000 letters from Irish rooters criticizing him for being one-sided toward Oklahoma but got nearly the same amount of mail from Sooners fans complaining of his Notre Dame bias. He had a similar experience with a 1957 Notre Dame-SMU game, another indicator that he was doing his job.

The New York Times actually called Mel's unbiased approach "unemotional" when it named him to its "Radio Honor Roll" in 1947. Mel was the only sportscaster on a list of personalities, stations, networks and programs that, in the words of *Times* writer Jack Gould, "made a contribution which ... was fresh and distinctive."

Wrote Gould: "Mel Allen of WINS, both in his seasonal coverage of the Yankees and in giving part of the World Series play-by-play, exhibited a dispassionate and unemotional reportorial ability altogether too rare in sports announcing." Mel thanked Gould in a letter for bestowing upon him "the most wonderful honor I have ever received in radio."

❖❖❖❖❖❖❖

When the Yankees played the Red Sox in their regular-season finale on October 2, 1949, Mel felt a special obligation to his listeners over the Yankees' Home of Champions Network. New York and Boston were deadlocked atop the American League. The winner that day would advance to the World Series. The loser's season would be over.

"We have had occasion to root for the Yankees during the course of the year, a very courageous team," Mel told his audience, "but today, against another great ball club, the Boston Red Sox, we're gonna give this broadcast the treatment that we feel both teams deserve—an equal treatment all the way through as if it were a World Series. ... Permit us to cast aside our partisan feelings to bring the broadcast, the most important of the year in the American League."

Sitting beside Mel in the booth, Gowdy noticed that his partner was completely calm. Mel lived for games like this one.

"We've been so full of tension all year long, that honest to goodness today I'm just forgetting about everything," Mel told listeners. "The Yankees have done an out-of-this-world job this year and the Red Sox have just been magnificent."

Throughout the ballgame, Mel, who had publicly predicted before the season that the Red Sox would win the American League pennant, echoed a consistent refrain: "The only tough part about it all is that one of these two teams has to lose."

Mel's descriptions were colorful and tight, his calls perfectly paced with the action, his transitions from one game sequence to another flawless. His voice was in constant motion, like an infielder before a pitch is delivered. Through Mel's words, fans saw Yankees third baseman Billy Johnson shade his eyes from the sun, Raschi squeeze the rosin bag and Henrich move to guard the line at first base. Mel described everything effortlessly: "Kinder into the windup, in comes the pitch ... Henrich swings, sends a ground ball out toward second—Rizzuto will score—Doerr up with the ball, throws to Goodman, one-nothing New York!"

Henrich's first-inning RBI groundout, which followed Rizzuto's triple, gave New York a 1-0 lead, to which the Yankees clung for seven innings. Leading off the bottom of the eighth, Henrich greeted new pitcher Mel Parnell, who had relieved starter Ellis Kinder, with a solo homer that increased the Yankees' lead to 2-0 lead. Two batters later, reliever Tex Hughson induced DiMaggio to ground into a double play. But Johnny Lindell singled and, after Stengel sent Bauer in to run for him, Billy Johnson followed with another single and Hughson deliberately walked Cliff Mapes to get light-hitting second baseman Jerry Coleman. Coleman gave the Yankees a 5-0 lead with a flair down the right-field line that cleared the bases. As Red Sox right fielder Al Zarilla dove and missed Coleman's dying quail by a couple of inches, Mel's voice and the roar of 68,000 fans rose to a fever pitch: "Swung on, little looper into short right field ... Zarilla comes fast and he CAN'T GET IT! Here comes Bauer! Here comes Johnson! Here comes Mapes digging for the plate ... and Mapes scores ... !"

After Coleman was thrown out trying to take third base, Mel went over his hit from Boston's angle.

"Zarilla tried desperately for the shoestring catch!" he said. "He almost got it and he didn't quite make it!"

Mel again attempted to stay impartial during a furious ninth-inning comeback bid. With Junior Stephens on second and Ted Williams on third and one out, Bobby Doerr drove a Raschi pitch to deep right-center.

"DiMaggio racing way back, the ball is OVER his head!" Mel screamed. "And there's two runs coming in and there's Doerr racing for second—he'll go for three. It's a three-base hit for Bobby Doerr and it's a 5-2 ballgame, and only one out. ... And the Red Sox are jamming at Yankee Stadium."

Boston got as close as 5-3, but with two outs, Birdie Tebbetts, representing the potential tying run, hit a foul popup just behind first base. As the ball rose, Mel's partisan feelings spilled out over the airwaves as Coleman and Henrich both called for it: "Look out now! Look out now! Henrich says he's got it ... Tommyyyy ... has and the Yankees win the PENNANT! And we're gonna have a special broadcast for you, ladies and gentlemen. … I'm gonna go downstairs to the clubhouse right now. Curt, take over!"

Gowdy recapped the game for a few moments before the floor was Mel's again.

"Hello there everybody. We're down here—Casey!—we're down here in the clubhouse ladies and gentlemen, I want Casey Stengel to say a word after that terrific victory. Casey, how ya feel, buddy?"

"I never felt so great in all my life," said the teary-eyed Stengel, a manager with a .436 winning percentage over nine major league seasons before taking the Yankees job. "This is the greatest thing that ever happened to me since I was born."

"I want to get Phil Rizzuto," Mel continued. "Hey Phil! Hey Phil, you and Tommy come here! Here's Phil Rizzuto, the real sparkplug of the team. Phil, you and Tommy Henrich are both in line for the most valuable player award—you did a terrific job. I don't know which one of you might get it—I hope one of you do—but whichever, I'd like to give you about four awards. … "

"Give it to the whole team, Mel," Rizzuto said. "No one guy ever one this pennant for us."

Many of Mel's interviewees used his now-trademark expression to describe the game.

"How about that one!" backup catcher Charlie Silvera yelled. Others were speechless, and Mel spoke for them, the weightless manner in which he bounced from player to player capturing the room's frenzied emotion.

"And here's the guy who gave his all out of the sick bed the last few days and did a tremendous job, Joe DiMaggio … !"

"And here's the guy who has played sensational ball all year at second base and was a sparkplug today, Jerry Coleman … !"

"Eh, here's Johnny Lindell!"

"And here's the Chief, Allie Reynolds!"

Mel had a special request of his pal Henrich. "How 'bout a little song, Tommy!?" he shouted. Several Yankees howled their approval. Henrich often led impromptu, barbershop-style numbers after victories, and this day's version, long and rollicking, was like the grand finale at a concert. "How 'bout that," Mel interjected in the middle of the song, as if on cue.

Boston manager Joe McCarthy, the Yankees' former skipper, waded through the crowd to congratulate Stengel. The men embraced right in front of Mel.

"Joe, would you just say a word?" Mel said. "People love ya! Joe, they love ya in New York! … Say a word here, buddy … "

"Well, I want to congratulate Casey Stengel," McCarthy said. "I think he's done a wonderful job this summer in handling the Yankees. And I feel bad that we both couldn't win but it's one of those things and Casey, good luck in the Series."

"Thank you, Joe," Stengel said. "You win so many, it's nice for you to allow me to have one."

Mel belly-laughed. "That's very nice!" he gushed, his voice overpowering the din of victory.

"Well, just movin' around and Vic, I haven't heard you say a word," he continued, settling next to Raschi. "Here's the guy, ladies and gentlemen, that pitched the Yankees to the pennant today with his 21st victory, Vic Raschi."

"Thank you, Mel," Raschi said. "It's a real pleasure to win this one, the best victory I've ever won."

"Thanks ever so much, Vic, and I'm so happy for ya."

"Freddy Sanford, how 'bout a word?" Mel said to another Yankees pitcher.

"Boy, this is the happiest day of my life, I'll guarantee you," Sanford replied.

"I know it is, Fred, and everybody feels that way."

Just when Mel appeared to have talked to everyone in the locker room, from players to Yankees coaches to co-owner Del Webb and the Red Sox's Yawkey to Bill Corum and other sportswriters, he found someone else.

"I guess we got about everybody ... except Mr. Webb's father! This is Mr. Webb's father. ... How do you like that? Your son did a pretty good job, didn't he?"

"Yeah," the senior Webb said. "What do we know about baseball and go Yankees!"

"Thank you very much, sir," Mel said, chuckling. "That's swell of ya."

"I guess that's about all, friends," Mel said finally, beginning to sign off. "We could keep going around and around here all evening."

He made sure to squeeze in one final thought.

"It was a great ball club that lost the pennant, the Boston Red Sox, a magnificent team, one that your heart went out to in defeat—Joe McCarthy, a good personal friend of mine, as are all the Boston Red Sox players. ... " he said. "Naturally, broadcasting with a team and living with them day after day and in a season like this, you always get a little more excited for the home team. But never at any time did we ever minimize anything that the opposition ever did."

CHAPTER 10

Mel Allen Day

On August 27, 1950, the Yankees lauded another team icon in the tradition of Gehrig, Ruth and DiMaggio. Fan donations helped the club accumulate $65,000 for the occasion, and before a game with the Chicago White Sox, the Yankees showered their honoree with hundreds of gifts, including a midnight black Cadillac sedan, a television set and a rack of ties. Mel was noticeably absent from his usual role as emcee on this Saturday afternoon, Mel Allen Day at Yankee Stadium.

Julius and Anna sat among the crowd of more than 45,000. They came to Yankee Stadium often. Anna had surprised her son one morning during the previous summer's furious pennant race with Boston by asking him, "How many games are the Yankees ahead of the Red Sox now?" This was the woman who thought he played too much baseball as a boy.

Julius was an even more frantic fan. As the Red Sox mounted their last-ditch comeback bid in the ninth inning of the final game of the 1949 season, he couldn't stand to listen anymore. He grabbed his hat and went outside for a walk as Esther, who was visiting her parents, started to cry. But when the Yankees pulled the game out, she ran to front door and yelled, "You can come back in, Daddy! The Yankees have won the pennant!"

Larry was at his usual post in the broadcast booth on Mel Allen Day. He was in good spirits as he got ready to watch the Yankees hail his brother with team honors previously unprecedented for a broadcaster. Just before the day's proceedings began, however, Mel killed Larry's festive mood.

"I gotta run downstairs," Mel said. "Take over the mike."

Larry didn't know whether to laugh or cry. He had virtually no broadcasting experience. Mel had let him call an inning here and there, but the younger Allen hadn't handled a special event before.

"I was so annoyed with him," Larry says today. "I was thinking, 'What am I gonna say? What am I gonna do?' Mel did certain things like that with me. One

minute I'd think he didn't have a lot of confidence in me and the next minute
he'd make me feel like I could do anything in the world."

Mel certainly didn't favor his brother. If Larry made a mistake, Mel shouted at him as much as anybody in the booth. "He'd kill me," Larry says. When
Larry had an opportunity to join the Indians' broadcast team the next season,
Mel gave him few pointers and little billing. Mel also wanted his brother to make
it on his own.

Larry found the year with Cleveland harrowing. The Indians' expectations
were enormous and a feud among sponsors doomed the experience. Larry
returned to his job as Mel's statistician the following season of 1952, spending
the rest of his career in his brother's domineering shadow.

Larry's voice lacked the resonance of his brother's, as did most everybody's.
But like Mel, Larry had a warm, conversational on-air style, which might have
made him a fine baseball announcer in his own right had he stuck with broadcasting, even if he doesn't think so.

"I didn't have the desire," he says.

Even while frazzled on Mel Allen Day, Larry spoke in an easy, enticing
Southern drawl similar to his brother's.

"Hello there, everybody," he said to begin the Yankees' broadcast. "It's three
ring time. This is Larry Allen speaking to you for the makers of Ballantine Ale
and Beer. Mel Allen and Curt Gowdy are absent from our Ballantine booth
today as we greet all you folks out on the Home of Champions Network. You all
know today is Mel Allen Day and, of course, Mel will be down on the field as
the hour-long ceremonies in his honor begin."

Larry deftly surveyed the situation surrounding the Yankees' "four-way
fight for the pennant" with the Indians, Tigers and Red Sox, who were all within 4 1/2 or fewer games of one other. First-place Detroit had just snapped
Boston's 11-game winning streak.

"All of this calls to mind the brilliant dash the Red Sox made the last two
years, just failing to win the pennant both times—and you can never tell, this third
time may be the lucky one for them, the lucky charm," Larry told listeners.

Larry handed the airwaves to Gowdy, who introduced Master of Ceremonies
Eddie Cantor, an actor, singer, entertainer and comedian famous for his work on
Broadway, Hollywood and vaudeville. Cantor and Mel, who were friends, had just
attended an area hospital together to entertain some war veterans.

"I'm happy to be here today for Mel Allen, who is a great American, a great
sportsman and a great guy," Cantor told the crowd in his hearty New York
accent. "And besides, this is the way I could get in free … " The jests of Cantor
and the jubilance of the live music from Tommy Dorsey's band and a choral
group comprised of members of the Lambs Club, an acting fraternity to which
Mel belonged, christened the sun-splashed day with a merry mood. Before the
festivities ended, Cantor snatched a handful of Mel's gifts and ran as if trying to
heist them. For effect, a nearby guard chased him as fans shrieked.

The fans cheered even louder when another of Mel's friends, James Farley, who served as Mel Allen Day's chairman, introduced the guest of honor. Mel wore a dark sport jacket, light-colored slacks and a tie displaying images of baseball players in action. Tall and dashing at age 37, he waved to onlookers, catching the longing glance of Jeanne Williams of New York's Columbia Diamond Rings. Representing some in Mel's swooning sisterhood of female listeners, Williams presented him with a $1,000 diamond ring certificate for "The Future Mrs. Mel Allen," who wasn't yet determined. Williams, an attractive blonde woman, wore a low-cut, V-neck top and checked skirt. She had a noticeably bare ring finger.

"They couldn't get her off the field," Larry remembers. "She's in almost all the pictures."

Mel, who knew how to play to the crowd and camera, kissed Williams on the lips to the whistling delight on fans. Mel also had a special smooch for his mother, the woman treated most royally on Mel Allen Day. Farley presented her with a chest of assorted sterling silverware "that really fits a queen." Amid applause, Farley said, "Mrs. Allen, take a bow."

Meanwhile, Julius, a cigar lover, was given a humidor in which he could store a year's supply of White Owls, donated by the General Cigar Company, makers of the smoke his son made famous. Larry, always rushing around to keep up with his brother's hectic life, received a Longines watch to help him stay on schedule.

In addition to his own array of gifts, Mel received $14,000 in cash, which he used to set up scholarship funds in the names of Lou Gehrig at Columbia University and Babe Ruth at the University of Alabama. Yankee Stadium's ushers, Mel's college fraternity of Kappa Nu and Scranton, Pennsylvania's Little League announced contributions to the scholarship funds. Groups from various other outposts along the Home of Champions Network—such as Passaic, New Jersey, Buffalo and Watertown in upstate New York, Yonkers in Westchester County and New Haven, Hartford and Bridgeport in Connecticut—also contributed.

"You oughta run for office," Farley said to Mel while watching this endless parade of guests.

Mel had actually just been elected as Sports Broadcasters Association president. The organization sponsored Mel Allen Day and Jimmy Dolan, with whom Mel later worked New York Giants football games, presented him with a plaque and hailed him for "the glory that your achievements have brought to our profession." One of Mel's closest broadcasting comrades sent his own wishes via telegram:

> Realize I was next to best announcer in baseball during three years with the Yanks. May big moments of past 10 years be small compared to those of tomorrow.
>
> Russ

Mel received scores of cables with similarly warm sentiments like the ones from Hodges. Another wire arrived from the former U.S. Supreme Commander of Allied invading forces on D-Day and the current president of Columbia University:

> Columbia has appreciated your continuing interest in our varsity sports at Baker Field through the years and your many fine reports of our games. Your generous gesture on the Lou Gehrig Memorial Scholarship is new evidence of that feeling and of deep interest in real sportsmanship. The Gehrig Scholarship helps to bring to Columbia other boys with Lou Gehrig's strength of character and will to win. We shall be more than ever thankful. Columbia wishes you well.
>
> Dwight D. Eisenhower

When Eisenhower later became president of the United States, Mel served on his advisory committee on the fitness of American youth. As a member, Mel was asked to consider and evaluate government and private measures that contributed to "a happier, healthier and more completely fit American youth."

Mel worked in a similar capacity for President Kennedy. He also promoted the participation in sports among youths internationally. Another cable Mel received on Mel Allen Day came from the Israeli government. It commended him for his involvement with Children to Palestine, a Christian-Jewish committee dedicated to helping young Jewish refugees in the brand new state of Israel. As a volunteer for the organization, Mel appealed for sports equipment for these children.

As he was saluted at Yankee Stadium's home plate, Mel thought about the many times he assumed the same spot while fans paid tribute other Yankees heroes.

"I was thrilled to the very marrow at just being able to stand here and introduce them and be behind them," he said in an approximately eight-minute speech to fans. "That was a lot of fun but standing here with the shoe on the other foot, I feel quite overwhelmed. My heart is really filled to overflowing with sincere appreciation for how nice and generous you people are and always have been. Having come from another part of the country in the South to take residence here, it only proves what wonderful neighbors and what wonderful, warmhearted people there are in this part of the country. I shall always be grateful for it."

During his speech, Mel shared the story of his 1940 encounter with Lou Gehrig in the Yankees dugout, when Gehrig mentioned how uplifting Yankees broadcasts were to a dying man.

"I've never forgotten that and that's why I'm proud that today, we're able in some small measure on behalf of you fans, who have made it all possible, to pay this bit of a tribute to Lou Gehrig," Mel said. Fans responded with a rousing hand.

Mel devoted most of his speech to recognizing individuals he felt made his career possible and enjoyable, such as "Mr. Ed Barrow" ("under whom I broke in in the ballparks") and "Mr. Dan Topping," "Mr. Del Webb" and "Mr. George Weiss" ("who have been so cooperative and helpful and generous"). Mel also thanked "Mr. Horace Stoneham," "Mr. Craig Smith of Gillette" and his old mentor, Frank Thomas, "who sort of gave me my start." He praised partners Joe Bolton, Arch McDonald, J.C. Flippen, Connie Desmond ("one of the happiest associations I've ever had"), Hodges ("one of the greatest guys that ever worked behind a microphone"), Gowdy ("one of the finest fellows I've ever had to associate with on any broadcast") and "good ol' Diz," Dizzy Dean. He acknowledged the hard work of brother Larry and WINS engineer Al Werner. He thanked *Birmingham News* sports editor Zipp Newman, another proponent of Mel's broadcasting work in the earliest stages of his career, for making the long trek from Alabama. He saluted the Sports Broadcasters Association and sponsors White Owl and Ballantine for their warm relations and commended Farley, Cantor, Dorsey and Dick Contino, the renowned accordionist who also played on his day, for their assistance.

For a final gesture of homage, Mel turned to Julius and Anna. "Without them," he said as his voice cracked with emotion, "I could never enjoy such a wonderful day. Mom and Dad, thanks."

Mel composed himself and went on with his speech.

"Someday when I'm old," he said in conclusion, "perhaps have a grandchild, have him sitting on my knee, and maybe point to some of these pictures in a scrapbook … I'll show him what a great day—the proudest day of my life—that I've had. And about all I'll be able to say to him is, 'How 'bout that.'"

The crowd gave Mel a long, lasting ovation. He embraced his parents, then went up to the broadcast booth to call the game with the White Sox. Fittingly, Tommy Henrich delivered a pinch-hit, 10th-inning, bases-loaded smash that one-hopped the wall to score DiMaggio and give the Yankees a 2-1 win. Hobbling on a bad knee, Henrich was reduced to a backup role in 1950, his final major league season. But on Mel Allen Day, he had played "Old Reliable" for his pal one last time.

❈ ❈ ❈ ❈ ❈ ❈

Mel had united Alabamans behind their football team as a college student and enlivened Allied troops as a serviceman. But his most unifying broadcasting role involved the national pastime.

"If you listened to Mel Allen … you knew that you were hearing baseball at its finest," Bob Wolff, the former voice of the Washington Senators and NBC's *Game of the Week*, said while attending Mel's funeral in 1996. "It didn't become baseball unless Mel was there at the microphone. For years and years, he personified everything that was good about the sport. And the fact that right now, you remember that voice so distinctly, it brings back all those happy days when baseball was really a sport you admired in every sense."

During Gillette's long association with the World Series, which began in 1939, the company, with the blessing of baseball's commissioner, routinely used the senior announcer for each participating team to broadcast the games. As the Yankees qualified for baseball's championship round almost annually in the late 1940s through mid-1960s, Mel became a mainstay in America's living rooms. He called a combined 20 World Series and 24 major league All-Star Games for radio and television.

"In my neighborhood, growing up in St. Louis, it wasn't even October until we heard that great voice of Mel Allen from Yankee Stadium," says Joe Garagiola, who would take Mel's spot on the Yankees broadcasting team in 1964.

Mel received fan letters addressed to "Mel Allen, The Voice of Baseball." He narrated baseball documentaries and All-Star Game and World Series preview shows and highlight reels. He recorded a reading of "Casey at the Bat" for Simon & Schuster's Golden Records and made radio and live appearances to read Ernest L. Thayer's poem. (As dramatically as he paused to say, "Three and two, what'll he do?" during a ballgame, Mel hushed at the poem's denouement before uttering, sadly, "mighty Casey has struck out.")

Mel supplied the audio for a television commercial pitching Transogram Co.'s "Roger Maris Home Run Trainer," a batting device for youngsters bearing the name of the Yankees outfielder who hit a then-record 61 homers in 1961. (Retail price: $3.98.)

"Mel Allen's Baseball Game," packaged in a record sheath showing off a picture of Mel at a microphone, sold in major league parks for $1.98. "Mel calls the plays, you play the game," maker RCA Victor advertised on the toy's cover. As with actual major league baseball, the action flowed through Mel's voice. Grooves on a two-sided record contained dozens of Mel's calls, which arbitrarily determined the fates of lineups children dreamed up. The recordings of Mel weren't from actual games, but they contained his well-known lines like, "How about that," "Going ... going ... gone," and "Around comes the right arm."

"How about that" and "Going ... going ... gone" were American idioms, due, in part, to Mel's vast national exposure. During the 1950 World Series, in which the Yankees swept the Phillies, Mel and Philadelphia announcer Gene Kelly's broadcast reached close to 100 million listeners in the United States, Canada, Latin America and overseas via Mutual and Armed Forces Radio. The audience for the 1951 Series, which Mel also called for Mutual, following the Yankees' six-game win over the Giants with Al Helfer, was an estimated 170 million, the dramatic rise a result of an exploding television industry.

The number of owners of TV sets in the American homes had increased from approximately 325,000 to 13 million between 1948 and 1951. Beginning in 1951, the Yankees began to broadcast games over television station WPIX ("Channel 11" to New Yorkers), an association that would last 47 years. Art Gleeson, who called Oakland (California) Oaks games when Casey Stengel led the team to the Pacific Coast League title in 1948, helped Mel broadcast over

WPIX and the Home of Champions Network. The next season, Bill Crowley, better known for his work with the Red Sox later in the decade, joined Mel and Gleeson in the booth. In hopes of jazzing up its early-1950s telecasts, WPIX used Joe DiMaggio and movie actor Joe E. Brown to host pre- and postgame shows. Both men were short-lived experiments. DiMaggio, so graceful as a center fielder, appeared as stiff as a board before the camera.

Mel broadcast his first World Series for television in 1952, partnering with Barber over NBC as the Yankees played Brooklyn in the Series for the third time in six years. Allen and Barber had called each of those Subway Series together for Mutual, the latter coming in 1949 when the Yankees dumped the Dodgers in five games. Research organization J.A. Ward, Inc., reported in 1952 that 31 million American homes contained a television set, radio receiver, or both, and that more than 49 percent of the TV households tuned in to the World Series.

Americans saw the words "A Gillette Cavalcade of Sports Presentation" on their TV screens and heard the NBC program's catchy jingle. *Dun ... dun ... dun ... dun dun dun dun dun ... dun ... dun ... dun ... dun dun dun dun dun ...* Allen and Barber appeared in black and white wearing smiles and dress hats. The announcers worked merrily along with Sharpie the parrot, Gillette's animated animal who debuted on the 1952 Series. "How are ya fixed for blades?" was the musical refrain during Gillette's commercials. "Better check!" Sharpie squawked. Mel and Barber then told viewers that a Gillette dispenser holding 20 blades cost just 98 cents.

Though effusive Allen and reticent Red had broadcasting styles that resisted one another, the announcers proved in 1952 how harmoniously they could work together. Like an alto complementing a soprano and vice versa, Allen and Barber, who each did half of the innings, harmoniously conveyed the drama of the seven-game series. While Red tactfully told listeners how Game 7 was "just as tight as a brand new pair of shoes on a rainy day," Mel boomed, "It's fairly cool today—it's topcoat weather. But you could be sure—as far as those men on the diamond are concerned, it's mighty hot."

NBC showed the 1952 World Series from a camera angle above and behind home plate. A magic technology Mel called "superimposition" displayed a split screen of the pitcher and first basemen holding on base runners. As the camera jerked through the collection of men in hats and business suits in the Ebbets Field stands or zeroed in for a fuzzy shot of Yankees owners Topping and Webb in their field box, it could easily make its audience dizzy.

Viewers often saw the picture much more clearly while listening to Mel. His voice had a charisma that the insipid early days of sports broadcasting before him, when mundane, matter-of-fact accounts were the norm, had lacked.

"Tension, as they lean forward, occasionally moving around, shifting positions, slapping hands together," Mel said as the camera found Stengel and other Yankees players crouching on the bench during Game 7. "No more baseball after today. This is it ... EVERY pitch is it."

As batters, who wore just their caps without helmets at the plate, stepped out of the box or pitchers shook off signs from their catchers, Mel gave rapid-fire summaries of the game: "Two balls, one strike, two down, last of the fifth, two-two the score."

When the action resumed, he gripped his large desk microphone tightly and held it close to his chest. He made calls precisely as the action unfolded and a split-second before the crowd erupted: "There's a line drive—grabbed by Rizzuto for the out!"

Because Barber's voice wasn't as clamorous and commanding as Mel's, the Ol' Redhead relied on a quick, decisive delivery and melodious, song-like tone. After Roy Campanella grounded weakly back to pitcher Eddie Lopat in the second inning of Game 7, Barber said, "No powah the-yah. Nubbah to mound."

Barber said the words sardonically, because the 1952 Series was actually a showcase of power. The Yankees and Dodgers combined for 16 home runs. Snider smacked two solo blasts in Game 6, but the Yankees' big bats neutralized him. Introduced as "Lar-ry Ber-ra" in the crackling baritone voice of Ebbets Field public address announcer Tex Rickart, Lawrence Peter "Yogi" Berra hit a ball over the Schaefer beer scoreboard in right field in the seventh inning. Mickey Mantle hit another solo homer, this one into the left-center field stands, in the eighth to carry the Yankees to a 3-2 victory.

Mantle, batting third in the lineup in his first full season with the Yankees, had replaced the just-retired DiMaggio as the team's regular center fielder. The year before, the zinc miner's kid from Oklahoma wowed at spring training camp in Phoenix (the Yankees had swapped spring sites with the Giants) as an unproven phenom. "That boy hits balls over buildings!" Stengel raved.

Mel believed it in Game 7 of the 1952 Series when Mantle crushed a 3-1 pitch from the Dodgers' Joe Black for a solo home run in the top of the sixth inning. Mel was at the microphone: "There's a fly ball out to right field that ball is going, going, it is gone! And the Yankees are back out in front 3-2 in the battle of the home runs." The ball landed across Bedford Avenue, which ran beyond the wall. Young Mantle, who hit .345 in the Series, struck again in the seventh inning when he turned around to bat right-handed against Dodgers left-hander Preacher Roe. He rapped an RBI single to give the Yankees their winning margin of 4-2. "The magnificent Mickey, just 20 years old, drives in his second run—his fifth in the series—and his 10th base hit," Mel told listeners.

In the bottom of the seventh, second baseman Billy Martin's game-saving play gave Mel another chance at a memorable call. With the bases loaded and two outs, Stengel, operating on one of his inexplicable yet ultimately successful hunches, kept left-hander Bob Kuzava in the game to face right-handed hitting slugger Jackie Robinson. Robinson worked Kuzava to a full count.

As Kuzava delivered his payoff pitch, Mel crouched to make his call: "It's a high popup—who's gonna get it? Here comes Billy Martin digging hard and he makes the catch at the last second! How about that?!"

Blinded by the sun, Yankees first baseman Joe Collins had lost the ball as it hung in the air between first and second base. While the wind blew it toward the pitcher's mound, Mel's voice traveled with Martin. The Southern sound jumped to a higher volume as the second baseman lunged forward to make a knee-high, last-second basket catch in the webbing of his glove.

The Dodgers didn't threaten again. Brooklyn fans' blood boiled as they heard Mel call captain Pee Wee Reese's flyout to the Yankees' Gene Woodling to end the game: "There's a fly ball hit out to left field … Woodling getting under it … and the Yankees are champions! And look at Berra—piggyback riding Bob Kuzava! The Yankees, for the fourth consecutive time—and boy they're pounding Kuzava for a tremendous relief job. Look at 'em go! They've always won the big one, and again they did it. … "

✺ ✺ ✺ ✺ ✺ ✺ ✺

Nineteen fifty-two marked the last year Red Barber called a World Series. After the Yankees dispensed the Dodgers in Game 7, Gillette paid him and Mel $1,400 each, its customary $200 a game. Barber steamed as he looked at his check.

"In television, that is peanuts," he wrote in *Rhubarb in the Catbird Seat*. "And for televising the biggest sporting event in the world—not for one day but for seven—it was worse than peanuts."

Barber vowed that if the Dodgers qualified for the 1953 World Series, he wouldn't broadcast it unless he could negotiate his own contract. Sure enough, when Gillette informed the Ol' Redhead that he and Mel were NBC's announcers for the 1953 Yankees-Dodgers Series, which had a potential audience of 75 million people for a single game over a TV network that stretched to 105 stations in 100 cities, Barber asked to negotiate his fee. Craig Smith, the company's esteemed, all-powerful advertising director, was aghast. Nobody crossed Craig Smith.

"You will get the same as you got last year," Smith said to Barber through an intermediary. "Take it or leave it."

Barber left it, and Gillette gave the vacant announcing slot on the 1953 Series team to Vin Scully, Barber's young Dodgers assistant.

While Barber brimmed at the pinnacle of his career during the 1952 World Series, his national notoriety began to dim after his dispute with Gillette and further flamed out after a spat with the Dodgers. Meanwhile, Mel's celebrity, which had likewise risen to a meteoric level, radiated across the country for the next 10-plus years.

Mel was America's pre-eminent baseball and college football announcer, his voice resounding from the World Series, the Rose Bowl and weekly scholastic football sites from every section of the country. He was a mainstay as a color commentator for horse racing's Triple Crown—the Kentucky Derby, the Preakness and the Belmont—as he described the races and worked the winner's circles interviewing victorious trainers, jockeys and owners for television and radio.

Mel appeared in movie theaters across the country as the voice of sports shorts for Fox Movietone News. (Mel narrated over 2,000 newsreels during his career.) He popped up all over television and radio and in newspapers and magazines as he pitched beer, cigarettes, razor blades, oatmeal, cars, soap, gasoline, lip balm and more in commercials and advertisements.

"Show 'em, Whitey; wash, lather—a Gillette Super-Speed razor that matches the face," Mel said to Whitey Ford in one commercial as the pair stood by a mirror and the pitcher fastidiously shaved.

In another televised ad, Elston Howard whistled after an inning-inning ending play. Almost preposterously, Mel, clad in a suit, walked into the picture to meet him at home plate.

"Now I have a chance to tell you about those quick, clean shaves. Easy too," Howard said to Mel.

"That's what they all say, Ellie: Quick, easy, clean," Mel replied, paternally clutching the catcher's arm as they walked toward the dugout. "And those Super Blue blades are double-edged for economy, too."

"Mel, I'll see you in the clubhouse real soon," Howard said. "You'll get a bang out of the way the rest of the fellows shave."

Handsome and stylish, Mel was a natural on television. He anchored numerous programs that were seen around the country, including CBS' White Owl-sponsored *Sports Spot*, which ran Wednesday evenings after the network's *Pabst Blue Ribbon Bouts* boxing broadcast. Mel reviewed hot issues in the sporting world and interviewed celebrities from former heavyweight boxing champion Joe Louis to Giants center field sensation Willie Mays to Henry Cabot Lodge Jr., the grandson of the famous American statesman who became a Republican Senator from Massachusetts, a U.S. ambassador, and a vice presidential candidate. White Owl also sponsored *Call the Play*, a program on which Mel showed game footage and asked Americans to try to outguess the decisions of professional managers and coaches for a shot at a $100 U.S. Savings Bond.

On national radio, Mel did sports commentary for NBC's *Weekend* news show and handled his own sports programs several times a week during baseball's off-season. These included NBC's *Sports Daily*, a roundup show, and ABC's *Mel Allen's Sports Report*, on which Mel called sportscasters in a round-robin style.

As Mel met some of these colleagues in press boxes across the country, they closely inspected his football spotting board, which he used to identify players, and measured his tiny baseball scorecard for secrets. The six-by-nine-inch scorecard was ideal for Mel. He had 20-20 vision. Mel also scored simply—for example, a hit was "H," a hit to right field was "H9." But as other announcers tried

HOW ABOUT THAT!
The Life of Mel Allen

Melvin Israel was born
on February 14, 1913,
in Birmingham, Alabama.
He is approximately two
years old in this picture.

Photo courtesy of the Mel Allen estate

A youthful Mel Israel
(top row, third from
the left) joins his
fraternity brothers
on the steps of the
Kappa Nu house at
the University of
Alabama in
Tuscaloosa. Mel
entered the
University in 1928
when he was 15
years old.

*Photo courtesy of
the Mel Allen estate*

Main Street in Cordova, Alabama, in August 2003. Allen's father, Julius Israel, ran a general store here in the 1920s.

Photo by Stephen Borelli

In August 2003, Larry Allen observes the view of Main Street in Cordova, Alabama, near the approximate spot where his family's general store once stood.

Photo by Stephen Borelli

HOW ABOUT THAT!
The Life of Mel Allen

Now going by the name Mel Allen, he clowns around with other CBS staff announcers in New York in the late 1930s. Allen is on the far right.

Photo courtesy of the Mel Allen estate

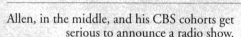

Allen, in the middle, and his CBS cohorts get serious to announce a radio show.

Photo courtesy of the Mel Allen estate

Allen began broadcasting New York Yankees and New York Giants baseball games over CBS flagship radio station WABC in 1939.

Photo courtesy of the Mel Allen estate

Allen served in World War II from September 1943 through January 1946. He rose to a rank of staff sergeant in the infantry and worked for the Armed Forces Radio Service.

Photo courtesy of the Mel Allen estate

Allen interviews a U.S. soldier for NBC's *Army Hour* during World War II. The show highlighted weapons and equipment in an attempt to boost Americans' support and enlistment numbers for the war.

Photo courtesy of the Mel Allen estate

HOW ABOUT THAT!
The Life of Mel Allen

Allen takes a break from Army duty to play a familiar game.

Photo courtesy of the Mel Allen estate

Allen poses for a publicity photo after he returned to the Yankees from Army service in World War II.

Photo courtesy of the Mel Allen estate

The New York Times once described Allen and Red Barber, respectively, as fire and ice. "Barber was white wine, crepes suzette and bluegrass music," baseball broadcast historian Curt Smith says. "Mel Allen, hot dogs, beer—Ballantine naturally—and the United States Marine band." The two called the World Series together for both the Mutual Broadcasting System and NBC.

Photo courtesy of the Mel Allen estate

Allen teamed with Russ Hodges, second from left, on Yankees broadcasts from 1946 through 1948 before Hodges became famous as the voice of the New York baseball Giants. "He was such a wonderful guy to work with," Allen said. Allen's brother, Larry, their statistician, is at left in this spring training photo from St. Petersburg, Florida.

Photo courtesy of the Mel Allen estate

HOW ABOUT THAT!
The Life of Mel Allen

Allen, (center) in a light-colored suit, and Cardinal Francis Spellman, to Allen's left, listen to the Babe speak on Babe Ruth Day, April 27, 1947, at Yankee Stadium. Allen was the day's master of ceremonies.

Photo courtesy of the Mel Allen estate

New York's Tobias and Lewis Music Co. dedicated a song entitled "Babe" to Babe Ruth in 1947. Ruth gave this copy of the sheet music to Allen and wrote a message on it toward the middle of the page. "To My Pal Mel Allen," Ruth penned, "From Babe Ruth." The pair got to know one another in 1946 and 1947 as Allen escorted Ruth to functions, where he introduced the Bambino to adoring fans.

Photo courtesy of the Mel Allen estate

Allen introduced Ruth one last time during the celebration of Yankee Stadium's silver anniversary on June 13, 1948. The Yankees also retired Ruth's No. 3 that day as they honored their 1923 team that inaugurated "the House that Ruth Built." When Allen asked the Babe if he wanted to say a few words to the fans, Ruth replied, "I must" in a raspy voice ravaged by throat cancer. Ruth died about two months later.

Photo courtesy of the Mel Allen estate

Allen partnered with Curt Gowdy, left, on Yankees broadcasts in 1949 and 1950 before Gowdy become the voice of the Red Sox. Allen took Gowdy under his wing and schooled him in big-league announcing. "Where would I be without Mel Allen?" Gowdy says. "I don't know. Maybe a fishing guide in my native Wyoming."

Photo courtesy of the Mel Allen estate

Julius and Anna Israel join their son, Mel, at a 1940s game at Yankee Stadium. Allen lived with his parents much of his life, caring for them both until their deaths.

Photo courtesy of the Mel Allen estate

HOW ABOUT THAT!
The Life of Mel Allen

Allen watches Boston Red Sox manager Joe McCarthy congratulate Yankees manager Casey Stengel after New York defeated Boston 5-3 in a winner-take-all game to decide the American League pennant on October 2, 1949.

Photo courtesy of the Mel Allen estate

Allen called Frank Thomas, left, "the greatest friend I ever had." The famed University of Alabama football coach helped get him his first job in broadcasting. In this photo, "Coach Tommy," once a pudgy man but now ill and frail with heart problems, accepts a check from Allen for the Babe Ruth Scholarship fund Allen set up at Alabama with money he received from Mel Allen Day.

Photo courtesy of the Mel Allen estate

Allen is joined by, from right to left, big band musician Tommy Dorsey, actor/comedian Eddie Cantor and Jeanne Williams from Columbia Diamond Rings on "Mel Allen Day" at Yankee Stadium on August 27, 1950. Williams presented Allen with a certificate good for a diamond ring for "the future Mrs. Mel Allen." Allen never redeemed the certificate.

Photo courtesy of the Mel Allen estate

Allen moved into this Colonial-style, 10-room house in Bedford Village, New York, in 1951 and lived here with his parents until his mother died in 1965. The house is located in Westchester County approximately 40 miles northeast of Yankee Stadium. Edward R. Murrow visited Allen and his family here in 1957 for a segment of his CBS celebrity interview television show, *Person to Person*.

Photo by Stephen Borelli

Allen used his Bedford Village house as a retreat from the bustle of New York City. "The minute I open the door, everything seems calm and serene," he wrote in an article for *Perfect Home* magazine in 1960.

Photo by Stephen Borelli

The Bedford Village house sat on 18 wooded acres and had two brook-fed lakes behind it. Allen's father loved to fish for the bass, perch, trout and bullheads that swam in the lakes.

Photo by Stephen Borelli

HOW ABOUT THAT!
The Life of Mel Allen

Allen detailed the mammoth home runs and 1956 Triple Crown season of Mickey Mantle. "He was the most exciting player since Ruth and DiMaggio, a big-leaguer in every way," Allen said.

Photo courtesy of the Mel Allen estate

Allen hosted a 1950s CBS television show called *White Owl Sports Spot*, which followed the network's coverage of Wednesday night boxing matches and featured celebrity sports guests. Here Allen interviews Hall of Fame golfer Sam Snead.

Photo courtesy of the Mel Allen estate

Allen often dazzled at the annual writers baseball game at the Bear Mountain Inn, located on the Hudson River about an hour's drive north of New York City. "He was by far the most feared hitter of our group," late *New York Times* sportswriter Leonard Koppett said.

Photo courtesy of the Mel Allen estate

Heavyweight champion Rocky Marciano officiated Allen's coronation as "king" of the 1955 winter sports carnival at The Grossinger Hotel & Country Club in the Catskill Mountains. Boxers often trained at Grossinger's, which celebrities frequented.

Photo courtesy of the Mel Allen estate

HOW ABOUT THAT!
The Life of Mel Allen

Among Allen's most avid admirers were women and boys. Both waited for him in droves at the Yankee Stadium press gate. Here he takes time to sign autographs for some boy scouts.

Photo courtesy of the Mel Allen estate

Allen said he was proud to serve on President John F. Kennedy's Citizens Advisory Committee on Fitness of American Youth. When the President was assassinated in 1963, Allen read a five-minute radio tribute to Kennedy for NBC, praising the President's sportsmanship. "I still thrill to a long run, a solid block or a good tackle," Allen quoted Kennedy as saying. "I'm like a lot of other Americans who never quite made the team but loved the game."

Photo courtesy of the Mel Allen estate

"If you played lousy or something, he never would say that," Yogi Berra says of Allen. "He was a good guy—everybody liked him. A hell of an announcer, too. And he praised the other guys even on the other team, too."

Allen and a delegation of major league stars including Stan Musial, Hank Aaron, Joe Torre, Harmon Killebrew and Brooks Robinson visited American troops in remote outposts in wartime Vietnam in November 1966. Here, President Lyndon Johnson congratulates Allen at the White House upon the delegation's return.

HOW ABOUT THAT!
The Life of Mel Allen

Allen was one of the hosts of NBC's off-the-wall weekend news radio show, *Monitor*, during the 1960s. "Today marks the date—117 years ago—that Florida was admitted to the Union," Mel said during a 1962 show. "The date: March 3, 1845. And the sun has been shining there most of the time ever since."

Photo courtesy of the Mel Allen estate

Allen and Mantle broadcast some SportsChannel Yankees cable telecasts together in the mid-1980s. After a previous Yankees regime dismissed Allen in 1964, George Steinbrenner brought him back in the late 1970s and 1980s to do Yankees cable games.

Photo courtesy of the Mel Allen estate

HOW ABOUT THAT!
The Life of Mel Allen

This is the face of Mel Allen that a new generation of baseball fans got to know as the jovial host of the television show, *This Week in Baseball*.

Photo courtesy of Phoenix Communications

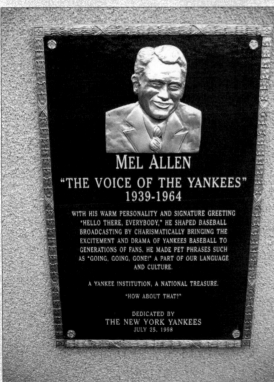

MEL ALLEN
"THE VOICE OF THE YANKEES"
1939-1964

WITH HIS WARM PERSONALITY AND SIGNATURE GREETING
"HELLO THERE, EVERYBODY," HE SHAPED BASEBALL
BROADCASTING BY CHARISMATICALLY BRINGING THE
EXCITEMENT AND DRAMA OF YANKEES BASEBALL TO
GENERATIONS OF FANS. HE MADE PET PHRASES SUCH
AS "GOING, GOING, GONE!" A PART OF OUR LANGUAGE
AND CULTURE.

A YANKEE INSTITUTION, A NATIONAL TREASURE.

"HOW ABOUT THAT?"

DEDICATED BY
THE NEW YORK YANKEES
JULY 25, 1998

Allen joined Yankees immortality on July 25, 1998, when his plaque was dedicated in Monument Park at Yankee Stadium.

Photo courtesy of Christopher Campbell

to use a scorecard the size of Mel's, they squinted to read their own handwriting. When they gave up on scoring Mel's way, they checked his microphone for magic dust.

This was a man who was billed in advertisements promoting his appearances as "America's No. 1 sportscaster." Walter Winchell, the nation's most famous columnist who wrote for the *New York Daily Mirror* and was syndicated to papers across the country, called Mel "tops in sports reporting."

Look magazine, in its second lengthy profile of him, pegged Mel as "the most famous voice in baseball—and probably in all of sports."

Mel backed up such statements by winning hundreds of sportscasting awards. He annually racked up top honors from in the major "best sportscaster" polls, included ones conducted by the Radio and Television Academy of Arts & Sciences (from whom Mel received a "Michael," equivalent to the movies' Academy Award, for sports telecasting and announcing) and publications like *Look, TV Radio Mirror, Radio Daily/Television Daily* and *Fame* magazine.

Mel graced the glossy pages of *Fame* 14 consecutive times as he was honored for its award, which *Motion Picture Daily* and *Television Today* chose by polling U.S. television editors, critics and columnists. In 1961, that same panel chose Mel as one of the top moneymakers in the television business. Its other honorees included Perry Como, Dinah Shore, Garry Moore, Carol Burnett, Alfred Hitchcock and Hugh Downs.

Drifting in such celebrity circles had been commonplace for Mel for quite some time. In the late 1940s, he and Como appealed to Americans over NBC's airwaves for a March of Dimes campaign against infantile paralysis and worked together on the *Chesterfield Supper Club*, an NBC radio show. On this program, Mel read Chesterfield cigarette commercials and introduced Como's sweet swing music. In 1947, Mel called part of a Yankees game with similarly famous singer and actor.

"There's two outs, there's men on first and third and Joe Page is pitching to Ted Williams in the first half of the sixth inning ... the Red Sox leading four to nothing," Bing Crosby told listeners over the Home of Champions Network. "Ted stands up there with that wide stance, steady, calm, cool, collected, flexes that big mace and here's the pitch to him ..."

"Bing is here, incidentally, friends, with owner Del Webb of the Yankees," Mel chimed in after Williams flew out, "and they're very good friends ... "

Bing and Mel sounded like they were old pals, too. Like Mel, Crosby had an easy delivery and stored a wealth of baseball knowledge. Mel suggested to Crosby, a part owner of the Pittsburgh Pirates, that he could play Joe DiMaggio and Bob Hope portray Joe's ball playing brother Dominic in an upcoming movie.

Mel was also buddies with Hope. The two hosted a charity golf match together in Washington, D.C., and would run into one another at the Rose Bowl and Kentucky Derby. Once while sitting near Hope on a flight back to New York from Louisville, Kentucky, Mel witnessed his friend perform one of his famous monologues right in the aisle.

"He had the whole plane jumping," Mel said years later as his eyes brightened.

On a train back to New York from the Rose Bowl, Mel had another Hollywood moment. He walked past a celebrated actor and grinned, continuing on his way.

"Hey Mel? What's a matter!" John Wayne barked. "Come here. Don't you speak to people?"

In 1959, Mel interviewed Wayne on the air between games of a Yankees doubleheader about the actor's new movie, *The Horse Soldiers*.

"You find 'em to be just ordinary guys," Mel once said of his relationships with show business stars. "They were just wonderful people. And they wanted to talk about sports."

So did politicians. In between games of a 1958 doubleheader, Mel conducted an impromptu, 10-minute television interview with vice president Richard Nixon, who attended the Yankees-Senators games with his wife and children. Mel and Nixon discussed the vice president's recent South American trip and the prospect of major league teams touring Latin America.

Mel's heart usually pounded as he met these celebrities and public figures. "I couldn't call him 'Jimmy,'" he said about meeting actor James Cagney.

But Mel was calm and composed, even lighthearted, when he chatted with them. While umpiring a 1955 celebrity softball game at Yankee Stadium, he permitted Eddie Arcaro, a Triple Crown-winning jockey aboard both Whirlaway and Citation, to swing and miss at a half-dozen balls.

"He fouled it—anyway I want to see *him* run," Mel declared after each Arcaro whiff.

Mel sat and smiled cheerfully as the Friars Club "roasted" him in 1952 and the Lambs Club "lambasted" him in 1964 in the traditional rite of membership in the esteemed acting brotherhoods. Jack Benny, born on the same day as Mel, though 19 years earlier in 1894, playfully chided him with the Friars, while actor Jack Waldron led the The Lambs' lashing.

"This boy can really talk and if we could ever bandage his jaw we'd have another Boulder Dam," Waldron said.

Mel's stardom stretched much further than that of most athletes'. He was one of the nation's most coveted speakers on the lecture circuit and he had a Madison Avenue agent, Dick Rubin, to help him negotiate his swarm of radio and television assignment requests. He also received an Academy Awards vote because of his Movietone News work for 20th Century Fox.

The Music Corporation of America figured Mel's good looks and charming voice would help him go far in Hollywood and wanted to find him a movie contract. Mel turned that offer down, too.

"I'm not an actor," Mel told his family. "I might get away with playing a priest or something. But I could go out there and starve and give up the thing I love."

This sportscasting profession that Mel adored earned him a six-figure year-ly salary. Walter Winchell, who feasted on celebrity gossip, reported in 1957 that Mel's earnings for that year were around $230,000. Such a swelling figure, which was foreign to athletes, let alone sportscasters, wasn't far-fetched. Mel worked so often and so hard that he made this kind of money.

As early as 1950, Hal Boyle of the Associated Press reported that Mel's annual salary was between $150,000 and $200,000. In 1957, Leonard Shecter of the *New York Post* estimated that all of Mel's enterprises earned him $150,000 annually, while Ben Gross of the New York *Daily News* reported Mel's yearly earnings at $200,000. By 1962, Tom Anderson of the Knoxville, Tennessee, *Journal* reported Mel had earned more than $200,000 a year on several occa-sions.

Practically anywhere Mel wanted to lend his face or voice, he could make a buck, either for himself or for charity. He once raised $225,000 by emceeing a 17-hour telethon for the Arthritis and Rheumatism Foundation. Standard Comics sought Mel's name for profit in 1949 and 1950 when it printed two issues of *Mel Allen Sports Comics*.

The words "How About That!" blazed underneath a picture of cartoon Mel on the front of one issue, which depicted him covering Lou Gehrig's 1939 Yankee Stadium farewell. The other installment bragged on its cover about "The Story of Mel Allen 'The Voice of the Yankees.'" Inside, the issue illustrated how Mel became "your favorite sportscaster," beginning in his college days. "Young Allen's a smart lad—and only 22!" thought a stodgy-looking law school profes-sor as Mel and other classmates took an exam. In later frames, a coach (who was-n't identified as Frank Thomas) asked Mel to cover college football games, Mel aced an audition with CBS, he dazzled while covering a rain delay of the Vanderbilt Cup auto race from a plane ("that boy can announce sports for me any day," said a CBS suit tuning in), he slogged through infantry camp and cov-ered baseball, football and boxing. The final frame showed Mel at the height of his career, smiling at a WINS microphone.

That face appeared in photographs in publications from coast to coast that profiled him. It was pictured by artist Mo Leff broadcasting a Yankees game in the popular sports comic strip *Joe Palooka*. It arrived at Downey's restaurant at 8th Avenue and 49th Street in Manhattan to present the championship trophy of a charity Broadway softball league to Sammy Davis Jr. and actors playing on the "Mr. Wonderful" team.

Mel's face grinned from a throne beside figure skating gold medalist Billie English, Mel's "queen" for the winter sports carnival at Grossinger's resort in the Catskill Mountains. During the 1955 ceremony, Mel wore a crown and royal robe as heavyweight-boxing champion Rocky Marciano officiated his coronation aboard a float.

When Mel emerged from Yankee Stadium's press gate, fans surrounded him, swooning as he signed his autograph in neat, looping cursive writing. When he hopped into a cab in Omaha, Nebraska, and said, "The Sheraton, please," the driver's head twirled around like it was on a swivel.

When he and Yankees broadcast partner Jim Woods and Joe Gallagher, a Yankees statistician, had to stop at the Canadian border on a drive from Detroit to Cooperstown, New York, an elderly worker for the Immigration and Naturalization Service reacted similarly. The man asked each of the three men where they were born, and Woods and Gallagher dutifully answered.

"I was born in Birmingham, Alabama!" Mel piped in. "Aren't you going to ask me?!"

It was pitch dark outside, and the man hadn't immediately recognized Mel's face. He sure knew the voice. "The guy's eyeballs got as big as grapefruits," Gallagher says.

Woods was formerly a minor league baseball announcer before joining Mel in the Yankees broadcast booth in 1954. He said he knew he was in the majors when he witnessed a phone conversation between Mel and Joe DiMaggio about Marilyn Monroe. Woods, who worked alongside Mel, Red Barber, Russ Hodges, Bob Prince and Jack Buck during his career, thought Mel was the best sportscaster of them all. Mel was certainly the most famous member of the group.

CHAPTER 11

The Bachelor

They mailed him marriage proposals, love letters, neckties, hand-knitted socks and scarves, bottles of shaving lotion, roses, cakes, pies, poems and invitations to dinner.

"You'd blush if you knew what I do to you when you appear on my TV screen," one of them wrote. "I might as well tell you: I kiss you, and kiss and kiss and kiss and kiss you. You don't even appreciate it. You just keep right on talking."

They formed fan clubs bearing his name from the Bronx to Trenton, New Jersey, and flocked to Yankee Stadium to see him on "Ladies Day," when they were admitted free to the ballgame.

"He is a knight on a white horse, a dreamboat, a lover boy—and to prove it, one recent Ladies' Day, a swarm of them waited outside Yankee Stadium after the game and mobbed him, ripping his clothing, stealing his pocket handkerchief and finally, in passionate triumph, knocking him down," one syndicated columnist wrote in 1953. "Valentino never had it so good."

Born on Valentine's Day, this heartthrob was one of the most eligible bachelors in America. According to five of the country's most glamorous unmarried women of 1958, Mel Allen was even chosen as one of "the 10 Sexiest Bachelors on Earth." Actresses Joan Collins, Zsa Zsa Gabor and Tina Louise, who later played sultry "movie star" Ginger Grant on *Gilligan's Island*, helped compile the list. Musicians Frank Sinatra and Sammy Kaye, FBI chief J. Edgar Hoover and Democratic presidential hopeful Adlai Stevenson were also among the "sexiest."

Two years later, Kaye, vice president Richard Nixon, chief justice Earl Warren, movie star Rock Hudson, TV actor Robert Stack, Yankees owner Dan Topping and others joined Mel as the Custom Tailors Guild of America's "Best Dressed Men in America." Mel received a similar distinction from *Esquire* magazine. He was meticulous about matching jackets, shirts and ties or, on those warm, summer afternoons at the ballpark, comfortable short-sleeved, open-collared dress shirts and slacks. He wore smart blue business suits and gray felt hats while traveling with the Yankees, who always looked formal on the road. Whatever he was doing, though, Mel preferred dress jackets to coats and he never donned jeans or shorts.

He wore conservative colors that set off his dark brown hair and fine hazel eyes, wrapping his snappy wares around a bear-like, 200-pound frame. Mel towered to nearly 6 feet, 2 inches tall, but his warm smile melted away any thoughts that he might be menacing. His thinning hairline, which began its retreat in the late 1940s, and mashed-in nose further humanized his celebrity status. And his voice, which sounded soft-spoken as it talked to women, could be disarming.

"I don't know a thing about baseball," *Motion Picture Daily* quoted one Long Island woman as saying in 1954. "I just watch because I love to hear Mr. Mel Allen's voice."

Wrote another of Mel's female followers in a *New York Times* "Letter to the Editor": "My interest in baseball was on the lukewarm side until Mel Allen made me feel that he reserved the seat next to him just for me. He also made me feel that no matter how many dumb questions I asked, he *wanted* to answer them all. He became my friend [although I never met him]."

The letter, from a woman in Manhattan, ran in *The Times* on October 17, 1971, seven years after the Yankees dumped Mel from their broadcasting team. Another woman from Pleasantville, New York, was similarly nostalgic in 1987.

"For years I have been wanting to write to tell you how much your knowledge, enthusiasm, and professionality have meant to me in my life," she penned in a personal letter to Mel. "As a young girl, I listened to you as you announced Yankee ball games on radio. Your descriptions of the game, and your explanations taught me all the baseball I know. ... One of my big fantasies was to be your 'side-kick,' announcing a play-by-play right next to Mel Allen! If I had a choice of meeting *any* baseball personality including my hero, Joe DiMaggio, I would opt for meeting you, just to thank you for teaching me baseball, to thank you for the enjoyment of listening to the games, to thank you for sharing your love of the games with me, and of course, for your marvelous stories."

Knowing that thousands—if not millions—of women from teenyboppers to grandmothers were listening to him, Mel patiently explained baseball rules over the air as game situations merited.

A 1949 nationwide "homemakers survey" conducted by Mrs. America Inc. determined that his sports commentary was "the best understood on the air today." As they tuned in to Mel's Yankees broadcasts, housewives and single women alike became baseball fans for life.

One irate man scolded Mel in a letter for ruining his wife's cooking, but another wrote to Mel about how he had drastically improved married life. "I used to hate coming home and listening to all the female gossip," the second man said, "but since you started doing the games it's a pleasure. Now my wife meets me at the door with the scores."

Mel especially charmed the wives of Yankees players.

"Mrs. Rizzuto, Phil is all right," Mel would say over the air. "He was just shaken up a bit. You don't need to have to worry."

When the Yankees were about to return home after a long road trip, Mel told the wives exactly what time the team was set to arrive in the New York area. Off the air, the wives liked Mel just as much. He was so polite and, unlike the ballplayers, he hardly ever swore, instead using expressions like "Jiminy Cricket," "dad gummit," and "gosh darn." "What a nice guy!" *Look* magazine quoted one Yankee wife as saying in 1949, "He's more considerate than most married men already."

Women who knew him only by his looks and his voice thought so, too. Nearly half of Mel's fan mail—which could reach 1,000 letters a week—came from "the high-heel set" or "the fair sex," as he called his female followers in two different instances. Some of the women were so sure that they wanted to slide a wedding ring down one of Mel's long fingers that they proposed to him in writing.

"It makes for nice reading," Mel said in 1950 about his flood of wedding proposals. "I'm just hoping one of these days I'll get one that I can take home and read again."

But Mel tended to shy away from forward females. Some of them spooked him, especially the ones who crawled into the back seat of his car and popped up as he drove home, or those who tailed him as he traveled with the Yankees. Though Mel would sometimes register as "Allen Melvin" at hotels and stay still and silent as he heard knocks on the door in the middle of the night, some stalkers still reached him. Once Mel opened the door of a hotel room and found a naked woman waiting for him.

"Get outta there!" he yelled, wheeling around and running down the hall.

She was one of Mel's regular pursuers, who thought she was going to court Mel and win his heart, Hollywood style. She sat in seats near him at Yankee Stadium, offering him and his booth mates fried chicken. She did publicity and reporting work to weasel her way even closer, writing an article entitled "My Boss, Mel Allen," in a prominent magazine.

"I wanted a job as his Girl Friday," she wrote. "Instead of asking about my qualifications, Mel tried to impress me."

Mel wanted nothing to do with her. After the woman appeared in the buck in his hotel room, Mel spoke to a lawyer, who arranged with her father that she would stay away from him. Mel felt bad about this. He was always concerned about hurting people's feelings, which is why he chatted with most of the Mel-crazed maidens who called him in his Yankee Stadium his office.

"If he'd only just hang up on one of them, just once," his secretary, Elsie Kurrus, said in 1949.

But Mel always kept the fanatical female fans at arm's length. The flock of women among the daily throng of 20 or 30 fans awaiting Mel after a game always concerned him. Such mobs alone were disconcerting to a mega celebrity.

In 1954, for instance, Mel received a call at his Detroit hotel room threatening violence if he broadcast a Yankees-Tigers game at Briggs Stadium later that day. The youthful male voice said that 400 gang members planned to storm Mel's booth and use his microphone to "tell the people how police are misusing Detroit youths." (The city's police had been cracking down on teenage gang activity.) The caller also told Mel he wanted an autograph for his girlfriend, "Cleo." Mel, who thought the call might be gag, still chatted a while, saying he would meet the caller and Cleo at the Yankees' dugout at Briggs Stadium before the game. Instead, he alerted authorities, who staffed the stadium with 50 more uniformed policemen than usual and placed officers outside Mel's booth.

"There was no real threat," Mel said after the game, which had no interruptions. "You might just call it a threat by innuendo. But I don't know why anyone would want to harm me."

Mel stayed cautious, and single. He went on only a handful of dates a year. Still, he always seemed to have a different gorgeous gal on his arm at galas. "Here comes Mel Allen with the future Miss Jones," sportswriter and friend Tom Meany once cracked while observing Mel escort another stunner to a Yankees victory party. Just by being famous, Mel had become a notorious bachelor. "Girls," Walter Winchell wrote in a 1954 column, "baseball broadcaster Mel Allen is shopping for a new Girl Friday."

Mel always laughed off his "eligible bachelor" status.

"If I don't hurry, I'll soon be declared ineligible," he liked to say after his age crept into the 40s.

But realistically, Mel could have chosen just about any bride he wanted. He knew Dinah Shore, a Southerner like himself who struck gold as a singer and actress. He had met Shore way back when she attended Vanderbilt University and made singing appearances at the University of Alabama. Mel got to know her again when the two were starting out their careers in New York, but Mel never showed much interest.

To Mel, dating another celebrity often meant unwanted publicity, like what happened when Dagmar, a bosomy, flirtatious starlet with a dumb blonde routine, stole a kiss from him when he appeared as a guest on one of her television shows. Observing the harmless gesture, a gossip columnist hatched a faux romance. Mel's cronies at a Sports Broadcasters Association meeting gave him a good ribbing about his "conquest" the day the column appeared.

"He should have been tickled about the story or at least understood that when you're a public figure and unmarried, there'll always be gossip items in the papers," *Park East* magazine quoted an unnamed sportscaster as saying in 1952. "Instead, he was angry as a wounded bull. It didn't do any good talking to him, advising him to laugh it off—the man was just beside himself."

Park East also quoted Mel about the matter.

"I don't want to sound like a preacher, but I just can't allow myself to get mixed up in loose gossip or notoriety," he said. "I feel the sport I'm connected with is one of the purest and finest things in the world, and I want everything that bears on my reputation to be kept just as clean. You get involved in any way with some showgirl, and before you know it, people are saying things about you which don't do you a bit of good."

When Mel did go on dates with public figures, it was usually with respected leading Jewish women like Caral Gimbel, the department store heiress.

"Oh, wouldn't that be wonderful if he married the Gimbel girl?" Mel's mother mused.

"What's wonderful about it?" Mel would say. "All she's got is money."

Caral Gimbel married another Jewish catch, Hank Greenberg.

"What was wrong with her?'" Mel's sister, Esther, once asked her brother.

"Oh, Esther," he replied. "She's like all the rest of the rich girls they introduce me too. She didn't make me feel anything. I just didn't care for her."

Mel often told Esther he probably met every wealthy Jewish girl from New York to California. He found most of them awfully aggressive. So he waited—and waited—for that girl who would meet his terms for love. This wouldn't be someone who actively pursued him. A chevalier to his core, Mel wanted to do the courting. As he noticed more and more women show up to watch the Yankees during the 1950s, he longed for the old-fashioned girl who stayed home.

"Men enjoy seeing women at baseball games, but don't like to hear them shouting catcalls," he was once quoted as saying. "It detracts from their charm and femininity."

Mel told another publication he wanted "a sort of throwback to the basic conception of a woman who looks forward to motherhood and takes pleasure in the simple things in life." He said his bride would have to be a good homemaker, cook and companion. She would be someone who didn't glob on makeup or dress just to impress.

"I'm sure there is an unsuspecting girl, unknown to me at this moment, who could convince me it's time for a change," Mel said in 1953. "She'd have to be wholesome, reasonably attractive, have ideas of her own but be sympathetic to mine as well. She would like sports, recognize responsibility and should 'wear well.' She'd never be able to settle down, for I spend my life traveling. I guess I never stay long enough in any one place to get used to a girl. So I stay single, but I'm hoping some day some girl will twist my arm."

Mel always said his intentions to marry were noble. When Jeanne Williams of New York's Columbia Diamond Rings presented him with his $1,000 gift certificate to be redeemed by "The Future Mrs. Mel Allen" on Mel Allen Day at Yankee Stadium in 1950, Mel said, "My goal in 1951 is to use it."

Six years later, Mel was dining with Ben Gross of the *Daily News* at Toots Shor's when Gross asked the $1,000 question: Why aren't you married? "Because my girl married someone else when I was in the Army during the war," Mel responded.

On several other occasions when he was asked about his stag status, Mel also referred to his "girl before World War II."

Mel missed an opportunity with Miriam Rosenbloum, his college girlfriend whom he decided not to wed before he entered the war. Mimi wound up marrying a New York doctor, whom she later divorced, but always remained fond of Mel. She wrote him the following letter dated February 14, 1948:

> Dear Mel,
>
> I've skipped Feb. 14 some years—but whether or not I've sent a card—I always remember that St. Valentine's Day is also—and most especially your BIRTHDAY.
>
> Hope this will be the very best birthday yet!
>
> It was good to hear you New Year's Day—even though the Sugar Bowl game was a sad day for our Alma Mater. [Alabama lost to Texas 27-7 in the 1948 Sugar Bowl.]
>
> Here's hoping you can get to Chattanooga someday—when you travel South again. It would be mighty good to see you again!
>
> Meantime, best regards to all your folks—and more good wishes for an extra special birthday!
>
> Mimi

Like so many of Mel's personal letters, Mimi's sat on his desk at Yankee Stadium as he was out enduring a life dominated by appearances, appointments and assignments. Elsie Kurrus, Mel's secretary, wrote Mimi a response.

"That boss of mine is out of town on another speech-making junket but he is due to return tomorrow and your letter is on top of the heap for his personal attention," Kurrus wrote.

But Mel never made his social life his highest priority.

"The thing I want most in the world is to find the right girl and marry her, but there's nothing hot in that department right now," he said in 1953. "Sometimes I wonder if I'll ever find time. This sports whirl—well, it's mostly a stag business, as you know. And you're on the road with the ballclub, in and out of town, from March to December. Even when you're home, you're lucky—if you're me, with newsreel and nighttime telecast commitments—to get a free Saturday or Sunday to go to a show and dinner."

When a second shot at marriage danced before his eyes—this time with a titian-haired musician who taught at Vassar College in Poughkeepsie, New York—Mel allowed his work to get in the way again.

"Yankees announcer Mel Allen is on Cloud No. 7 with Vassar music teacher Mildred Goldberg," Walter Winchell wrote in a gossip column on November 24, 1949.

Mel introduced his honey to his friends and family, something he rarely did with girlfriends. He even invited her to dine with him and his brother Larry.

Perhaps nervous about meeting Mel's girlfriend for the first time, Larry squeezed lemon juice into her eye as he tried to drown his shrimp.

But Mel, not Larry, was the one who doused his shot at marriage with the music teacher. As Mel showed signs to his brother and sister that he might propose to this girl, he maintained his indefatigable work schedule.

"I don't figure I'm serious about anybody, because when I am out of town, I think more about baseball than anything else," he told a reporter from *Look* magazine curious about his relationship with the Vassar music teacher. Months could pass in between Mel's calls to his steady. Finally, one day, her father answered the phone.

"Mel, you're too late," he said.

The woman had given up on Mel and, like Mimi, ended up marrying a doctor. On the set of *This Week in Baseball* nearly 50 years later, Mel would tell writer Ouisie Shapiro about being left on the doorstep of marriage with a broken heart.

"He just kind of carried that one around with him," Shapiro says.

❖❖❖❖❖❖❖

After missing opportunities to wed, Mel wasn't about to let Larry lose lovely Marjorie Martin when the younger Allen dated her in the mid-1950s.

"If you don't marry that girl, I will," Mel told his brother.

Margie, as she is known to friends and family, grew up in Stamford, Connecticut, about 10 miles south of the Allen's house in Bedford Village, New York. Mutual friends fixed her up with Larry.

"He's Mel Allen's brother," they said.

"Who's Mel Allen?" she replied.

Margie was more concerned with Larry, who, in between flying around the country to assist Mel on baseball and football games, dated her for two and a half years without popping the question.

"What is it with this Allen boy?" Margie's mother asked her. "Is he just taking advantage?"

When Larry proposed to her, Margie was so angry she said, "No."

"I told him he was too late," she says.

But unlike Mel's girl from Vassar, Margie gave Larry one last chance. "I was so sick that night and I said, 'Maybe I made a mistake.'" Margie recalls. "I was 23 years old. I was an old maid already going on 24."

She called Larry and asked him to lunch.

"Is that offer still open?" Margie said. "I think I'll take you up on it."

Forever the best man but never the groom, Mel stood beside Larry as he married Margie in 1956. Larry had stopped to catch his breath amid a hectic working life, unlike Mel.

"You gotta rest sometime," Larry says. "He was going 90 miles an hour. I could never do what he did. How he did it, I don't know."

While Larry returned home from press boxes around the country to Margie, his wife of nearly 50 years with whom he raised two children, Mel often just flew off to another stop on his endless itinerary.

"What girl would want to follow the kind of schedule that rules my life?" Mel said.

Forget marriage. Mel's strenuous schedule barely allowed him to maintain friendships. Mel's closest friends often fell into one of two categories: Elders in positions of prominence who had helped him along in the early stages of his career and those he saw as he worked. People like Frank Thomas, University of Alabama speech professor T. Earle Johnson and prewar Yankees president Ed Barrow fell into the first group. New York City Police Lieutenant Tom Maxwell, who was in charge of detail around Yankee Stadium, broadcast partners Hodges and Gowdy and sportswriters Milton and Arthur Richman were some who comprised the second category.

After games, Mel could easily grab dinner with Maxwell, who was stationed at the press gate, or Hodges or Gowdy. Or he could attend services on Jewish holidays with Milton Richman, who worked for United Press International, and his brother Arthur, who wrote for the *Daily Mirror.*

Other times, Mel just ran off to another engagement in his calendar, which overflowed with baseball and football games, Fox Movietone News narrations, TV and radio shows, commercial tapings, charity work and several appearances a week across the United States and Canada on the banquet and lecture circuits. Mel didn't even have an "off season." After the World Series, he immediately shifted into full-time football mode. In fact, in 1962, after the Yankees nipped the Giants, who had moved West by this time, in Game 7 of the Series for NBC television, Mel flew directly from San Francisco to his home state to call Alabama-Tennessee for CBS-TV.

As the busiest broadcaster in sports, Mel often crisscrossed the country several times a week.

He began one particular 10-day span in November 1953 with a Friday night flight from New York to Los Angeles, which took 11 hours in those days, for a USC-UCLA football game. He called the game Saturday, then immediately flew back to New York to do a Washington Redskins-New York Giants NFL game as the Redskins' play-by-play man, a role in which he served in 1952 and 1953. On Monday, after handling his *Sports Daily* NBC radio show, he flew to Salt Lake City to prepare for a Brigham Young-Utah football game on Thanksgiving Day. But on Wednesday, he jetted back to New York do his *Sports Spot* TV show, then returned to Salt Lake City the same night to get a few hours of sleep before Thursday's game. On Thursday night, he flew back to New York, then quickly caught a train to Philadelphia to prepare for a Saturday Army-Navy game. On Sunday, he was in Pittsburgh for a Redskins-Steelers game.

Mel's schedule could get even more chaotic in September and early October, when he traveled for both baseball and football games, studying his football rosters in between Yankees broadcasts. Mel's duties as the sports narrator for Fox Movietone News were almost always in the mix, too. With some exceptions due to schedule conflicts, Mel reported to a studio on the West side of Manhattan from wherever he was in the country every Monday and Thursday night between 1946 and 1964 to write and narrate his Movietone News reels.

During Yankees road trips, Mel would fly back to New York on Sunday and Wednesday evenings, do his newsreel work, spend the night at an airport motel and jet off to the Yankees' next location.

Mel could fly close to 100,000 miles during his busiest years. By the early 1960s, he had traveled an estimated two million miles in the line of duty and *Sports Illustrated* reported that he appeared on radio and television 600 hours a year. As his assignments blurred together, Mel pushed himself harder, obsessed with his work but never completely satisfied with it.

"He used to worry he wouldn't do the All-Star Game or the World Series," Gowdy says. "He did them every year."

After winning one of his countless "best sportscaster" awards, Mel's reaction was: "It's nice, but what if I don't win it next year?" Or, he would say, "If the New York Yankees had been an eighth-place team all the time I'd been with them I'd be an eighth-place announcer."

Mel packed his schedule full of assignments hoping that every last one would add to his reputation as a sportscaster and prevent a pink slip for at least one more day. His was a competitive field with limited opportunities, and Mel worked almost in fear that his current contract was his last. He thought if he slacked off, his career could crumble or, at the very least, someone would take his job.

"I have as much security in this business as a light switch going on and off," he said in 1957.

By staying busy most days and nights of the week, Mel attempted to combat his insecurity.

"He never stopped being a broadcaster," colleague Vin Scully says. "All of a sudden you look up and you're 45 years old. In some ways, I always feel a little sad when I think about Mel. I always thought of him as a good-natured man who was consumed by the business. I always looked at Mel as a warning to me that I never wanted to get so caught up in being an announcer that I forgot I was a man."

❀❀❀❀❀❀

Because Mel never took a wife during a much more traditional time than today, some wondered if he was homosexual. His brother and sister knew better. Larry has a vivid image of driving home from an event with Mel and a girlfriend, who sat in the front seat next to him.

"I was lying down in the back 'cause we had a long ride home and they were necking," Larry says. "Mel wasn't trying to hide anything from me."

Esther, meanwhile, recollects taking her children, Risa and Billy, to Washington to visit Mel during a road trip and noticing how well the female hotel staff knew her brother.

"I never saw so many grabbin' hold of Mel and saying, 'Oh, you haven't been back in a long time' and 'We had such a good time' and 'Do you remember this?' and 'Do you remember that?'" Esther says. "I thought to myself, 'Boy, he had a time in Washington.'"

But Mel was never one to kiss and tell. He didn't think his personal life was anybody's business.

"I just wouldn't get any peace of mind in behaving like a wolf, keeping a woman or running around town," *Park East* magazine quoted him as saying in 1952. "Sex is all right in its place, but there's a time and place for everything."

Some time after Mel and his sister moved in together in the late 1970s following her husband's death, Mel found the time and place appropriate to share with Esther a rare morsel of his private life.

"You know, I once lived with a woman for 15 years," Mel said to Esther as she cleared off the dinner dishes.

"You did?" Esther said, startled. "Did I ever meet her?"

"No."

"Did Mother and Dad ever meet her?"

"No."

"Was she an actress?"

"No, she worked for the Metropolitan Opera Company."

The woman was in costume design. For 15 years, Mel managed to maintain a residence with her separate from his "home" address, which was with his parents. Esther regrets not learning more about this affair, but she never thought she should pry.

"I felt that if he wanted to tell me about her, he would," she says.

Mel never said any more, although he mentioned the mystery woman to Esther's daughter Risa once as uncle and niece drove home from temple. At the time, Mel was in his 60s and Risa was a young adult. Risa remembers her uncle saying that this woman was Swedish and much older than him. "I think he was attracted to non-Jewish women," Risa recalls. "And I think he had a guilt about that because I think he didn't feel like he could marry a non-Jewish woman. When they bought the house in Bedford, she gave him an ultimatum about getting married. And I think the relationship broke up."

His niece's account explains why Mel's family doesn't remember him having many steady girlfriends. Mel felt a strong connection to Judaism, and his parents always hoped he would marry within the faith. The two girlfriends his family knew about—Mimi and the music teacher from Vassar—were Jewish. Yet how serious was Mel about either one of them if Mimi lived in Chattanooga and the music teacher only heard from Mel every once in a while?

Esther connects Mel's 15-year affair to calls her brother used to receive in Bedford Village from an unknown woman. Mel's sister remembers her mother complaining about them sometime after Mel moved himself, his parents and Larry into their Westchester County house in 1951.

"She's always calling up wanting to talk to Mel," Anna would say to Esther. "Does he talk with her?" Esther would ask her mother.

"Yes, he does," Anna would say. "She's constantly on the phone with him."

Anna Israel had always been Mel's main squeeze, and she loved it. She dressed up to go watch Mel work at Yankee Stadium. When he got home, she cooked for him and doted over him. After dinner Mel might take her out to movies.

"She took care of all the wifely things except sexually," Risa says. "I question whether she would have liked to have seen him get married. I sometimes wonder if my grandmother really would have wanted to share the limelight with somebody. I think my grandmother really enjoyed the spotlight and being the sports mother of the year."

The American Mothers Committee named Anna as its "Mother of the Year in Sports" for 1951. She and the "mothers of the year" in other categories were honored during a breakfast at New York's Waldorf-Astoria. At the end of the event, one of the other women tried to leave with Anna's umbrella. She was also Russian, so Anna told her off in their native tongue.

"You can pull that in Russia, but you can't do that in America," Anna said. "In the old country, it was your umbrella, but it America, it's my umbrella."

Anna Israel was a pistol. She was charming and sweet but also forceful, demanding and even a little bawdy. "Did you notice that her eyes were crossed?" she might joke to other family members when Mel occasionally brought a girlfriend by the house.

Tommy Henrich remembers another comment Anna made to him about one of Mel's dates for a party at the Israel home.

"I don't know what he sees in that little girl,'" Henrich recalls Anna saying. "She's so small. I don't know he'd find her in the bed."

Mel's girlfriends never heard Anna's remarks, which were more casual than critical. Mel's mother always tried to make the women feel welcome, though her queen-like exterior of beauty, glamour and feistiness was rather intimidating.

"Mel had a very talented, very able mother," Esther says. "I always used to say, 'Mel can't find a girl that matches up to his mother.' That's just my observation, which may not be true. I had a mother—she could sing, she could act, she threw parties. She was a lively person. Whatever she did, she did better than anybody else."

Margie Allen, who admittedly hated the kitchen before marrying, remembers her sinking feeling about following Anna Israel as Larry's caretaker.

"Believe me, I was nervous about it," Margie says. "She was a dynamo— that woman could do anything. And not only could she cook but she was beautiful. She walked into a room and everyone's head turned."

Margie had nothing to worry about, though. Anna told her to be blunt about anything she did that bothered her. Margie never had a problem with her mother-in-law, who always stuck up for her. When Anna saw the engagement ring Larry had bought Margie, she told him it was too small and sent her son back to the jeweler to pick out a more elegant one.

"I got news for you," Anna would say to her son. "You're always gonna be wrong and she's always gonna be right because she's the daughter-in-law."

After Larry and Margie got married in January 1956, Anna turned her attention to Mel, who was pushing age 43.

"I'm not gonna be here always," she told her eldest son.

Like any good Jewish mother, Anna wanted her children to get married and present her with grandchildren. Such instincts overtook any faults she might have found in the women Mel dated.

"I wish I could rid of both of my boys," Anna told Margie.

When Mel continued to stay single after his brother married, Anna would complain that he "never married anybody but those New York Yankees."

In an interview with *Look* magazine in 1960, she lamented about how dramatically Yankees losing streaks weighed on her eldest son's mind and how night games and doubleheaders wound him up so tightly that he stayed up all night uncoiling.

"He has no time for a private life, so how will he ever meet a nice girl and settle down and get married?" she said. "He's in love with sports instead of a woman."

Two years later, when Anna voiced similar sentiments to *Sports Illustrated,* a reporter asked her if she was even happy about the fame her son had achieved. Anna shrugged her shoulders and said, "I wish he was a shoemaker. A married shoemaker."

But while Anna urged Mel to marry, she also contributed to his bachelorhood. Not so much because of her aura of perfection or the critical eyes she could cast but because Mel so was utterly devoted to she and Julius. With Larry and Esther both married and Julius in frequent states of ill health, Mel felt responsible for his parents. Instead of marrying, he lived with and took care of his mother and father until they both died.

"I am a bachelor by circumstances rather than design," Mel said in 1957.

Esther gets teary-eyed when she thinks about what those circumstances were.

"Mel supported his mother, his father, his brother," Esther says. "Larry couldn't have gone to college if it wasn't for Mel. I wouldn't have had a wedding if it wasn't for Mel. He paid for my [appendicitis] surgery. He took care of his family and everybody in it at one time or another. When some people wanted to say, 'Why didn't he ever marry?' I wanted to say to them, 'He always had family!' He had a complete family around him all the time."

CHAPTER 12

Uncle Mel

About 40 miles northeast of Yankee Stadium, amid woodlands and estates of Westchester County, was Mel Allen's oasis. Here in Bedford Village, New York, he lived in a grand, white house that had three floors and 10 rooms. The Colonial-style home sat on 18 acres of property where deer, otters, beavers, snakes, frogs and all sorts of other wildlife could be found.

True to his Alabama upbringing, Mel preferred this wide-open country to cluttered New York City living, which was only a quick commute away. Once he left Yankee Stadium, Mel met no stoplights as he drove up the Major Deegan Expressway and Saw Mill River Parkway and over his narrow, snaking, dirt-and-gravel road. In an hour or so, Mel was home, where his insular family life always awaited.

"The minute I open the door, everything seems calm and serene," Mel wrote in an article for *Perfect Home* magazine in 1960. "Thoughts of business leave my mind."

Inside his house, Mel found his mom's delectable meals and his dad's practical advice. He might see his nieces and nephews in the spacious, pine-paneled den, where everyone always gathered. The room had a fireplace, but it projected its own natural familial warmth because Esther and Danny frequently brought over Risa (born in 1946) and Billy (born in 1949) from Long Island, and Larry and Margie often came up from their apartment in Riverdale with Carolyn (born in 1958) and Andy (born in 1961).

After bouncing the children on his knee, Mel could play with Bama, his large, frisky Weimaraner with a tannish-gray tint and green, beady eyes. Or he might adjourn up the circular staircase to his bedroom. Though he was usually loud and loquacious in public, Mel could be more private and reclusive when the spotlight and microphone were away from him. He loved to close his door and curl up with a book. Mel was an avid reader. He devoured everything from biographies about famous figures like Franklin Delano Roosevelt and Winston Churchill to mystery novels to book-of-the-month selections.

From his bedroom window, Mel could look out on one of the two brook-fed lakes on his property. His family often swam and fished in them. Julius would go out there looking for bass, perch, bullheads and trout. When Mel's father brought his catches inside, he gave them to Anna, who fried them up for him and Mel. Mel knew no better cook than his mother, who never used recipes, let alone teaspoons or tablespoons, and made everything from scratch.

"You just throw it in," Anna would say as she tossed together ingredients, a pinch of this and a pinch of that.

In no time, out of the skillet or oven came fluffy buttermilk pancakes or biscuits, crispy fried chicken, sweet-and-sour stuffed cabbage, or a succulent pot roast. (The meat was kosher, of course.) On the side, Anna could easily whip up pickled potato salad, which she layered and then adorned with rosettes. For dessert, she made strudels that buried any bakery version and pies filled with blueberries she picked in her backyard. Mel had a man's appetite, and Mom could always satisfy it with a seven-course meal from soup to nuts.

Sometimes, Easter Bellamy, the Israels' live-in housekeeper, would fill in admirably as cook. She made a famous fruit cake and luscious lamb shanks and veal chops. Or she'd buy a large, smoked calf's tongue and slice it up for sandwiches, which Mel found scrumptious.

"He would always tell me, 'You cook more like my mother than anybody I know,'" Bellamy recalls. "I thought that was a compliment."

Mel's family knew him better than anyone. He could lean on them whether he was friendly or grouchy, quiet or chatty. Mel worked so hard and so often that he enjoyed nothing more than to come home and energize in his familial comfort zone, where there were no preconceptions. Mel didn't have to feel guilty about sleeping in after a late game. When he awoke and came down to the breakfast nook off the kitchen, his mother would be waiting to serve him a cup of coffee.

"Home is contentment in a busy world," Mel wrote in his 1960 article for *Perfect Home* magazine. "Without a home, and the happiness within, a man misses the greatest satisfaction in life."

America saw just what Mel meant on an April night in 1957, when Edward R. Murrow visited with him and his family on the CBS television program, *Person to Person.*

Person to Person opened up the living rooms of public figures and sports and Hollywood celebrities for the nation's enticed eyes. Wielding a cigarette from the studio, Murrow informally chatted with his subjects in their homes.

"Where are you Mel?" Murrow asked as his black-and-white screen revealed one of the Allen lakes in Bedford Village.

Mel casually rowed into the right side of the TV screen in a small boat.

"How about that!" Murrow exclaimed, erupting into a smoker's cackle. Mel Allen and his yacht."

"Hello Ed," Mel said is his friendly, Southern fashion.

A few moments earlier, Mel's dog Bama had spotted his master on the lake and dove in to join him. The horse-like animal's wake nearly capsized the boat. A cameraman retrieved Bama before he interrupted the show, but got drenched when the dog shook himself off.

Mel weathered Bama's plunge and looked sleek in his suit as the CBS cameras caught him. He skillfully turned his boat toward a nearby dock.

"Pull hard on the left oar—you aren't going to make it!" Murrow yelled.

"Oh, I'll make it," Mel said.

"What are you doing in a boat at this time of night?" Murrow asked.

"Well, isn't everybody doing this sort of thing?" Mel replied.

As casually as he responded to Murrow's questions, Mel docked his boat and hopped ashore.

"You're not trying to make a getaway, are you?" Murrow asked.

"No Ed," Mel said, picking up a fishing rod and casting its reel into the lake. "I was out trying to see where some of these fish are my daddy always catches out here."

As he continued to talk to Murrow, Mel reeled in his fishing line. He walked from the dock on to his lawn and around a small stone wall that separated the higher ground on which his house sat from the lawn and lakes. He climbed a stairway leading to a side door of the house.

"Uh, Mel, do you ever get bored of doing ballgames day after day?" Murrow asked Mel as he walked.

"No I don't, Ed, because each day presents something new, and every game you find different personnel in it," Mel said. "You never get bored with it because there's not a script written in advance. As you know, the excitement of wondering what's going to happen gives you a brand new thrill every day."

Mel walked through a door at the top of the stairs and into his kitchen as a CBS camera finally caught a close-up of his athletic frame. His face was a little full from Anna's home-cooked meals. Mel walked into the dining room, where he found his mother. Anna's hair was neatly done up and she wore a dark, elegant dress and white pearl necklace.

"Ed, I'd like for you to meet my mother," Mel said, taking Anna's hand and leading her into the picture.

"How do you do, Mr. Murrow," she said uneasily.

"Good evening, Mrs. Allen," he replied.

"We're so glad that you're visiting us this evening," she continued. "We're all proud that you thought enough to come and visit us."

Sensing his mother's nerves, Mel jumped into the conversation and introduced the other members of his family, who sat at the dining room table to the right of where he and Anna stood. Esther, Danny, Billy, Risa, Larry and Margie were dressed in semi-formal attire.

"Good evening, Mr. Murrow," they all said.

Esther beamed as she swung her head around to look at everyone's expressions as Mel named them on national television. Her husband, the Long Island urologist, wore dark-framed glasses and looked more serious. Their children twitched timidly and excitedly. Larry and Margie, a younger couple without children yet, smiled nervously. Melded together, they all formed a wholesome family portrait of varying personalities and ages.

"C'mon, Mom, we'll go see dad, the fisherman," Mel said, ending the Rockwellian moment. "He's probably thinking about the one that got away, Ed."

Mel led his mother on a short walk to the living room, where Julius sat.

"Dad," Mel said, "I'd like you to meet Mr. Murrow."

"Good evening, Mr. Allen," Murrow said.

Julius's warm, noble face, which resembled his son's, appeared on screen.

"How are you, Mr. Murrow?" he said softly in his Southern accent.

"Mr. Allen, Mel didn't have much luck at the pond," Murrow said. "He tells me that's because you hook all the fish while he's out working. Is that right?"

"Yes," Julius replied calmly. "I have more time and I do most of the fishing. That's why I catch more. Probably have more patience, too."

"That's right," Murrow said. "Tell me, do you ever regret that Mel gave up the law to become a sports broadcaster?"

"Well, at first, when he mentioned going to New York, I was very apprehensive," Julius replied. "I thought that he had a very bright future as a lawyer in the state of Alabama. But because he loves his work so well, and because it turned out as it has, I have no regrets."

Murrow turned his attention back to Anna, looking refined but a little stiff as she sat on the couch.

"I've known Mel very seldom to be at a loss for words," Murrow said to her. "Did he start talking at a very early age?"

"As a matter of fact, Mr. Murrow, he started walkin' at nine months of age and commenced talkin' words, you know, and at one year, why, he could almost talk to you, you know, he formed phrases," she said in an accent that contained subtle hints of the South and Russia. "And when he was two years old, my husband took him to a ballgame against my wishes. Ever since then I knew that I was gonna live with baseball all my life—as long as I live."

The family had been worried how gentle, unassuming Julius would fare in front of the glare of the CBS cameras, but Anna turned out to be the one who seemed a little shy. She had been frazzled about the show from almost the moment Mel mentioned to her that an army of crewmen was coming to her house.

"What can I give them to eat?!" Anna said to her son. "It's Passover!"

Mel's mother wanted to play hostess for anyone who came into her home. But during the week of this Jewish holiday, she faced serious cooking restrictions.

"How could they come up at this time?" she asked Mel.

"Mother, that's the time they scheduled it," he said. "I can't do anything about it."

Bound to only unleavened bread, Anna baked a half-dozen round Passover sponge cakes, which Esther helped her prepare without flour. She also ordered a large plate of meats from the deli, which she served along with a special spread. When the team of 18 men or so from CBS arrived, they had a feast waiting for them on a table in the finished basement. The crewmen not only loved the food, but they told Anna that on previous assignments, no one had bothered to give them as much as a cup of coffee. The crew left Bedford Village contented, a feeling Mel knew very well.

❈ ❈ ❈ ❈ ❈ ❈

Each year for a month or so, the Israel hearth moved south to Florida. As Mel, Larry and the Yankees prepared for the upcoming baseball season during spring training, the rest of the family vacationed.

Before 1952, they stayed in Pat Sergi's cottages on Lido Beach, not far from where the Yankees worked out at St. Petersburg's Miller Huggins Field. Anna's siblings and their families sometimes came down from the cold of the North to join their relatives at Sergi's, where sportswriters and Yankees players also lived during spring training. Joe DiMaggio would walk past the Israel cottage on his way to the ocean just as the laughter of lively conversation, the screams of children and the clamor of mini-disputes were drifting out.

DiMaggio stopped one day to listen some more and say hello to Julius, who was outside.

"You know Mr. Allen," DiMaggio said, "every time I pass your cottage, it gives me a feeling of longing for my family."

With those words, DiMaggio was off to ponder his failed marriage to Dorothy Arnold. He was retreating, from newspapermen and from life. As he walked off to a quiet corner of the beach, Esther's daughter Risa would run after him. DiMaggio didn't like to be bothered, especially as he lounged in the sun, but he always played with Risa. He'd lift her up and let her bury his feet in the sand as her father took pictures. DiMaggio knew he could trust these people. They were relatives of Mel Allen, who had sat with him for hours in that hotel coffee shop in Chicago and listened to him moan about Dorothy.

More than a decade after she played with DiMaggio on the beach, Risa remembers seeing the Yankee Clipper in the stands at Yankee Stadium during a World Series game. DiMaggio waved when he spotted her with Anna and Julius. Being Mel Allen's niece had its perks. Risa got to sit in the "Peanut Gallery" of children next to host "Buffalo Bob" Smith on *The Howdy Doody Show*, too.

"Peanut Gallery" tickets were in such high demand that parents wrote for them months before their children were even born. But Uncle Mel landed spots on the show for Risa, her brother Billy and her friend Gail in no time. The three children even got to shake hands with the puppet that portrayed Howdy Doody.

"Of course, I was the star at 'show and tell' in school the next day," Risa recalls.

She enjoyed what happened after Howdy Doody time even more. That's when Uncle Mel took everyone to Toots Shor's, where they could celebrity-watch.

"I thought that my uncle kind of gave stardust to our family," Risa says. "We were a nice, Jewish family, but I think having him as our uncle kind of gave us a little more stature among our friends. He was always kind of larger than life and drove a Cadillac and he'd have big parties and invite the Yankees over. It was very glamorous to a child."

When Risa was in her early 20s, Mel made last-minute arrangements for she and her parents to sit right under the stage at Caesars Palace as Frank Sinatra opened the latest Las Vegas show. When Risa attended George Washington University, Mel invited her to a White House ceremony President Lyndon Johnson held for him and a contingent of major league baseball players who visited American troops in Vietnam with him in 1966. When Risa attended the University of Alabama for two years before she transferred to George Washington, Mel introduced her to Bear Bryant, who invited her to dine with him and Mary Harmon at their home.

Thanks to Uncle Mel, Bryant also gave his niece Carolyn, Larry and Margie's daughter, a personal tour of his office when she visited Tuscaloosa as a potential student.

During a trip with Uncle Mel to Williamsport, Pennsylvania, for the Little League World Series, Carolyn's younger brother, Andy, got to play softball with Ernie Banks and catch one of the Hall of Famer's fly balls. Mel and Andy also spent a morning with Joe DiMaggio.

"He was always nice to my uncle and he was very cordial to me," Andy Allen recalls.

So was George Steinbrenner, the Yankees owner who invited Mel and Andy to watch a game with him in his box.

"I sent Steinbrenner a 'Thank you' note and he wrote me a letter back," Andy says.

While he and Andy were at Yankee Stadium, Mel took his nephew down to the locker rooms, where he met 1970s stars Catfish Hunter, Reggie Jackson, Thurman Munson, Roy White and Mickey Rivers. A decade and a half earlier, security guards let little Carolyn practically have the run of Yankee Stadium. She often found her way into the broadcast booth and onto Uncle Mel's lap.

"That's where my dad and my uncle went to work," Carolyn says. "We have a little kids' view of that. We were around ballplayers and stuff, but they were just people."

When they saw him get swarmed for autographs, Mel's nieces and nephews realized their uncle was no ordinary person. Carolyn remembers seeing hundreds of kids crowd around her uncle at once as he emerged from Yankee Stadium. Mel's niece, who was just a tot at the time, was so terrified of the mob scene that she was afraid to run over to her uncle. But Carolyn knew she would have her time alone with Uncle Mel. He would occasionally stop by Larry and Margie's Riverdale apartment after games to play with her. Or, when she visited Bedford Village, he took her on rides in his car and, when it was snowing, pointed to the white branches hovering above.

"I don't ever think that I remember a time where he really didn't have time for us kids," Carolyn says.

Esther knew she could count on Mel to escort three-year-old Risa on a train to Florida in 1949. Mel's sister had just given birth to Billy and skipped her annual spring training trip. But Risa was raring to go. After she waved goodbye to her parents, she immediately turned her attention to Mel.

"Uncle Mel, would you please take my hat and coat off and hang it for me?" she said.

Risa grinned from ear to ear along much of the ride.

"Egads, Philmadelphia!" she said after hearing the conductor announce a stop.

Mel was fascinated when his niece talked to herself in the mirror.

"It was the darndest thing," he said at the time.

When Risa got bored, she asked Uncle Mel to tell her stories.

"She wound up being my mother and I was the little boy," Mel said. "She never gave me a bit of trouble, except that she wouldn't let me read my book."

Risa was hardly a distraction compared to his newborn nephew, Andy, during spring training of 1962. Margie had planned to stay home with Andy, who was only a couple of months old, but Anna called her from Florida and insisted they fly down. Margie warned her mother-in-law that Andy cried all the time. "He needs more to eat," Anna said, continuing to push her daughter-in-law to visit.

When Margie decided to go, Mel agreed to fly to Florida with her and the baby. Andy squealed for almost the entire flight and day and night once they arrived at the family's rented house in Margate. The racket was so bad, Mel checked into a motel.

Perhaps parenthood wasn't for Mel, but he still always made his family a top priority. He devoted so much time and effort to work and family that there wasn't room left in his life for much else.

"Mel had this strong sense of obligation," Risa says. "I always felt like he felt he had to take care of everybody. I sometimes think he did more for us than we did for him."

When Risa's first husband, an art dealer, got into legal entanglements with importing, Mel's letter helped bail him out of trouble.

Uncle Mel's help wasn't as welcome when he wrote another letter on behalf of Billy in hopes of gaining his nephew admission to Georgetown University Law School and tried to intervene for Andy as his nephew was applying to medical school at the University of Alabama at Birmingham. Billy didn't want to go to law school in the first place and dropped out almost immediately. Andy, who had straight A's as an undergraduate at Vanderbilt University and solid MCAT scores, thought Uncle Mel might do more harm than good.

But that was just Mel's way. He had always helped out his family in any way he could. Whether it was his cousin Elmore Rayman, Aunt Betty's son who sought financial help for his schooling, or his nieces and nephews, Mel's relatives all knew they could lean on him in a pinch.

"You didn't have to ask him," Andy says. "He always put everybody up into a situation where he was the financer. He was sort of like the father figure taking care of everybody else and making sure everybody had what they needed. 'Don't worry. I'll take care of everything.' That was his whole thing."

Mel didn't just intervene when family needed his help. He sometimes spoiled his relatives with surprises. Mel gave Risa and her first husband a prenuptial dinner at New York's esteemed Algonquin Hotel. On a separate occasion, he took the couple out for a bottle of champagne to celebrate their engagement at the Friars Club, where he later arranged to have Carolyn's rehearsal dinner.

"He was just a wonderful uncle," Carolyn says, pausing in thought, "and probably closer than an uncle. He was a dad."

CHAPTER 13

A Game Guy

Mel Allen had a perfect pour. In between innings of Yankees telecasts, he showed off his talent by draining a bottle of Ballantine into a glass.

"At the end of the first half of the first inning, then, Washington nothing and the Yankees coming to bat," he might say. "And I'd like to go to bat for the Crisp Refresher."

As Mel poured, the frothy head of his beer would rise right to the tip of the rim but never over it.

"Ballantine beer is the Crisp Refresher," he said as the head settled. "You can prove that by pouring yourself a cool, foaming glassful. Look at it and see how golden and clear it is. Then taste it. Taste how smooth and delicious it is."

Mel Allen also had a secret. Off camera just before these commercials, he would grease the inside of the rim of his glass with butter to prevent overflow.

If Mel's millions of fans had known about his trick, they would have reacted with similar horror to the pre-teen who once waited patiently for Mel outside the Yankee Stadium broadcasters' booth, only to see him fire up a cigarette as he emerged.

"Mr. Allen," she said, "I thought you only smoked White Owls."

"Darling," Mel replied, "you've just learned something very interesting about life."

Mel was not that slick-pouring, cigar-puffing, self-assured guy that America saw in commercials and on broadcasts.

A better glimpse of him came at the end of Edward R. Murrow's *Person to Person* show from Bedford Village. Standing in front of his grand fireplace, over which several of his trophies disguised an often-insecure man, Mel read a prayer to America:

Dear God, help me to be a sport in this little game of life. I don't ask for any place in the lineup; play me where You need me. I only ask for the stuff to give You a hundred percent of what I've got. If all the hard drives come my way I thank You for the compliment. Help me to remember You won't let anything come You and I together can't handle. And help me to take the bad breaks as part of the game. Help make me thankful for them.

And, God, help me always to play on the square, no matter what the other players do. Help me to come clean. Help me to see that often the best part of the game is helping the other guys. Help me to be a "regular fellow" with the other players.

Finally, God, if fate seems to uppercut me with both hands and I'm laid up on the shelf in sickness or old age, help me to take that as part of the game also. Help me not to whimper or squeal that the game was a frame-up or that I had a raw deal. When in the dusk I get the final bell, I ask for no lying complimentary stones. I'd only like to know that You feel I've been a good guy.

The author of *A Game Guy's Prayer* was never known, but he might as well have been Mel Allen, a man who could be kindhearted, a little corny and never fully at ease with his enormous celebrity.

❖ ❖ ❖ ❖ ❖ ❖

Mel was tickled that Murrow featured him on *Person to Person*, a show that also dropped in on the homes of President Truman, Marlon Brando and Marilyn Monroe. Mel was also flattered that thousands of people wrote to him and to CBS for a copy of *A Game Guy's Prayer* after the show. He had the prayer printed onto cards, which he mailed out en masse.

Mel never took a single fan for granted. He always tried to reply to each of the 1,000 people who might write to him on a given week, no matter how illegible their handwriting was.

"I am practically the only New York Yankee fan in my place of employment," a woman from Leeds, Massachusetts, penned to Mel in 1961. "I asked a Red Sox fan for a pencil and he said write to Mel Allen—he probably will send you one … " Mel mailed the woman a Yankees pencil and told her to "hang in there" at the office.

That same year, a man from West Haven, Connecticut, wrote to Mel wanting to know Roger Maris's ethnic background. Mel dutifully replied in writing to tell him it was Austrian and German. In 1962, a man from South River, New Jersey, asked Mel in a letter if Mickey Mantle had ever pitched during a regular-season game. Mel wrote back to say that Mantle had not, but added, "Incidentally, he does have one of the best knuckleballs in baseball."

Larry often researched answers to trivia and rule-related questions that fans submitted to his brother, while Mel's full-time secretary typed the reply letters.

Even when Mel didn't craft the letters himself, he made sure they contained a personal touch:

> Dear Jimmy:
>
> I wish there was something I could say to lessen the disappointment of not being able to comply with your request for a ball autographed by Bill Skowron and Yogi Berra. We receive thousands of requests such as yours and since it is absolutely impossible for us to take care of them all, we have made it a practice not to grant any of these requests.
> Your kind consideration in your postscript made us feel real good. Young fellows such as you serve always as an inspiration for us to try and do a better job. May the Good Lord bless you with many years of health and happiness.
>
> Cordially,
> Mel Allen
>
> PS: As a small consolation to you and your brother I am enclosing some pictures of the team with their printed autographs on the back.

Mel especially anguished over his responses to negative fan mail. He would routinely receive letters, sometimes on the same day, asking him not to "dwell obsessively on the sterling qualities of the opposing team" and telling him he was "95% partial to the Yankees." Taken together, the criticisms should have told Mel that he was doing his job as an impartial announcer. Yet both accusations— and any other criticisms fired at him—bothered Mel profusely.

"I know that there is much about our broadcast that can be improved," Mel would write in responses to fan critics. "Obviously there is no intention to irritate people, and when that happens we feel even worse than the listeners."

Mel took each individual complaint extremely personally, such as one in 1948 from a Long Island woman who listened to his WINS disc jockeying show. "It is needless for me to say that your listeners know now that you are not a Christian, or you most certainly would have known that Wednesday was Ash Wednesday," she wrote. "Your remark about people in New York 'walking around with smudges on their faces which must have been caused by soot,' was not very intelligent. But then what can you expect from people who are not intelligent!"

Mel immediately replied to the woman:

> Thanks ever so much for your letter of February 12th. You may be sure that I sincerely regret having said anything over the air that might be construed as being in the sacrilegious vain. I am terribly sorry that

I forced you to take the attitude that you did since there was absolutely no intention on my part of making anyone angry. Actually I merely intended a good-natured indication of our being aware that it was Ash Wednesday. You may be sure that it was not a lack of intelligence, on my part as you indicated, but rather, at most a mistake in judgment. Although the fact that yours was the lone letter of complaint to reach this desk might indicate that not too many people thought as you did.

All I can say is that I was deeply aware of the fact that it was Ash Wednesday. I did not intend any disrespect. I am no heathen. I may be an awful announcer, in which case I can't blame you for not tuning me in, but please be assured that I am at the front among those who believe in religion. I believe in God just as you do. Again, permit me to say that I intended no harm but that if what I said was out of order, I offer my sincere apology.

> With best wishes, I remain,
> Cordially,
> Mel Allen

Mel never thought much of his own ability. Even when he rose to become America's foremost sportscaster, he credited his fame to the games he broadcast.

"I think I'm the luckiest guy alive, to get paid for doing the work I love, and so handsomely too," he once said. "This job is a vicarious summation of all of my dreams. Like most kids, I thought of being a ballplayer. But, in a sense, it's better this way. Here you play nine positions and you're at bat, too."

Even while broadcasting the most intense of sporting events, Mel flashed his audience constant reminders of the sheer joy his announcer's role brought him. "Man it's been a great series," he said during NBC's telecast of Game 7 of the 1952 World Series between the Yankees and Brooklyn Dodgers. "It still is. We've got two innings at least to go!"

Mel even set his love for his trade to music in a 1950s rock-and-roll tune entitled *Play Ball, You All,* which he arranged with Walter Bishop, a young musician whom he knew from Fox Movietone News' studios, for Red-E records. Mel left the singing of *Play Ball, You All* to a group called El Rojo and the Left Fielders, but the song's lyrics had his prints all over them:

> *Bases loaded like a gun,*
> *Anxious for that extra run*
> *Grand slam bounces off the bat,*
> *Going, gone! How 'bout that!*

Mel never uttered his catch phrases to attract attention to himself. *He* wasn't the story. He illustrated that point in two books he co-authored with sportswriters: 1959's *It Takes Heart* with Frank Graham Jr. and 1964's *You Can't*

Beat the Hours with Ed Fitzgerald. The books drew solid reviews (Richard Nixon publicly endorsed *It Takes Heart*) while barely mentioning Mel. They were anthologies of inspiring sports tales he had gleaned over the years.

"The history of the sports world is full of stories that tell of the remarkable accomplishments of individuals gifted with exceptional courage and spirit and unflinching desire," Mel wrote in the foreword to *It Takes Heart*. "It is these very people who have persevered to change the course of history. But nowhere else do you find examples of heart more dramatically portrayed than in the sports world."

Mel's narratives told of figures who overcame long odds against them to excel on the fields of sport, like Joe DiMaggio returning from a heel injury and a 65-game absence to stir the Yankees to a three-game sweep of the Red Sox in 1949.

"Joe will live in the memories of baseball fans for many, many reasons," Mel wrote. "But no other memory will erase that of the crippled star, coming out of the dugout when he was most desperately needed, to turn back the surging Red Sox. That is what every sport is all about."

Mel weaved humor and pathos into other stories. "They took pictures of my head," he quoted Dizzy Dean as saying after getting nailed in the noggin on the base paths, "and the X rays showed nothin'."

About Roy Campanella, the Dodgers' catcher who was rendered a quadriplegic and robbed of his stellar playing career in a 1958 car wreck, Mel wrote: "The wonderful world that Campy had constructed for himself had just dissolved in the sickening crash of the rented convertible he was driving." But Campenella's story was still one of triumph because, as Mel detailed, Campy maintained his easygoing nature and sense of humor. "Laughter, too, can shed light on a great heart," Mel wrote.

Mel devoted much attention in his books to athletes like Campy who fell short of winning, but still persevered, often overcoming personal tragedy to do so.

"Only time could beat a team like Southern Methodist and a player like Kyle Rote," Mel gushed about the SMU back who stepped in for injured stalwart Doak Walker in 1949 and nearly led his team to an upset over Notre Dame.

Seven years later, 39-year-old Sal Maglie, the Brooklyn pitcher who opposed the Yankees' Don Larsen in Game 5 of the World Series, was, in Mel's words, "as heroic in defeat as he had been all year in victory." This fateful day of October 8, 1956, may have moved Mel more than any during his sportscasting career.

❋ ❋ ❋ ❋ ❋ ❋ ❋

Yankees teammates called Don Larsen "Gooney Bird," and the pitcher exuded a goofy image to back up his nickname. He had large ears that jutted out from underneath his baseball cap and, while he stood six foot four, he threw his

220-pound body around awkwardly as he pitched. Larsen's windup was so flawed that Red Sox coach Del Baker detected that the right-hander tipped his pitches. To erase this deficiency, Larsen switched to a no-windup delivery late in the 1956 season, and his new style made him look more like he was playing a game of catch with Yogi Berra rather than actually pitching.

Larsen hadn't nearly harnessed his immense physical ability by 1956, the year he turned 27. In 1954, Larsen mustered only a 3-21 record for Baltimore. Probably his most memorable feat as a Yankee before the 1956 World Series was emerging virtually unscathed after wrapping his car around a telephone pole at 5:30 in the morning during spring training in St. Petersburg. The incident furthered Larsen's reputation as a carouser and night owl. "The only thing Don Larsen fears is sleep," Jimmie Dykes, his manager in Baltimore, once said.

Larsen's Yankees manager, though, believed in him. "See that big feller out there: He can throw, he can hit, he can field, he can run," Casey Stengel said. "He can be one of baseball's great pitchers any time he puts his mind to it."

Larsen's mind had been elsewhere in Game 2 of the 1956 Series, when the Yankees gave him a 6-0 cushion in the top of the second. Larsen promptly helped blow New York's lead in the bottom half of the inning, and the Yankees ended up losing the game. But based on another enigmatic Stengelese hunch, Larsen got a second Series start in Game 5.

As Mel prepared for his television broadcast for NBC, he thought about Stengel's strange affinity for Larsen. How could he pitch Gooney Bird in such a critical spot? As Larsen rang up zero after zero on the scoreboard on the right-center-field wall, everyone at Yankee Stadium saw that the Ol' Perfessor had made another genius calculation. For at least one day, Larsen's no-windup delivery was an awesome weapon. The pitcher's slow, easy motion kept the Dodgers off-balance and disguised a sneaky fastball that he pumped past Brooklyn's most potent hitters. "He's outta there," Mel told listeners, his voice tinged with surprise as he watched Larsen strike out Gil Hodges in the second inning.

Of course, Larsen also received the requisite gift from the baseball gods that seems to go along with every feat of pitching perfection. Leading off the top of the second, Jackie Robinson ripped a grounder to the left of third baseman Andy Carey. Carey could only get the edge of his glove on the hot shot, but he inadvertently deflected the ball to shortstop Gil McDougald, who stood deep in the hole between third and short. McDougald snagged the ball and fired it to first baseman Joe Collins to get Robinson by a step.

"McDougald grabs it off ... annnnnd ... they get him!" Mel said, startled by the lightening-fast play. "How aabout that! An assist for Andy Carey, tremendous alertness on the part of Gil McDougald, a great throw and a fortuitous turn of events."

Larsen had to be a little lucky to beat Maglie, who matched nasty stuff with veteran guile. "Strike three called!" Mel exclaimed as Maglie K'd Collins in the fourth. "Man, we're lookin' at some pitchin'!" Larsen was so superb, however, that *The New York Times'* John Drebinger, a seasoned baseball scribe, wrote after the game that only four of Brooklyn's batted balls that afternoon had a chance of falling in for hits.

The Yankees' hitters did just slightly better. With two outs and nobody on base in the bottom of the fourth, Mantle pulled a Maglie pitch down the right-field line. The clout paled in stature to some of the Mick's behemoth blasts during his Triple Crown regular season, in which he batted .353 with 52 homers and 130 RBIs. This ball barely cleared the outfield wall, Mel's voice following it as it hooked around the foul pole: "There's one—if it stays fair! It is goingggggggggggg, going GONE!" In the top of the fifth, Mel's voice traveled with Mantle to Yankee Stadium's "Death Valley" in left-center, where the outfield wall stood 457 feet from home plate: "There's a drive into left-center, Mantle digging hard, still goin', still goin', GREAT CATCH! HOW ABOUT THAT!" The voice exploded upward just as Mantle, in an all-out sprint, lunged and made an over-the-shoulder, one-handed catch of Hodges's blast to the edge of the warning track. The next Brooklyn batter, Sandy Amoros, sent a towering shot to right that curved just foul.

"There's a drive to deep right field!" Mel screamed. "It is a … foul ball! Two umpires called it. Ed Runge and then Hank Soar, who let the fans know at once. It was mighty close! Sandy Amoros came within … well, let's say a foot of tying the score … maybe inches."

Feet and inches were pushing Larsen toward history, something Mel sensed after Mantle's home run. "One to nothing, New York," he said. "Each pitcher had retired every man he had faced until just now." Mel was far too superstitious to utter the words "no-hitter" or "perfect game." Eight years later, when he was informed that the San Francisco Giants' Jack Sanford was no-hitting the New York Mets, he would tell listeners over the Home of Champions Network: "In the seventh inning, Jack Sanford is pitching the type of game every pitcher dreams of having." *Sports Illustrated* called Mel's evasive language during no-hitters-in-the-making "downright irritating." The *New York Mirror*'s Bill Slocum Jr. also criticized Mel in print on this subject in 1959.

"Mel is charged with making the ball game as interesting as possible to the average listener," Slocum wrote. "Many listeners are not aware of the rarity and drama of a potential no-hitter. Nor are they all aware of the childish superstition that keeps some announcer from mentioning it."

But Mel had allies in Bob Wolff and Vin Scully. Wolff, who was calling his first World Series in 1956, felt that perhaps 15 percent of his listeners were superstitious. He didn't want them to blame him for jinxing Larsen. "The crowd is very aware of everything that is happening here, as far as the score and other important matters are concerned," Wolff told his Mutual radio listeners in the eighth. During the same inning, Wolff said, "I'm sure you who are listening are well-informed of the drama that Larsen holds right within his pitching grasp." Like Wolff, Mel also gave his listeners lots of hints that a pitcher was tossing a no-hitter or perfect game. "Well, at the end of five innings it's the Los Angeles Angels five runs on seven hits and no errors," he might say. "In fact, the Angels not only have all the runs but all the hits."

During the Larsen game, Mel just started counting the consecutive outs. Scully followed his partner's lead upon taking over NBC's telecast midway through the fifth inning. "Don Larsen is spinning quite a web today," Scully told listeners in the sixth. "He's retired 16 men in a row." In the Yankees' half of the sixth, Hank Bauer singled to score Carey, giving Larsen a 2-0 lead. By this time, the Yankee Stadium crowd was bustling with nervous energy. Could Gooney Bird do it? "Mister Don Larsen, through seven innings, has retired 21 men in a row," Scully said. Sitting beside his partner, Mel rooted for Larsen, though he bottled up his feelings within the professional confines of the press box. As butterflies floated through his stomach, Mel squirmed in his seat. "Well, all right," Scully said, "let's all take a deep breath, as we go to the most dramatic ninth inning in the history of baseball."

After Larsen retired Carl Furillo and Campanella to begin the ninth, Dale Mitchell emerged from the Dodgers' dugout to bat for Maglie. Mel winced. The man standing between Larsen and the first perfect game in World Series history was a pesky, left-handed slap hitter—a great candidate to spoil the day. Larsen worked the count on Mitchell to one and two. After Mitchell fouled off a fastball into the left-field stands, Larsen fired another fast one that Berra caught low and a tad outside. From center field, Mantle thought the pitch was a ball. But home-plate umpire Babe Pinelli raised his right fist to signify strike three. Larsen had done it.

"Got him!" Scully yelled. "The greatest game ever pitched in baseball history by Don Larsen!"

The crowd of more than 64,000 erupted, as did Mel. "The tension had broken everywhere, and suddenly I found myself cheering for Larsen like all the other fans," he recalled later. "There was a live mike in front of me, of course, but the cheering drowned everything out." Mel shouted so much that he was hoarse for Game 6. "It was worth it," he said. Larsen's pitching prize helped propel the Yankees to a seven-game victory in the World Series.

"We weren't cheering Larsen because he had an 'NY' on his uniform," Mel said. "A lot of the people standing weren't even Yankees fans. We were applauding someone who did something that had never been done before."

❈ ❈ ❈ ❈ ❈ ❈ ❈

Four years after Larsen's perfect game, Mel found himself at the brink of another World Series first. But at this moment—in Game 7 of the 1960 World Series—his Yankees faced a much more precarious situation. They were tied with Pittsburgh in the bottom of the ninth inning as the Pirates' Bill Mazeroski stepped to the plate.

"Mazeroski beat out a bunt in the second inning, popped to short and grounded to short into a double play," Mel told his NBC viewers. "Ralph Terry on the mound, sudden death now—last of the ninth, 9 to 9."

Mazeroski took a ball outside. "C'mon, Billy, just get on," cried a Pirates fan sitting near Mel's broadcasting perch. The light-hitting third baseman did better than that. He launched Terry's next pitch, a slider, into the residential area behind the vine-covered outfield wall at Forbes Field.

"There's a drive into deep left field!" Mel roared. "Look out now! That ball is going ... going, gone! The World Series is over! Mazeroski hits it over the left-field fence for a home run and the Pirates win it 10 to 9 and win the World Series! ... and the fans go wild. ... "

Mel was mum as Mazeroski rounded the bases, pushing past overjoyed teammates and spectators on his final approach to home plate. Mel remained silent for about 40 seconds. Where was the Voice of the Yankees? Had New York's excruciating defeat rendered him speechless? After all, Mel's team had outscored Pittsburgh 55-27 in the Series and blown a 7-4 eighth-inning lead in Game 7. Maybe Mel was so disgusted he had left the booth. But actually Mel hadn't gone anywhere. He thought that by allowing the clamor of the crowd to envelop the airwaves, he would best capture the chaotic scene.

"The Pittsburgh Pirates are the champions of the world!" he boomed to break his silence. As he recapped the game, Mel sounded as enthusiastic as he had when he called Mazeroski's fatal blow.

"And now to wind up this 1960 World Series telecast, let's switch cameras to pick up Bob Prince and some of the victorious Pittsburgh Pirates," he said. "Take over, Bob!"

"Thank you very much, Mel Allen, and hi everybody," Mel's partner said casually before drifting into several casual clubhouse interviews.

Not only had Mel remained composed during perhaps the most devastating loss in Yankees history, but he had prevented a partner from crumbling, too.

Before Game 1, Prince had a classic case of mike fright. When he thought about the millions upon millions of people who would be listening to him, "the Gunner," as Prince was known, turned as white as a ghost.

"Bob," Mel said, noticing his partner was nervous, "do you know who in our broadcasting team here is the most nervous of all right now?"

Prince only managed to mumble a response.

"Well," Mel continued, "we're now only 20 seconds from air time, and can you imagine how long that dad-gum peacock has been waiting to spread his lovely feathers?"

Prince saw that Mel was pointing to the NBC-TV symbol, and he nearly fell out of his chair. When Prince finally stopped laughing, he was relaxed enough to broadcast.

Mel had been a similar tonic for trembling, 25-year-old Vin Scully in the 1953 World Series booth. A mere three years before that, Red Barber had hand-picked Scully fresh out of Fordham University to be his assistant on Dodgers broadcasts. When Barber refused to call the 1953 Series unless Gillette offered him more money to do so, Scully found himself handling NBC's coverage of a

Yankees-Dodgers Subway Series with Mel. On the morning of Game 1, Scully, who lived with his parents in New Jersey at the time, was so nervous he said he "up-chucked" the breakfast his mother prepared for him.

But Scully eased into his first World Series assignment after he saw Mel bound into the Yankee Stadium booth with a knowing grin on his face. Mel had just chatted with the Dodgers' owner.

"Walter O'Malley asked me to take care of his boy," he said to Scully. "Don't you worry about a thing."

Five years later, Mel helped prop up Curt Gowdy, too. A bad back had kept Gowdy, then the voice of the Red Sox, from broadcasting most of the Boston's games during the 1957 season. Gowdy was still grappling with his ailment in 1958 when Tom Gallery, NBC's sports director, asked him if he wanted to work the network's telecast of the 1958 Series between the Yankees and Milwaukee Braves with Mel. Giddy about his first World Series assignment, Gowdy flew to Milwaukee, where he spent a miserable night trying to sleep through his pain.

"Mel, this is terrible," he said to his friend the next morning. "My back is killing me, and I don't think I'm going to make the game this afternoon."

"You'll make the game if I have to carry you myself," Mel said sternly.

"I don't think I can do it," Gowdy told Mel as he loafed outside to their cab for County Stadium.

"You'll do it," Mel said. "Now come on and stop griping."

Gowdy worked all seven games of the Yankees' win over the Braves, largely because Mel willed him to do so. Mel aided old friends like Gowdy instinctively. After Bear Bryant led his 1959 Alabama football team to the inaugural Liberty Bowl in Philadelphia, Mel treated the coach and his players to a meal at Mama Leoni's in New York, famous for its savory seven-course Italian dinners.

Mel also often gave friends tickets to Yankees games, even during the World Series, when he had to pay for the tickets himself. In 1957, Mel ordered two sets of box seats for Tom Parise, a pal who ran a steakhouse in Thornwood, New York. Parise's was a convenient stop along Mel's route home to Bedford Village from Yankee Stadium. Mel sometimes dropped by for one of Parise's thick, juicy steaks, which were so large they filled up two people. If Parise's was "closed," the Italian family invited Mel into their home, which doubled as their restaurant, to dine with them. Mel never forgot the generosity of the Parises or of any of his friends.

"You don't make a friend, you recognize him," Mel liked to say.

❊ ❊ ❊ ❊ ❊ ❊ ❊

Just before he worked the 1958 World Series with Gowdy, Mel made a trip to Freehold Raceway, the New Jersey horse track and home to the "Mel Allen Pace," to make some race presentations. While Mel took a break in the track's publicity office, an official from another New Jersey town approached him.

"We were looking for a speaker for the dedication of a boys club in Lodi, October 19, and I thought, perhaps, that you could make it," the man said.

Mel faced a daily barrage of offers to speak. He also knew he had to call a college football game that weekend at a site yet to be determined. But still, Mel considered the man's request.

"Don't count me out," he said. "Keep after me, and if we'll be around that area, I'd be glad to make it."

"It will be a real big affair," the man replied.

"I didn't ask you how big it will be, did I?" Mel said softly. "If I can possibly make it, I'd be honored to help you out."

Mel was a sucker for youth organizations and charitable and religious causes. He attended father-son breakfasts at churches of all denominations, youth baseball dinners, junior high assemblies, high school football banquets and Lions Club gatherings. He thought nothing of talking at such affairs in small towns like Warren Township, New Jersey, and Hazleton, Pennsylvania. Mel helped Hazleton rebuild and attract new industry after a hurricane ransacked it 1959.

"I sincerely enjoyed every minute of your presence and again must confess that I rate you as the finest human being I have ever had the opportunity to meet," Phil Sarno, the sports editor of the town's two newspapers, wrote in a letter to Mel that year.

If he believed in a cause, Mel would speak for free despite the hefty fee he could command. He also volunteered his services to a seemingly endless number of goodwill organizations. He spearheaded the "Fight for Sight" campaign for the National Council to Combat Blindness for a decade, recruiting fellow celebrities for a fund-raising benefit he hosted at Carnegie Hall. Mel also served as chairman of sportscasters for the United Cerebral Palsy Foundation and national sports chairman for the Multiple Sclerosis Society. He devoted his time to the Salvation Army and to B'nai B'rith, a Jewish association that defended human rights and fought discrimination throughout the world. Mel also joined national and international efforts to combat cancer, muscular dystrophy, polio, infantile paralysis and juvenile delinquency.

On the anniversary of Mel's 20th year as Voice of the Yankees in 1959, New York City Mayor Robert Wagner and New York Governor Nelson Rockefeller wired him their congratulations for his philanthropy over the years. In 1963, Mel received the prestigious Dr. Raphael M. Dansker Humanitarian Award for his service to mentally disabled children. Mel usually didn't get this much notoriety for his charity work. He quietly visited orphanages, veterans' hospitals and even a yard full of inmates at the Indiana State Prison.

"Words cannot express the appreciation that the inmates and the staff of this institution have for your appearance here," Alfred Dowd, the Indiana prison's warden, wrote to Mel in a letter dated August 5, 1959. "The place is still buzzing over your being here and the informative and entertaining talk you gave to the men. ... The men will always have a warm place in their hearts for you and they realize, as the members of the staff and I do, that you put yourself out considerably to be here with us, and for this we are extremely grateful. ... "

Mel drew inspiration to see prisoners from Pope John XXIII, whom he met in Rome in 1959. The Pope surprised everyone with a visit to Rome's Regina Coeli prison on the day after Christmas soon after he was elected in 1958. Romans nicknamed the pontiff "Johnny Walker" because he not only was known to make surprise trips around Rome but also joined the people on foot for the stations of the cross during Lent. Upon his visit to the prison, John XXIII said, "Why shouldn't I go to see the prisoners? They can't come to see me."

The words of another prominent Catholic prelate, Cardinal Francis Spellman, the Archbishop of New York, also motivated Mel. Mel got to know Spellman personally when they ran into one another at New York's LaGuardia Airport. A close friendship formed during a cab ride back to Manhattan. Spellman, an avid baseball fan, asked Mel if he might find time to visit the homesick seminarians at North American College in the Vatican, and Mel turned the cardinal's request into an annual sojourn in the late 1950s and early 1960s. Sometime after his football season ended on New Year's Day and before spring training revved up in early March, Mel would take highlight reels of the past year's World Series to Rome to show to young men studying for the priesthood.

"Those kids are the nicest, politest young men I ever met," Mel told Bill Slocum Jr. of the *New York Mirror* in 1959. "They even stood up when I entered the hall. Man, I wished the folks in Birmingham could have seen that."

Mel's parents got to see him speak at North American College in 1961, when he took them and Esther to Europe and the Holy Land on the occasion of Julius and Anna's 49th wedding anniversary. In Rome, Archbishop Martin O'Connor, the rector of North American College and a good friend of Mel's, arranged for the four to sit directly in front of John XXIII during an audience. Afterward, Anna told O'Connor: "Those were great seats, Monsignor. Right in back of home plate."

Mel liked to recite his mother's line to friends, but he usually remained low-key about his interfaith work abroad. It was a labor of love that he mostly kept to himself, much like his own Jewish faith. Long before the public stir Sandy Koufax caused by declining to pitch in a World Series game on Yom Kippur in 1965, Mel was privately burdened by the prospect of announcing a Series contest on this Jewish Day of Atonement. He met with a rabbi, who agreed that broadcasting the World Series was an opportunity Mel shouldn't pass up. Though Mel tried not to work on Yom Kippur, he decided to call the Series a couple of times on the culminating High Holy Day, but not before he spent a few hours of reflection with his prayer book.

Mel traveled overseas with a similar sense of duty. Though his leisure trips were rare (his 1961 voyage to Europe marked his first vacation of more than two weeks since his sportscasting career began), Mel always took time during them to promote sportsmanship. He planted a "Mel Allen Sports Tree" in Tel Aviv and showed World Series films to Israelis and to U.S. military personnel in Italy, France, Germany and the Caribbean. He received a hero's welcome wherever he appeared. As Mel emerged from a limousine at his hotel in Rome in 1958, a bellman asked, "Who is that?" A doorman replied: "Don't you know? That's Mel Allen, the king of baseball." While staying in Tel Aviv in 1961, Mel got word from the states that he had won 1960's *Radio Daily/Television Daily* award proclaiming him America's top television sportscaster. When they heard the news, Israelis showered him with acclaim, a gesture that thrilled Mel more than winning the award.

Another of Mel's most memorable traveling experiences took place in 1963, when he and Larry visited American troops and their families at the U.S. base at Guantanamo Bay, Cuba. Over three days, Mel and Larry shared Series footage and talked sports, which Mel called "a vital wedge" against the Communist thought that overwhelmed the island nation. Sports are an activity, Mel said, in which everyone can participate, regardless of their race or creed.

"The world of sports offers a great code of living—sportsmanship," Mel would say in a message he preached throughout his national and international lecture circuits. "We can keep the spirit of sports alive by giving youngsters an opportunity to play and watch the action. In this way the youth of America learn the meaning of teamwork and to respect each other. It's these youngsters who are going to take the big step forward and preserve our democracy."

Mel declared that the major leagues' opening day should be a national holiday for schoolchildren. Lawmakers in Washington never went for that idea, but many of them shared Mel's Cold War outlook.

"These kids, like those in the Little League, learn to appreciate each other as human beings," Mel told an audience at the Pittsfield (Massachusetts) Boys' Club in 1960. "They know the true meaning of the brotherhood of man under the fatherhood of God."

At the same function, Mel spoke of an "insidious ideology of Communism" in the Soviet Union, a country, he said, that put money and resources into its Olympic teams to flex its power in front of the world. "We don't ever want that to happen in the United States," Mel said.

A large man with a loud yet overly friendly demeanor, Mel could captivate speaking audiences young and old, whether he was making his anti-Communist spiel or telling a tale from Yankeeland. His somber voice cracked as he spoke of a cancer-stricken Babe Ruth offering Yankees fans a final farewell. In almost in the same breath, he laughed aloud while relating a conversation between two of Ruth's old teammates where the Babe lay in state inside a sweltering chapel.

"Boy, would I like to have a beer," third baseman Jumping Joe Dugan whispered to pitcher Waite Hoyt.

"Yeah," Hoyt said, "and so would the Babe."

Mel always spoke reverentially and respectfully about his Yankees, even after the 1960 season, when owners Dan Topping and Del Webb unceremoniously kicked his beloved Casey Stengel to the curb.

"Casey has not been well during the last two years," Mel said to the crowd at a youth baseball banquet in Scranton, Pennsylvania, "and the Yankees probably did not want to risk the chance of further impairment of his health." (Stengel would have told the gathering that he was fine and that the Yankees forced him to "retire.")

The previous off season, audiences bombarded Mel with inquiries about why the Yankees slipped to a meager 79-75 and finished 15 games behind the pennant-winning Chicago White Sox. "Yogi said that we lost because we made 'too many wrong mistakes,'" Mel would say to evade a negative-sounding response.

Mel's mind was a vast reservoir of lines and anecdotes, which he fed to audiences at the several dozen speeches he gave a year. With his cluttered schedule, he had little time to prepare for his talks, but as he waited to be introduced in an auditorium or banquet hall, he jotted preparatory notes on whatever he could find. He underlined, circled and checked names and phrases, filling up nearly all of the white space on programs, place cards, dinner napkins and hotel envelopes. Just before he was called to the podium, he might glance down and see he had written the words "proud" and "landing field." These were references to two jokes he liked to tell during speeches.

The first one involved two friends who hadn't seen each other in 25 years who bumped into one another. After they exchanged pleasantries, one revealed that he had a bed-wetting problem.

"What have you been doing for it?" his friend asked.

"Well, I went to the urologist for treatment, but I quit going to him because I've been going to a psychiatrist."

"Does he help you?"

"No, I still wet the bed, but now I'm PROUD of it."

The punch line would make crowds at men's club and press association functions hysterical. So would Mel's "landing field" joke, in which a man sat across from a woman wearing a gown that was cut low into a V shape. She also wore a diamond pendant that formed an airplane and hung down "at the V," as Mel described.

"Oh, I see you're admiring my airplane," she said to the man.

"Well no, madam," he replied. "To tell you the truth, I really was admiring your landing field."

In front of the appropriate crowd, Mel loved to tell a good dirty joke. When a group of sportscasting cronies were gathered around, he would talk about the time he was rattling off his lines during a fast-paced sports roundup show and said "a hide-farting Army team" instead of "a hard-fighting Army team." When he delivered his punch line, he belly-laughed so hard that tears rolled down his cheeks. Mel's buddies nearly fell over in giggling fits just watching him guffaw.

❊ ❊ ❊ ❊ ❊ ❊ ❊

Each August, on an open date for New York's major league baseball teams, Mel found himself in another spot in which he thrived among the fellows. He annually joined New York baseball writers for their gathering at the Bear Mountain Inn, located along the Hudson River about an hour's drive north of the city. Family members picnicked as the writers played a baseball game, which often pitted American and National League newspapermen against one another.

The sides notoriously trotted out ringers, who were usually players and, in one case, a broadcaster. At Yankee Stadium, Mel was known to one-hand foul balls that slashed into his broadcast booth. At Bear Mountain, he played center field, pitched and carried an awfully big stick.

"He was by far the most feared hitter of our group," longtime New York baseball writer Leonard Koppett recalled in 2002. "Whoever was pitching, he would kill it."

That is, except when Ryne Duren was on the mound. In 1959, Koppett, who was managing one team, called in Duren, the Yankees' relief ace, to face Mel with two on and two out in the sixth inning of a seven-inning game. Duren, a six-foot-four right-hander, wore thick glasses and a scowl that intimidated opposing hitters as much as his wild, explosive fastballs. Mel, who batted right-handed, stood a country mile from the plate as he faced Duren. Though Mel cocked his bat up behind his right ear like Joe DiMaggio used to do, his trembling hands defied the stone-cold resolve of Joltin' Joe.

Duren's first pitch hit the catcher on the heel and bounced about 100 feet up the mountain behind home plate. Fearing for everyone's safety, Duren lobbed the next one over the plate. As Duren delivered, Mel, who was expecting another wild heater, stepped out of the batter's box. But when he saw a lollipop drifting in, he lunged back into the box and swung. Because he was off balance, Mel managed to hit only a weak grounder to Koppett at second base. Koppett fielded the ball but threw it into center field, allowing the base runners to score and Mel to be the hero.

As he listened to his boisterous teammates cheer, Mel didn't care that he had had hit a dink instead of a drive against Duren. As his adopted creed, *A Game Guy's Prayer*, goes: "When in the dusk I get the final bell, I ask for no lying complimentary stones. I'd only like to know that You feel I've been a good guy."

For Mel, a man who just wanted to be liked, a prayer had been answered.

CHAPTER 14

Mr. Touchdown

Hello there everybody and fans around the world as well. This is Mel Allen speaking to you from mammoth Municipal Stadium in Philadelphia, today the scene of football's most colorful classic: the traditional Army-Navy battle ...

Hello there everybody. This is Mel Allen speaking to you direct here in Madison, Wisconsin, from Camp Randall Stadium ...

Hello there everybody. This is Mel Allen coming to you from the famed Rose Bowl in Pasadena ...

The voice didn't just represent the Yankees and the World Series. To millions of Americans, especially those in burgs of the South, Midwest and West, Mel was the sound of fall Saturdays and New Year's Day. Many of these people treated college football like a religion, and Mel's voice was as familiar as their pastors' voice.

In Baton Rouge, Louisiana, the *State Times* called his voice "the most recognized in sportscasting history" when Mel descended upon a 1960 LSU-Mississippi game.

In Columbus, Ohio, Mel was "America's foremost sportscaster" on programs for the Touchdown Club All-Sports Awards Dinner.

In Washington, D.C., the city's Touchdown Club invited him to host its gala and tell football tales to Senators and Supreme Court justices.

Mel covered hundreds of college games for radio and television, stopping at stadiums from coast to coast and partnering with a host of other announcing greats. They included Russ Hodges, Curt Gowdy, Al Helfer, Lindsey Nelson (one of the original New York Mets broadcasters) and Chick Hearn (the eventual voice of the Los Angeles Lakers). Students sniffed a big game when Mel appeared on their campuses in the 1950s and 1960s. In fact, Mel broadcast the "Big Game" itself between California and Stanford and most other major rival-ries of his day: Army-Navy, Oklahoma-Texas, Southern Cal-UCLA, Michigan-Michigan State, Alabama-Tennessee. Mel was NBC's top college football announcer for a decade and did both national and regional games for CBS and ABC as well. He was the play-by-play man for 14 Rose Bowls, five Orange Bowls and two Sugar Bowls and a weekly fall football presence.

Mel picked preseason All-America teams for *Sport* magazine and was a member of the panel that selected NBC's postseason All-Americans. He emceed *Look* magazine's awards dinner for its All-Americans in the wine cellar of New York's Mama Leone's restaurant and was coveted at most other national football affairs. All he had to do was say, "Hello there everybody," and the events became the virtual center of the sports world.

❈ ❈ ❈ ❈ ❈ ❈ ❈

The storied struggle of Army against Navy was an annual stop on Mel's football schedule. He called the game 14 times in an era when both schools were football powers. The Thanksgiving weekend contest, which had roots reaching back to 1890, carried the weight of an entire season. The underdog often pulled the upset as Mel worked in front of crowds that doubled the size of those at most baseball games he broadcast.

Cadets coach Red Blaik and Navy's Eddie Erdelatz had led their teams to top-10 national rankings before clashing at Philadelphia's Municipal Stadium in 1954. In the stray seconds of airtime before Mel signed on for NBC, commotion from cadets and midshipmen clogged the airwaves. That is, until Mel's megaphone voice met the clamor head on: "High jinks on the field by members of the midshipmen and the core of cadets, who are marching around the track, around the gridiron, engaging in the high jinks to add to the color of the most magnificent football game to be played anywhere, anytime, any year."

Not even the backdrop of blaring bullhorns and bellowing fans could overpower Mel. His voice came in resoundingly clear to radio listeners throughout this day that Navy scored an enthralling victory and Army felt an excruciating defeat.

"It is third and four for Army," Mel said during the first offensive series of the game. "Bob Kyasky at the left half, flanks out to the right against a 6-1-4 … and the handoff on the ride series goes to the right halfback—a fumble at the 28-yard line! Recovered by Navy! Jim Royer recovered it!"

Mel instantaneously adjusted to Navy's offense: "There goes Welsh on the keep play—he's to the 20! To the 15! He's downed on the 13-yard line!"

Mel's voice stayed right with George Welsh, Navy's lightning-quick, 5-foot-10, 160-pound quarterback who scampered, juked and passed while driving the Midshipmen to a score: "And so it is fourth and 14 for Navy on the Army 16 … Weaver flanks far out to the left, Welsh fades back on a draw play, keeps, fakes throws, completes it to Craig at the 10! To the five! He's OVER!"

Mel's words rolled off his tongue in brisk succession, as they did on John Weaver's extra-point attempt: "The snap, the spot, the boot and it is … good!"

Had listeners turned off their radios at this point in the game, they would have thought Mel was Midshipman at heart. But those who tuned in on Army's ensuing drive could have called him a Cadet: "It is fourth down and one for Army on the Navy 11, and this is the big play, Navy leads seven to nothing with two and a half minutes to go in the first period … a dive tackle—Uebel! And he goes, I believe, for the first down! … What a tremendous charge by the fullback, Pat Uebel, a six-foot, 197-pound junior with Flay Goodwin, the left guard, leading the charge as Uebel really BOLTED in there, exploded in there for the first down on the eight-yard line."

Mel often dotted his broadcasts with simple verbs like "bolted" and "drove" and ordinary adjectives like "sensational," "wonderful," and "tremendous." But the words Mel used didn't matter so much. His commanding voice engrossed his audience as much as what he said: "Weaver flanks out to the left, Welsh with the ball, fades, keeps, throws a pass, Smith in the end zone! He's GOT IT! TOUCHDOWN!" Nearly as quickly as he called the play, Mel recapped what he had just seen: "Earle Smith, the right end, went straight down and out. He was all alone as he went straight down, hit the goal line and flared out to his right and Welsh, who bootlegged the ball beautifully, hit him right in the bread basket."

Mel's sister Esther thought her brother had a photographic memory. This would explain how he could recollect picture-perfect images as players spilled from the line of scrimmage in all directions and describe furious football action with knee-jerk ease: "[Center] Billy Chance moves up over the ball, Army's ball, first and 10, on the Navy 43, 14-13 Navy, three minutes to go in the second quarter, and Pete Vann with the ball he … fakes to Uebel! Keeps! Throws a long pass, Kyasky's out there! He's got it on the nine! To the five, he's OVER! HE'S OVER!"

When one team scored, the other came right back, Army and Navy pounding one another like two heavyweight fighters going toe to toe in the middle of the ring.

"Ladies and gentlemen," Mel said after Navy's Welsh dove for another touchdown just before halftime, "all I can say about this game is, How aaaaaaaaaBout that!"

At the half, Mel could finally exhale and ponder Navy's 21-20 lead. "Well, ladies and gentlemen," he said in a hoarse voice, "sometimes, and you'll forgive me, but if being honest is a sin, then I am going to sin. Sometimes, a fellow behind a microphone likes to sort of move into a game on an easy style and fashion and not holler at you, but this game has been one of the most amazing we've ever seen. The action has been so sensational it's been at top speed. And to go with it, the reaction of 102,000 fans. You can understand why we have just been movin' along with 'em in that fashion. How 'bout that, Joe?"

"Mel," said his color man, Joe Crogan, "you're just one of the 102,000 yellin' their lungs out here."

Navy provided the only scoring of the second half and held on for a 27-20 win. As the game slowed down from its relentless pace, Mel's voice hummed more than hollered.

"The ball is on the eight," he said, introducing Army's last-ditch attempt at a score in the fourth quarter, "it's fourth and four for Army, 27-20 Navy, and now Army's got to go for it here as they line up with Johnson and Holleder at the ends, Vann … rolls out … tries to pass … it's knocked down! A great play by number … number … 36, Joe Gattuso, the left linebacker!"

✿ ✿ ✿ ✿ ✿ ✿

When he heard Mel momentarily struggle to identify a player, Larry was waiting with help. Mel's brother pointed to the player's name on their spotting board, which he had constructed with a large piece of poster board and small, rectangular stickers. Larry wrote the names of positions on the field across the top of the board and typed each player's name, number, height, weight, hometown and school year onto the stickers. He placed several stickers under each position on the board, according to team depth charts. Larry then stuck colored, glass-headed pins into the appropriate stickers to indicate for Mel which players were in the game.

The spotting board served as a check for Mel, who had memorized most of the players' names and numbers long before game time. He prepared for his football assignments as if he was cramming for an exam. During the week leading up to each game, he carried lineup cards in his pockets, studying them during slivers of spare time in his schedule. Meanwhile, Larry tried to arrive at game sites a few days before kickoff. He arranged for him and Mel to watch practices and game film and to meet privately with players and coaches. Mel tried to join Larry to do all this at least 24 hours before game time.

Unlike at baseball games, when Mel would stay on the field gathering color up until close to the first pitch, he completed most of his football preparation hours before kickoff. He liked his spotters and assistant broadcasters seated in the booth and ready to work an hour before the game began. This way, they picked up last-minute substitutions and announcements. An announcer was only as good as his next mistake-free broadcast. Mel knew this because he had once confused the jersey colors of Army and Navy for most of the first quarter, applying Army players to numbers he had memorized for Navy men. This was perhaps Mel's most embarrassing broadcasting moment.

But Mel was almost always on top of his assignments, poised to make effusive, accurate calls.

"Second and 12 for Iowa on the Oregon State College 49-yard line … balanced line, Wing-T right, Hagler on the wing … Dobrino and Nocera behind Ploen," he said early in his 1957 Rose Bowl telecast. "A keep by Ploen, and he's going … gets a good block! He's down to the 40 and to the 35 … and still on his way and driving. He's to the 15, to the 10, to the five and he's OVER!"

As he often did after calling a touchdown, Mel paused for 15 seconds or so. This allowed his audience to listen to Iowa's band blare and the 15,000-plus

Hawkeye fans who had journeyed to Pasadena cheer their team, which was making its first bowl appearance. Usually smitten with Rose Bowl fever himself, Mel knew exactly how they felt.

****

The Rose Bowl is football Heaven on earth. A grand parade down Colorado Boulevard, full of festive floats and brilliant flowers, proclaims the paradise of Pasadena, a city where the picturesque San Gabriel Mountains are in full view and a warm breeze blows while much of the country is covered in snow. The game itself, almost always played under drenching California sunshine in front of 100,000 fans, features two of college football's elite teams. Traditionally, a powerhouse from the East, Midwest or South met the best from the West, and the winner was considered the national champion. But in 1947, the Rose Bowl began featuring the champion of two power conferences, the Big 10 and the Pacific Coast Conference, whose original members now play in the current Pacific-10.

From CBS's radio booth, Mel called his first Rose Bowl in 1949, when California and Northwestern were locked in one of the most compelling struggles in the game's history. With Cal leading 14-13 with six minutes left, Northwestern drove 88 yards for a score in just three minutes, reaching the end zone on right half Ed Tunnicliff's 43-yard touchdown tear. Tunnicliff was the first Northwestern back to go in motion in the game. He fooled several Cal players as he took a lateral from left half Frank Aschenbrenner and ran around the right end for the score, powering Northwestern to 20-14 victory.

"The tremendous thrill of the Rose Bowl game still lingers with me," Mel wrote in a letter to Pacific Coast Conference commissioner Victor Schmidt after he had returned to New York. "It is a memory that I shall cherish forever. The honor of broadcasting the Rose Bowl game is a dream come true. I only hope that it all met with your approval." Mel also wrote to Craig Smith at Gillette's Boston offices. Smith was responsible for Mel's first Rose Bowl nod as well as his Boston Braves-Cleveland Indians World Series assignment the previous fall:

> Dear Craig:
> A belated Happy New Year and a billion thanks for having made 1948 my greatest year.
> I was thrilled beyond expression over the Rose Bowl assignment and am still pulsating from that wonderful experience.
> All I can say is, from the deepest recesses of my heart, thanks!
>
> Gratefully,
> Mel Allen

Mel would work 12 consecutive Rose Bowl telecasts between 1952 and 1963, calling the game's first coast-to-coast telecast in 1952 and its first remote football color telecast in 1962. He became a West Coast fixture leading up to the game as he attended press conferences at the Huntington Hotel, the lavish media center tucked amid palm trees in upscale West Pasadena, and emceed the Rose Bowl's Kickoff Luncheon at the Pasadena Civic Auditorium Ballroom. There he visited with the parade's Rose Queen and the co-the captains of both participating teams.

Mel and Larry often spent a week in California at the end of the year preparing for the Rose Bowl and the East-West Shrine Game. The East-West Game, played at San Francisco's Kezar Stadium a day or two before the Rose Bowl, featured college All-Americans who played for the benefit of Shriners Hospitals for Crippled Children. With a summer and fall chock full of baseball and football behind him, Mel felt refreshed out West even as he flew back and forth between San Francisco and Los Angeles to attend practices. Those sentiments changed in 1959, when he was asked to broadcast the Tournament of Roses Parade festivities, which began around 9 a.m. on New Year's Day, before he called the Rose Bowl in the afternoon. Mel was peeved because he always wanted to be well rested for his assignments, and he knew working the two-hour parade would sap him of vital energy.

After an early-morning wake-up call, Mel and Larry rode 10 miles northeast in a limousine from their Los Angeles hotel to Pasadena. There, Mel did television commentary of the 70th Rose Parade for ABC with Ronald Reagan and *Honeymooners* actress Audrey Meadows. ABC competed with NBC's coverage, featuring television personality Betty White and broadcaster Roy Neal. Neal later became known for his space coverage for NBC, which the parade's theme— "Adventures in Flowers"—foreshadowed. White pompons formed a rocket on the Long Beach, California, float "Adventures in Universe," while Gardena, California, contributed "The First Moon Shot." Another 10 Rose Parades would pass before Neil Armstrong and Buzz Aldrin made the actual "first moon shot" aboard Apollo 11.

When 1959's parade festivities ended around 10:30 a.m., Mel was already tired with hours to go until the Rose Bowl game. After a fried chicken lunch with Larry, he had an idea. The Allens went to a first aid station inside the stadium, where the staff let them and several NBC crewmen lie down on cots for a nap, invigorating Mel to call Iowa's 38-12 trouncing of Cal.

Alertness was indispensable for football, a game with dizzying substitution rates. Late in the 1956 Rose Bowl, Michigan State players rushed onto to the field as the Spartans attempted a game-winning field goal against UCLA.

As Michigan State lined up for kick, Mel and Larry hadn't yet identified the kicker's number. Suddenly, Larry turned to Mel. "It's Dave Kaiser," he said moments before Mel called Kaiser's 41-yard boot that gave Michigan State a 17-14 win.

"Go see if Al Helfer got that right," Mel said to his brother. Larry opened the door to the radio booth just in time to hear Helfer sign off. He had told listeners that Gerald Planutis, who missed another 41-yard field-goal attempt earlier in the game, booted the game-winner. When Larry checked with the press box, he found that everyone there had made Planutis the hero, too. They were wrong.

❀ ❀ ❀ ❀ ❀ ❀ ❀

Choosing Kaiser was a risky decision for Michigan State coach Duffy Daugherty. A leg injury had prevented the kicker from even attempting a field goal for his team before the 1956 Rose Bowl. But Daugherty still thought Kaiser was the Spartans' best long-distance kicker, something Larry gleaned from the pregame coaching meetings he and Mel were so adamant about attending. The Allen brothers got all sorts of tidbits from these conferences. Coaches even divulged trick plays they might use. Like Joe DiMaggio, they knew their secrets were sacred with Mel, who wouldn't dare tell the opposition about them. "Once you ever broke that confidence, man, you might as well go look for another job," Mel recalled in a 1970s interview.

Coaches liked and trusted Mel so much that they invited him to speak at team functions, where he quoted Knute Rockne. "The thing that lifts a man to be a champion is the emotional urge," Mel would say. Coaches saw such drive in the way Mel tirelessly applied himself to his job. They hoped Mel would rub off on their players, who intently listened as he spoke to them. "It is the general opinion that you were the best speaker that has ever appeared at one of our rallies," Donald Eckelbarger, Army's head cheerleader, wrote in a letter to Mel following Mel's speech at a 1958 "Beat Navy Rally" at West Point.

Notre Dame also invited Mel to talk at its pep rallies and banquets. (Mel did Irish telecasts from 1949 through 1951 for DuMont and NBC.)

"I want you to know that everyone connected with Notre Dame is deeply appreciative of your kindness in coming out to be the Toastmaster at our banquet," Notre Dame coach Frank Leahy, winner of five national titles during his Irish tenure, wrote to Mel in 1950. "You certainly did a marvelous job. Your closing comments impressed me very much. America needs more men like you at this time." Many other of college football's finest college coaches agreed. "I truly admire you—your sincerity and your ability," Bud Wilkinson, author of a 47-game winning streak at Oklahoma, once wrote to Mel. Woody Hayes, winner five national titles at Ohio State, penned a personal message for Mel on the cover of a playbook he gave him: "To Mel Allen ... A great sportscaster whose fairness and sincerity always shows through!"

In the city in which Hayes worked, Columbus, Ohio, Mel spoke annually at the Columbus Touchdown Club All-Sports Dinner, which benefited the United States Olympic Fund. "Columbus discovered America and then

Columbus discovered football," Mel said to more than 800 Touchdown Club members and guests to open the 1958 affair. Over the years in Columbus, Mel introduced Notre Dame's "Four Horsemen" and boxing heavyweight champions Jack Dempsey and Rocky Marciano to thunderclaps of applause. He also handed out awards for current sports achievement to an amateur golfer with a buzz cut and sheepish smile named Jack Nicklaus and to stilt-like University of Kansas basketball star Wilt Chamberlain. The top of Mel's head, nearly six feet, two inches from the ground, only reached the shoulders of the "Basketball Player of the Year" when they stood side by side.

Mel often told Columbus audiences that "no banquet in the country can compare with this one." Such praise convinced Sam Nicola, the Columbus dinner's general chairman, that making Mel master of ceremonies emeritus in the mid-1950s through mid-1960s gave his extravaganza legitimacy for continued success.

❉ ❉ ❉ ❉ ❉ ❉ ❉

Mel saw many of his old friends while journeying around the country for football, always making time for those who had helped him in the past. He visited Ted Husing, his old sportscasting mentor, while preparing for the 1960 Rose Bowl. Husing had developed a brain tumor in 1954 and, no longer able to work, moved to Pasadena to live under the care of his mother. He died in 1962 at age 60.

Mel lost Frank Thomas years before that to severe heart complications. Thomas had retired as Alabama's football coach after the 1946 season and become the school's athletic director. A near-death experience in 1950 kept Tommy from attending Mel Allen Day at Yankee Stadium. Just a week or so before those festivities, Tommy was elected to the Helms Hall College Football Hall of Fame in Los Angeles. Mel journeyed west to accept the honor on his behalf. In March 1951, Tommy lapsed into a coma for two days. When he awoke, he asked to see Mel, who rushed to his mentor's side. A doctor told Mel his presence was more beneficial to Tommy than any medicine or care, but Mel left Tuscaloosa knowing the coach was gravely ill. In November 1951, Mel wrote to University of Alabama president John Gallalee:

> Dear Dr. Gallalee:
> I hope you will not think me unduly presumptuous when I beg your indulgence for a moment in a matter both urgent and delicate.
> It is my sincere hope that you and those in command can find it convenient to retire Frank Thomas on a good salary commensurate with his tremendous contribution to the University perhaps retaining him only on an advisory capacity. No one has any greater love for the University then I and no one can exceed my zeal in wishing only the

best for Alabama. In my travels broadcasting football games at colleges all over the country I have been tremendously impressed with the manner in which the various schools show their appreciation to those who found themselves in the same situation now confronting Frank Thomas. I honestly feel, and strongly, that Coach Thomas not only has literally given his life to the University but in so doing has helped make Alabama a place of which all its sons and daughters are even prouder than ever. There are few men more deserving of this reward than Coach Thomas. Please do all you can to make his remaining time on this earth as pleasant as possible.

Again forgive me if I have stepped beyond any bonds of propriety but I am intensely eager to see the University again open its heart in a direction that will receive nationwide praise. You see I love Alabama. I also love Frank Thomas.

With deep gratitude for your kind consideration I remain
Most respectfully,
Mel Allen

Tommy fought off his illness for two and a half more years, dying of heart failure on May 12, 1954, at age 55. Mel received word while broadcasting a Yankees-Indians game in Cleveland. He was soon in Tuscaloosa to console Tommy's wife, Frances, and their children, with whom he rode during the funeral procession. A bright sun shone over the glorious spring day. It was the kind of weather in which Thomas loved to pick up a baseball glove and play catch with an assistant coach. Tommy's belly would protrude out of his white T-shirt as he threw. Mel smiled as he thought of his friend while reminiscing with some other famous members of the Crimson Tide family. One of them was Bear Bryant, now the head football coach at Texas A&M.

Tommy had given Bryant his coaching start as an Alabama assistant. When Bryant steered his Kentucky team to a berth in the 1951 Sugar Bowl against Bud Wilkinson and mighty Oklahoma, he sought out his old mentor for advice on solving the Sooners' Split-T offense. The Wildcats used two Thomas trademarks—opportunistic offense and an overly aggressive, pressuring defense—to pull off a stunning 13-7 victory.

Bryant's coaching heroics at Kentucky thrust him into the national spotlight. His first television experience came on *Sports Spot*, Mel's CBS show.

After asking Bryant a few football-related questions, Mel paused to light up a White Owl, inhaled and breathed out a cloud of smoke.

"It's wonderful," he said. "Would you like to try one of these mellow cigars, Bear?"

"Oh no," Bryant answered quickly, "I seldom smoke at all, and I never smoke cigars."

Fast-talking Mel, usually quick on his feet, was flabbergasted. He told viewers that the Bear had a reputation as a practical joker and prodded Bryant to try a White Owl.

"I don't see how anybody smokes these things," Bryant said, pushing the cigar away.

The cameras quickly faded to a commercial. When the show came back on, Bryant had wised up about the sponsor.

"I've changed my mind," he said. "How about one of those cigars, Mel?"

Mel and the Bear chatted about a more serious matter in November 1957 in College Station, Texas, before a Thanksgiving Day game between Texas A&M and Texas. After practice, Bryant, who was now coaching the Aggies, asked Mel to take a drive with him. The Bear had a greater burden on his mind than the Longhorns. Alabama wanted him to come back home to try and rejuvenate the Crimson Tide. Bryant was torn because the Aggie faithful adored him and he and Mary Harmon were quite happy in College Station. Bryant asked Mel what he should do.

"I don't know what to tell you, Paul," Mel said. "You've got a lot to keep you here. But there's nothing like being asked to come home."

Coaching in Tuscaloosa, Bryant almost immediately assumed a strong, imposing stature that epitomized to Alabamans the good qualities in a state that had a black eye from Governor George Wallace's opposition to integration. In 1961, Bryant led the Crimson Tide to a perfect season and their first national championship since 1941. President Kennedy visited Tuscaloosa to congratulate the team. Bryant and Allen, the proud faces of Alabama glory, posed for pictures with him.

Mel could claim a small stake in Bryant's success. While visiting with the Bear one fall football weekend, he wore a houndstooth-checked hat. Bryant removed the hat from Mel's head and tried it on.

"I like this," Bryant said. "I think I'll keep it."

Mel took the hat back.

"What size do you wear?" he said.

Mel sent Bryant the hat that would become a symbol of his coaching legend as he stalked Alabama's sidelines.

❈ ❈ ❈ ❈ ❈ ❈ ❈

During Mel's glorious college football era, the professional game was far less popular than it is today. So when Mel agreed to broadcast for the moribund Washington Redskins in 1952, the nation's capital was abuzz. *Washington Star* columnist Harry MacArthur even hailed Mel's arrival as a "miracle."

Mel was actually flattered when Redskins owner George Preston Marshall approached him with an offer in the lobby of the Shoreham Hotel. To Mel, this was another feather in his cap, not a second-rate assignment. Mel's main concern about the Redskins job was its potential conflict with his fall college football schedule.

"That's all right," Marshall told him. "We'll take a chance on that."

Mel broadcast Redskins games in 1952 and 1953, reporting to Washington's Griffith Stadium or wherever the Redskins played on the road the day after he broadcast his college games. Mel and color man Jim Gibbons, a longtime Washington radio personality, did a simulcast over dozens of radio stations from Massachusetts to Florida and some scattered TV outlets. They told listeners how "Slingin' Sammy" Baugh, who was then 38 years old, completed his first 11 passes of a game against the Chicago Cardinals. Despite the Hall of Famer's flash from the past, the Redskins went 4-8 that 1952 season under coach Earl "Curly" Lambeau. Lambeau, who founded the Green Bay Packers in 1919, led Washington to a 6-5-1 record in 1953.

Hoping to lesson the grind on his schedule, Mel passed on the Redskins in 1954, but the lure of the NFL tugged at him again in 1960. The league had begun to boom following Johnny Unitas's dramatic drive to win the 1958 NFL championship for Baltimore against the New York Giants. Played in front of national television audience in New York, the advertising capital of the world, "the game" featured the NFL's first ever sudden-death overtime ending. Afterwards, fans continued to pour into Yankee Stadium and other venues around the league. New Yorkers embraced their Giants: tackle Rosey Grier, who terrorized quarterbacks; left half Frank Gifford, who tore up the field with touchdown runs; middle linebacker Sam Huff, who delivered blistering hits on ball carriers.

Mel called the full 1960 schedule of Giants games over the entire CBS Radio Network, which strung from coast to coast. As Mel broadcast from Yankee Stadium, the deep, distinguished voice of Bob Sheppard, the building's eternal public-address announcer, echoed in the background, just as it did during baseball season: "Tackle by Grier and Robustelli." The commercials Mel read during Giants games also had a familiar ring:

> How many times you hear somebody say 'Christmas comes but once a year, thank goodness.' Chances are it's a woman shopper up to her ears in bundles, tired, trampled from the downtown mob scene. And what's worse, she can't seem to decide what to give her husband on Christmas morning. Oh, she's already got his big present but she's still looking for that little extra something that'll make this his best Christmas ever. Well, here's my tip to her and to all shoppers: Whatever else you give a man this Christmas, be sure to give him a box of White Owl cigars. You see, for a man, cigars are synonymous with red-letter days, festive occasions that just naturally call for a good cigar, and, believe me, White Owl's a mighty good cigar. Each and every White Owl is crammed full of quality tobacco that's been aged longer to make it smoke milder and taste better. So shoppers, for the man on your list, get the best: A box of wonderful White Owl cigars, economically priced from about a dollar and a half to around five dollars. You'll find them conveniently gift-wrapped and on display wherever fine cigars are sold.

Such advertising eloquence earned Mel 1960's "Salesman of the Year" honors from the National Association of Direct Selling Companies. White Owl and Ballantine, Giants sponsors in 1960, had lucked out again.

Jimmy Dolan was Mel's color man for Giants games, though sometimes Mel brought Larry in for commentary. As on Mel Allen Day a decade earlier, Mel gave his brother no forewarning.

"At the end of the game, he would turn to me, and suddenly, I'm on the air," Larry recalls. Most of the time, however, Mel flew solo over the Giants' airwaves, describing a roller-coaster season under coach Jim Lee Howell, who had led New York to the 1956 NFL championship.

The 1960 "football Giants," as Mel called the team on the air, raced to a rousing 5-1-1 record with a 27-24 comeback victory November 13 against the Pittsburgh Steelers.

"Gifford and Triplett in behind Conerly ... Schnelker, left end," Mel said in the first quarter of the game. "The ball is given to Gifford on a sweep, he's got blockers! HE'S GONNA GO! And he's OVER for the touchdown!"

Thunderous cheers shook Yankee Stadium.

"Darrell Dess and Jack Stroud pulled out and led the way and ... Rosie Brown," Mel said. "The Giants threw three rugged blockers out in front and they led the way. I believe I coulda scored there. Jimmy Dolan, all of us, Larry ... "

Mel had a way of sweetening esoteric football talk with a dab of Alabama honey. Of course, as Pat Summerall lined up to kick a potential game-winner with 30 second left in regulation, Mel relied on sheer emotion: "Conerly will hold, Summerall will try, there's the kick, it's up and it isssssss ... GOOD! IT'S GOOD!"

The Giants fizzled in the second half of their season. A win in their December 18 finale with the Cleveland Browns would have earned them only the Eastern Conference's spot in the Playoff Bowl, the NFL's consolation game between second-place finishers. Yet still, the Giants and Browns, bitter rivals playing for an opportunity to bask in the warmth of Miami, which hosted the Playoff Bowl, pounded at one another on the raw December day. New York's Dick Lynch intercepted Cleveland quarterback Milt Plum on the game's first play from scrimmage and dashed for a touchdown.

"First play is a pass," Mel told his listeners. "INTERCEPTED by Lynch on the 15, to the 10, to the five, he's over for the touchdown! How about that!"

The Giants led 34-21 in the fourth quarter when Cleveland, winner three NFL championships under Hall of Fame coach Paul Brown, came alive behind, another Hall of Famer, fullback Jim Brown. "Milt Plum, looking over the defense, gives the ball off to Jimmy Brown," Mel said. "He's got a hole, bolting through, down and OVER for a touchdown! ... Boy, he is hard to stop. He had a hole there and he carried men with him and moved in for the touchdown, and Cleveland has 41 points." The Browns would win 48-34. As Cleveland ran out the clock in the fourth quarter, fans who remained from a Yankee Stadium crowd that once swelled to 63,000 booed loudly. The jeers eventually ceased and Yankee Stadium fell silent. Mel wrapped up his broadcast and, like the Giants fans, disappeared into the dark winter's night. He would be back. The House that Ruth Built was always reborn in the spring.

CHAPTER 15

Dial 'M' for Murder

The Yankees had a distinctly different face as the 1961 season dawned. For the first spring since 1948, Casey Stengel wasn't directing the team from the dugout.

Owners Dan Topping and Del Webb had dumped him shortly after New York's seven-game loss to Pittsburgh in the 1960 World Series. The main reason the owners fired Stengel was because they didn't want to lose Ralph Houk. Houk, a coach on Stengel's staff, had proven to be a natural leader while managing the Yankees' American Association team in Denver from 1955 through 1957. A soldier who had earned the rank of major by the end of World War II, Houk was a master motivator whose teams loved him. He stuck by his regular players through slumps and stuck up for his entire squad no matter what. Several other big league teams coveted Houk, so Topping and Webb dropped Stengel, who had won 10 American League pennants in his 12 seasons with the Yankees, and promoted the "Major" to manager.

Houk, who was 41 years old when the Yankees installed him as manager, represented what Topping and Webb described publicly as a youth movement. Stengel was out, Topping told the media, because the Yankees were invoking an age-limit policy. Topping said Stengel's contract called for his "retirement" at 70. Topping and Webb also unceremoniously dismissed 66-year-old general manager George Weiss following the 1960 Series with the same public rationale. However, the 58-year-old face of Roy Hamey, Weiss's replacement, proved that Topping was only telling half of the truth.

"Call it a youth program or whatever you want to call it," Topping told the press at the Yankees' Fifth Avenue offices on the day Weiss announced his resignation, "but we've got to think of the future. No man can go on forever."

Cruel, cold-hearted decision making governed the years Topping and Webb co-owned the Yankees after Larry MacPhail sold off his interest in the team following the 1947 season. Weiss, a solemn, serious, impersonal man, had once embodied the Yankees' stone-cold arrogance. He drew up player contracts with a tight grip on the team's purse strings and negotiated salaries practically down to the last dollar. Ruling from the Fifth Avenue offices, Weiss never schmoozed with players. On the rare occasions he entered the Yankees clubhouse, he quickly ducked in and made a beeline for Stengel's office.

"If we saw him, somebody was gone," Yogi Berra recalls. "Everybody'd say, 'Uh oh.'"

Weiss, who joined the Yankees organization in 1932, was the architect of New York's incomparable farm system that served as the foundation for a dynasty. From 1946 through 1960, he set the standard for major league general managers by assembling a string of teams with unrivaled success. Weiss not only scouted and signed the best young players in the country, but he constantly orchestrated shrewd deals to sharpen the Yankees' major league roster.

Before the 1960 season, Weiss had pulled off a mega-deal with the Kansas City Athletics for rising outfield star Roger Maris. The general manager packaged Hank Bauer and Don Larsen, players he thought were no longer productive, in the seven-player deal. Weiss easily parted with these two indelible contributors to Yankees history knowing he was acquiring Maris, whose quick, powerful left-handed swing was perfectly suited for Yankee Stadium's short porch, located a mere 296 feet down the right field line from home plate.

In 1960, Maris's first season with the Yankees, he clubbed 39 home runs and won the American League's Most Valuable Player award. But Maris's MVP season paled next to his 1961 encore, when he clouted a then-major league record 61 homers.

That same 1961 season, Mickey Mantle, who batted fourth in the lineup behind Maris, locked his teammate in a heroic home run duel.

"Here come the M&M boys," Mel would tell Yankees fans over the air. "Dial 'M' for Murder."

Mel was playing off the name of a popular 1950s Broadway show turned Alfred Hitchcock flick as the sluggers staged their own thriller at Yankee Stadium. Mantle and Maris combined to hit 115 homers in 1961, breaking the major league record of 107 that Babe Ruth and Lou Gehrig set in 1927.

The Yankees ran away with the 1961 American League pennant. The only real competition they experienced was internal as Mantle and Maris swatted at Babe Ruth's single-season record of 60 homers. Mantle outhomered Maris 7-0 to start the season, but Maris went on a tear in May and June, homering 24 times in 38 games. Maris had 27 homers to Mantle's 25 by end of June. The Great Home Run Race was on. Like two thoroughbreds racing neck and neck, the M&M boys lunged back and forth for the home run edge for most of the remainder of the season as they chased the Bambino.

"That's swung on, there's a long drive to deep right field … that ball is gonna beeee going, going gone!" Mel roared during the first game of an August 13 doubleheader at Washington. "Mickey Mantle rocks one out for his 45th of the year."

Maris clouted No. 44 in the same game and followed with his 45th in Game 2.

"Swung on, there's a high drive deep to right field annnnd the ball is gonna be going, going gone!" Mel yelled. "Maris drives over the right-field wall—number 45—and Mickey, waiting at home plate, extends his hand in greeting."

Mantle and Maris were friends, but sportswriters and fans pitted them against one another. Most favored Mantle, the engaging, homegrown golden boy who embraced the energy of New York, to Maris, the shy outsider from Fargo, North Dakota, who sometimes bristled at the big-city pressure. Fans who tuned in to television station WPIX or WCBS at 880 on their dials, the Yankees' new flagship station that 1961 season, never heard a bias in Mel's voice.

"You know every time he comes up and man, all the photographers get up and crowd around the plate—11 of 'em," Mel told his listeners on September 17 as Maris batted against the Tigers in Detroit. "I know it bothers him—out of the corner of the eye … two away in the 12th. Four all. Terry Fox into the stretch. And the pitch … swung on, there's a drive hit to deep right-center field! Bruton going after it. That ball is gonna beeeee IN THERE for a home run! Number 58 for Roger Maris against the upper deck in deep right-center!"

❖ ❖ ❖ ❖ ❖ ❖

By mid-September, the flu had knocked Mantle from the home run race. But Maris had hit 58 homers by the time the Yankees played the Orioles September 20 in Baltimore. The day marked Yankees game No. 154, which baseball commissioner Ford Frick had circled for Mantle and Maris earlier in the season. The Babe had belted his 60 home runs during a 154-game season in 1927. The major league season had grown to 162 games in 1961 with the addition of the American League's ninth and 10th teams, the Minnesota Twins and Los Angeles Angels. Frick, a former friend and ghostwriter to the Babe, had declared that Mantle and Maris would have tie or equal Ruth's record in 154 games in order to avoid asterisks next to their names in the record book.

New York could wrap up the AL pennant with a win September 20, but that story was a side note. The Yankees had already put second-place Detroit away. The crush of reporters that crowded Memorial Stadium had come to watch Maris, who needed at least two homers to avoid a dreaded asterisk. Maris confronted young fireballer Milt Pappas and a stiff wind that remained after Hurricane Esther had swirled around Baltimore.

"A ball game between Minnesota and Washington scheduled to be played in the nation's capital has been postponed because of rain," Phil Rizzuto, who had brought his Brooklyn accent to the Yankees' broadcast booth in 1957, said over the Home of Champions Network. "Let's hope that it's not moving this way, though, if the wind's blowing northerly, that means it's comin' this way, right Joe?"

Rizzuto was speaking to Joe Ripley, who worked for the advertising agency that handled the accounts for the Yankees' sponsors.

"If Washington is to the south of Baltimore and the winds are northerly ..." Rizzuto continued. "Doesn't make any difference? No? ... Oh, I'd neva make a weathaman anyway."

The weather didn't seem so important after Maris clocked a 2-1 Pappas pitch in the third inning. The rising line drive sliced through the wind and landed in the right-field bleachers. The opposing crowd erupted, as did Rizzuto.

"DRIVE DEEP TO RIGHT!" he screamed in his high-pitched voice. "Way back there! Way back and there's number 59 for Roger Maris! Atta boy, Roger—59 home runs. And look at the photographers go—man, he really creamed that one."

Mel called Maris's shot for Yankees television station WPIX.

"There's one!" he said as Maris connected. "It is going ... it is going ... it is ... GONE! NUMBER 59!"

As if he were doing a poetry reading, Mel dramatically paused twice in the middle of his call. Rizzuto always marveled at how Mel could build up the importance of an event. When he sensed a big play unfolding, Mel gradually increased the volume of his voice to an excitable level. "Not like me," Rizzuto once said. "I'm up all the time. He'd go up and down. He got excited when it mattered most."

Like when Maris walked to the plate in the top of the seventh inning.

"And up comes Roger Maris," Mel told Yankees radio listeners, the words "Roger" and "Maris" ringing above the rest of his sentence. As the crowd buzzed with each pitch from Orioles reliever Dick Hall, Mel remained mostly silent, letting the fans tell his story.

"There's a strike," he said as a few cheers fluttered in the background. "Nothing and one."

Mel was quiet for 18 seconds as Hall checked for a sign from catcher Gus Triandos and delivered.

"There's a drive," Mel said, his voice elevating with a burst of crowd noise, "but it is gonna go foul." His voice lowered as the long fly ball landed out of play. "He got up under it but it went foul."

Mel waited another 15 seconds as the crowd stirred.

"Two strikes on him," Mel said, "and the pitch ... swung on, there's a high fly ball to right field, deep, and it's gonna beeeeee ... caught by Robinson."

Mel said the word "caught" sharply as Orioles right fielder Earl Robinson squeezed the ball in his glove. From the middling tone of Mel's voice, listeners could tell the ball never had a chance of clearing the wall. The wind had caught it and held it in the park.

"Rog gave it great try," Mel said. "He thrilled the crowd with his long fly to deep right and gets a hand as he goes back to the dugout. That could be his last time at bat in this game—4-2 New York, seventh inning—but we'll see. ... "

Maris would get one more shot. When Orioles manager Paul Richards saw that the slugger was due to hit third in the top of the ninth, he brought in nasty knuckleballer Hoyt Wilhelm to pitch. Wilhelm, who would one day be enshrined in the Baseball Hall of Fame, had no-hit the Yankees in 1958. If he could throw his knuckler for strikes, the right-hander was unhittable. At nearly 40 years old, though, the pitcher threw much flatter fastballs. Richards told Wilhelm that a fastball to Maris would cost him $5,000. After Wilhelm disposed of sure-hitting Bobby Richardson and Tony Kubek on four pitches, he tossed Maris two straight knucklers.

Batting with a backdrop of anxious chatter, Maris fouled the first knuckleball off with a check swing. Wilhelm fooled him again with his next pitch.

"A little tap, a roller down the line on a half-swing and Wilhelm tags him out," Mel said half-spiritedly, capturing the anticlimactic moment. "They give him a standing ovation here," he said, his voice livening again and the crowd cheered. "Of course, the ballgame is not over—it could go into extra innings, but they still give him a standing ovation. He got 59 homers."

That total was more than any other player not named "Babe" had amassed over a 154-game season. Unlike the punchy reporters who pointed out Maris's shortcomings to him all season, Mel chose to shower the slugger with praise in the visitor's locker room after the Yankees' 4-2 win, which clinched the AL pennant.

"Hey Rog, commere," Mel barked as he toted his television microphone around. "Congratulations!"

"Thank you very much," Maris said softly.

"Rog," Mel said, "I'm sorry you didn't get number 60."

These were probably the most docile words Maris had heard from a media member all year.

"Well, I was tryin', Mel," he said.

"I know you did," Mel replied.

With Mel's fatherly hand on his shoulder Maris, a shy man in the face of ferocious expectations, knew he could relax during this interview, which lasted a few minutes.

"You won't mind the asterisk, will ya?" Mel asked. Maris had heard this question over and over. But this time, he didn't feel antagonized.

"I sure won't," he said.

"Rog," Mel continued, "in this last month, I know you've been under severe pressure."

"That, you are right on," Maris said, tensing up again.

"Do you feel relieved?"

"Right now, yes, very relieved," Maris replied, exhaling. "The pennant's cinched and the 154-game limit is over."

"That was the main thing, winning the pennant, of course," Mel continued.

"That's right."

"God bless ya," Mel said, ending the interview. "Great team man, Rog."

"Thank ya."

"I remember the times you bunted to get the run home, too," Mel said, laughing out loud. "Wonderful. Gonna get a shot of ya here, Rog … "

A mass of photographers converged around Maris.

"Well I'll tell ya, they've got a lot of pictures—I'll tell ya that much," Maris said, making a rare attempt at a joke around reporters.

"They all promise ya copies?" Mel asked, not missing a beat. He had Maris on a roll.

"I think I've got enough pictures to wallpaper my house right now," the 59-homer man cracked.

Mel chortled again in his characteristic fashion as and he turned and continued his clubhouse interviews of Yankees players who drenched one another with Ballantine beer.

"Hey fellas, that's made to drink, not pour," Mel boomed. "The Crisp Refresher! Yessir."

Mel spoke with every player and team official he could find, though a prominent Yankee was noticeably absent.

"Is Mick here?" he asked, his voiced reverberating through the clubhouse. "Eh Mick?" he asked loudly a few minutes later.

"I'm sorry that Mick's heavy cold kept him from being on," Mel finally said, his voice falling more solemn. "He's got a very, very heavy cold and had to bundle up and get back to the hotel."

❊ ❊ ❊ ❊ ❊ ❊ ❊

If either Mantle or Maris had to break his beloved Babe's record, Mel privately preferred that Mantle do so. The Mick was a true Yankee, the successor to DiMaggio in center field who was destined for the Hall of Fame. Mel also admired the way the Mick always played hurt. After blowing out his right knee during the 1951 World Series, Mantle hobbled around for the rest of his career. Day after day, Mel watched him tape his leg from ankle to thigh to protect the knee, then take the field and impact almost every game with a monster homer, a running catch or even a stolen base. Mel called Mantle "the best one-legged ballplayer I ever saw."

When Mel watched Mantle drag with the flu, he asked the Mick if he had spoken to Sidney Gaynor, the Yankees' team physician. Mantle had, but still felt lousy. "Would you want to get a second opinion?" Mel asked him. When Mantle acted agreeable, Mel gave him the name of his East Side general practitioner, Max Jacobson. Jacobson administered mood-lifting, energizing "miracle" shots. The injections were concoctions of vitamins, enzymes, hormones and, as *The New York Times* exposed in 1972, amphetamines. This was an era when the public never questioned the words and actions of physicians. People assumed whatever doctors did was in the best interest of their health.

To his patients, Jacobson was just "Dr. Feelgood," whose shots seemed to work magic. "It was medicine, wonderful medicine," singer and entertainer Eddie Fisher wrote in his 1999 autobiography, *Been There, Done That*. Fisher was just one of dozens of the doctor's high-society patients. President Kennedy and his wife, Jacqueline, also saw Jacobson, who said he administered shots to the president before a 1961 Vienna summit meeting with Soviet Premier Nikita Khrushchev. Some of Jacobson's other clients included pop singer Johnny Mathis, writer Truman Capote, actor Cecil B. DeMille and playwright Tennessee Williams.

Jacobson was an inner-circle celebrity doctor. If you knew the right people, you met him. When Mel, a man who never got over being impressed by famous people, was introduced to Jacobson, he was sold on the doctor's star-studded list of clients alone.

"If the president and his wife go to him, well it was good enough for Mel Allen," his sister Esther says.

Esther's husband Danny, the urologist, told Mel he thought Jacobson was a quack. Dr. Kaufman was right.

In 1975, the New York State Board of Regents revoked Jacobson's medical license, citing 48 counts of unprofessional conduct. At the time, at least one of Jacobson's patients—Mark Shaw, a photographer for President Kennedy—had died from amphetamine poisoning, and the doctor was suspected of contributing to several other deaths. Jacobson's injections temporarily lifted the spirits of his patients but also caused a colossal crash after the effects wore off. The patients experienced bouts with depression, paranoia, severe weight loss, changes in personality, irritability and excessive talkativeness, just to name a few side effects. In his autobiography, Fisher details nearly four decades of super highs and pavement lows that Jacobson's shots caused.

Jacobson's 1950s and 1960s clients like Fisher didn't know he was injecting them with heavy doses of a deadly, addictive drug. Mel swore by Jacobson, so much so that he took his parents to see him, too. Before he met Jacobson, Mel had raced around at the top of his profession for years, staying one step ahead of the competition and his health. By the early 1960s, however, he had begun to slow down, and Max's magic injections seemed to help him.

The shots were an apparent cure-all for middle-aged ailments. Jacobson said he cleared up a case of President Kennedy's laryngitis prior to an address to the United Nations with a shot to the neck. Fisher says Jacobson's shots invigorated his failing voice for stellar singing performances at the Copacabana and Grossinger's.

"Max could cure the world," Fisher wrote. So why couldn't he fix Mantle's case of the flu?

When the Mick arrived at Jacobson's office off Central Park West, he immediately found the doctor a little creepy. With his white lab coat, dark-rimmed glasses, thick German accent and chemical-stained fingernails, Dr. Feelgood resembled Dr. Frankenstein.

"He used a syringe that looked as large as a bicycle pump, and then he injected me too high on my right hip with a needle that wasn't sterilized," Mantle wrote in his 1994 book, *All My Octobers*. "The pain was so bad, I swear I think he actually hit the bone. I said to him, 'Hot damn, that hurts,' and he assured me I would be all right momentarily. He told me to walk it off, don't catch a cab. I almost passed out on the street."

The area on Mantle's leg where Jacobson stuck the needle became infected, and the Mick developed a large, painful abscess. The combination of the injury and a high fever (Jacobson's shot hadn't even cleared up the flu) sabotaged the rest of Mantle's regular season. He would finish with 54 homers, seven behind Maris's record-breaking total of 61.

Mel, of course, had just been trying to help Mantle. But Topping was furious that his announcer had sent his star player to an unauthorized doctor. The owner even thought about firing Mel. But how could he? Mel was the Yankees' No. 1 spokesman, his name and voice synonymous with the ball club. Mel's radio and television accounts of the M&M boys' blows drew fans from faraway places to Yankee Stadium. Attendance was up by almost 1,000 fans a game from 1960. Some years, the tight-fisted Yankees only needed to draw an additional 10,000 fans for an *entire season* to make a profit. Mel wasn't going anywhere.

❖ ❖ ❖ ❖ ❖ ❖ ❖

During the Yankees' 158th game of 1961, Maris uncoiled his compact swing at a hanging curve from the Orioles' Jack Fisher. "There it is!" Mel told his Yankees radio listeners as the ball rose into the air. "There it is!" The ball seemed to sail in slow motion toward the right field-wall at Yankee Stadium. "If it stays fair … there it-is!" Mel's words "it" and "is" blended together as the ball banged off the upper deck and back onto the field. "NUM-BER 60!"

A sparse but hearty crowd stood for a standing ovation. Maris motored around the bases with his head down, his typical home run trot. His teammates, who had heard these same Yankees fans boo him as he dared to challenge their blessed Mickey to a home run derby, insisted on changing Maris' routine. They pushed him out onto the field a curtain call.

"And they're callin' him out of the dugout!" Mel yelled over the air. "This is MOST unusual!"

Maris reluctantly took off his cap and bowed.

"Now this IS something," Mel said.

Maris trotted past the Babe on the final day of the regular season, October 1, 1961. A daytime crowd of only about 23,000 gathered at Yankee Stadium for New York's game with the Red Sox. The crowd whistled and cheered loudly as Maris walked to the plate with one out in the bottom of the fourth inning and public-address announcer Bob Sheppard announced him in that deep, distinctive voice: "Numba nine … Roga Maris … centa field … numba nine." The decibel level rocketed even higher with Maris's drive off Tracy Stallard's 2-0 pitch.

The ball rose high into the air and dropped into the right-field stands, one section of the cavernous ballpark that was packed.

"Here's the windup," Rizzuto told Yankees radio listeners, "the pitch, fastbawl ... HIT DEEP TO RIGHT! THIS COULD BE IT! WAY BACK THEYA! HOOOOOLY COW, HE DID IT! SIXTY-ONE FOR MARIS!"

Mel was in the broadcast booth but taking a break from the radio and television microphones during the historic home run. Rizzuto and Red Barber, who had fled from Brooklyn to the Bronx in 1954 after a power struggle with Dodgers owner Walter O'Malley, recorded the calls for the Yankees.

"I told the fans to be prepayed, they'd never know it was a homa," Rizzuto said as he handed the radio airwaves to Barber after the fourth inning. "I said, 'Holy cow, theya's numba 61,' and I screamed and I got a headache."

"Still have it?" asked Barber, whose formal style would never allow him to share such personal sentiments with his listeners.

"I still got it, and I need somethin' right now, Red," Rizzuto said as he scurried over to the television side.

Barber painfully forced a laugh.

"Well ... " he said, then remained silent for several seconds.

Had Barber unleashed the venom he really felt, he might have lost his job. In 15 years, the Yankees broadcast booth had taken a 180-degree turn from the jovial Allen-Hodges years. Though Mel, Barber and Rizzuto, who teamed to handle Yankees radio and television broadcasts as a trio between 1957 and 1962 and in 1963 and 1964 as a foursome with Jerry Coleman, always sounded like they got along over the air, the three were not friends.

※ ※ ※ ※ ※ ※ ※

Barber's move to the Yankees in 1954 was an earth-shattering event. Fans on local and national levels perceived him and Mel as major rivals. Mel was the voice of the lordly Yankees, Barber the breath of blue-collar Brooklyn, teams that seemed to play annually in a Subway Series. Now the figureheads of these two rival franchises would work together.

"Even in ideal conditions, that's not a very good setup," says Ernie Harwell, who assisted Barber on Dodgers broadcasts in the late 1940s and Russ Hodges on Giants baseball games from 1950 through 1953. "It meant for a little acrimony."

Mel and Red always measured their words and actions carefully around one another.

"Am extremely happy to be once again broadcasting the Worlds Series with you," Barber wrote to Mel in a telegram dated September 18, 1947, "and wish to congratulate you on your assignment."

After the pair worked the 1949 Series side by side, Mel wrote his partner a similarly laudatory letter.

"Believe me," Mel told Barber, "it was a pleasure to have joined with you again on a World Series broadcast. Here's to hoping it happens often."

When he introduced Barber during the middle of Game 6 of the 1952 Series, Mel played off the words "shaving luxury" he had just used in a Gillette advertisement: "For a real telecasting luxury, plus the valuable benefits of so many years of covering sports in his inimitable fashion, let's use the Ol' Redhead, Red Barber." Replied Barber: "Thank you, Mel. That's another case of the pot calling the kettle black."

When Barber turned their 1952 NBC Series telecast over to Mel in the middle of Game 7, he said: "And moving over to the microphone, one of the brilliant broadcasters of our day—it is always a real privilege and a pleasure to be associated with him at any time, especially on a World Series for Gillette—is Mel Allen. Mel, how does this one look to you, Melrose?" Mel was silent. "That pause was meaningful," he finally said. "That's one that's tough to answer, Red."

Allen and Barber always smiled side by side when they knew the camera was running. But when they thought they were off the air after Game 7 of the 1952 Series, they sat silent and expressionless. Mel's eyes danced around the booth, looking everywhere but at Barber, who had his head down as he adjusted his microphone. When Mel glanced toward his producers for a go-ahead to wrap up the Series for NBC's viewers, he realized he and Barber were already on the air.

"Well Red," he said, snapping to attention, "the camera's back on and it was a tremendous Series."

When Barber heard what his partner said, he instantly flashed a grin.

"Congratulations, Mel, on a great job and congratulations to the New York Yankees," he said. As Barber praised Casey Stengel, Mel scratched his head, looking disinterested in what his partner was saying. When Mel took another turn to speak, Barber glanced down and around, as if similarly apathetic.

This postgame moment had encapsulated the relationship of Allen and Barber, which was always professional but also a little stiff.

"It was a thrill for me to work a World Series with a veteran like Red Barber," Mel told ESPN four decades after the 1952 Series. "But I never thought I was competing with him, except to this extent: I was always hopeful that I held my own against someone who was recognized."

In Barber's mind, no broadcaster could completely compare with him.

"Nobody," he wrote in *Rhubarb in the Catbird Seat,* "has ever worked harder in preparing for a broadcast that I have."

Barber was so fond of himself he even spoke in the third person, calling himself "the Ol' Redhead" on the air.

Barber liked to think he had contributed to Mel's astronomical fame. When he turned down Larry MacPhail's invitation to broadcast Yankees games immediately after World War II, he wrote in *Rhubarb in the Catbird Seat* that, "the track was clear" for Mel's career to take off in the Bronx.

"If I had taken MacPhail's offer and gone over to the Stadium, people might not have heard so much about Mel Allen," he wrote. "Perhaps I would have been known as the Voice of the Yankees."

But Mel was the one who had long held that title by the time Barber became a Yankee in 1954. Barber didn't try to challenge Mel for his role as the Yankees' top broadcaster. Though he made the same Yankees salary ($50,000) as Mel, he accepted a much less prominent role in the Bronx than he had had in Brooklyn. He handled a pre- and postgame interview show and called some play-by-play innings here and there at home games. He rarely traveled with the team. Nevertheless, Barber said, he worked alongside Mel as "a colleague, as an equal, but with different duties."

Mel always acted cordial around Barber and certainly never treated him like an underling.

"No one could have been more cooperative and agreeable than Mel was," Barber wrote in *Rhubarb in the Catbird Seat*.

To avoid confrontation at Yankee Stadium, the two men often simply stayed out of each other's way. If they broadcast the same game together, they worked independently.

During these days before booth analysts existed, baseball broadcasters called their allotted radio innings by themselves. If a partner wasn't handling the team's telecast, he sat silently next to the radio guy. He wouldn't speak unless the on-air man asked him a question or introduced him for commentary. During slow games, broadcasters might attempt to banter back and forth with their partners, but Allen and Barber rarely did this.

"They would separate, totally and completely," says Coleman.

Jim Woods, a Yankees broadcaster from 1953 through 1956, provided a helpful buffer between Allen and Barber. A good ol' boy from the Midwest with a gravelly voice, Woods was known as "the Possum." Enos "Country" Slaughter came up with the nickname while surveying Woods's tattered, gray-haired buzz cut.

"I've seen better heads on a possum," Slaughter said.

Woods laughed off the pet name in the same amiable fashion he approached his role in the booth. He was the quintessential No. 2 man, a fine baseball broadcaster who always seemed to be stuck behind a more esteemed colleague. Woods welcomed his role as secondary player to Allen and Barber, working wherever and whenever he was needed without complaining.

"Mel and I never had a coolness between us, and Jim helped what could have been a sticky situation," Barber wrote in *The Broadcasters*.

Barber once declared that Mel, Woods and himself comprised "the best baseball broadcasting trio in history." But after three seasons, the Yankees split up the threesome.

Their breakup process began on Old Timers' Day in 1956, when New York cut Phil Rizzuto, who was nearly 39 years old and had been reduced to a role player. Ballantine president Carl W. Badenhausen and his sons, Rizzuto's golf partners, at a New Jersey country club, didn't want to lose the Scooter to another organization. Rizzuto had a gregarious nature and name recognition that could potentially sell an awful lot of beer. As the president of Ballantine, the

Yankees' chief sponsor, Badenhausen had significant influence over the club's selection of broadcasters. After the 1956 season, he ordered the Yankees to fire Woods and hire Rizzuto.

Mel was outraged that Ballantine and the Yankees would dump a pro like Woods for an ex-ballplayer with virtually no broadcasting experience. Mel tried to save Woods's job, and, when he couldn't do that, he helped find the Possum a position in the Giants' booth with Hodges for the team's final season in New York.

"Mel," Woods wrote in a letter to his ex-partner dated March 10, 1957, "I just want to thank you from the bottom of my heart for everything. For the loyal friend you have always been and for being such a wonderful guy to work for and with. If in the future plan of unforeseen things I would have the opportunity to return to the Yankees, I know the determining factor would be you a great deal more than the ball club. There are a lot of things you feel about a person that you just can't put into words, but I hope you know how I feel."

Woods said he learned more from Mel than any of his other partners, including Barber, Hodges, Bob Prince and Jack Buck. Before coming to New York, Woods had been a sports broadcasting bigwig in Atlanta the way Curt Gowdy was in Oklahoma City. Woods was well known around town for his coverage of college football (the University of Georgia), professional baseball (the Atlanta Crackers of the Southern League) and appearances on local television shows. He actually had to take a pay cut to take the Yankees job.

"I thought I was pretty good when I joined the Yankees," Woods once told author Ted Patterson, "but Mel soon took that misguided opinion away from me."

As Woods worked one of his first Yankees exhibition games from St. Petersburg, he made what he thought was a routine call: "Mantle swings ... there's a foul back on top." Sitting beside Woods in the booth, Mel snapped his fingers, as he often did when a junior partner displeased him.

"What?" Woods said, looking at Mel.

"On top of what?" Mel asked.

"The roof," Woods replied.

"Well then say the roof," Mel growled. "Complete your sentence."

"Little things like that made better announcers out of all of us who ever worked with Mel Allen," Woods told Patterson.

Mel gave his partners on-the-job tutorials in baseball broadcasting. During an assistant's first spring training with the Yankees, Mel might leave the booth for a couple of innings to allow him to work alone.

"That's to let him know he's on his own and I have confidence in him," Mel said in 1953 as he prepared to break in Woods. "If I stay there he'll know I'm listening to every syllable and he'll get nervous."

The tactic had the opposite effect on Rizzuto, who struggled mightily to fill the dead air without Mel's help.

"Holy cow!" Rizzuto recalls. "That was torture."

Rizzuto knows, however, that he would never have gotten into broadcasting, his profession for 40 years after he retired as a player, without Mel's prodding. When Rizzuto was sitting on Stengel's bench during his last couple of Yankees seasons, Mel would invite him up to the booth to do an occasional half-inning of play-by-play.

"Maybe it's the ham in me, but the more I did it, the more I loved it," Rizzuto recalled later.

Mel encouraged Rizzuto to work on his broadcasting skills at home by watching Dodgers and Giants games on television with the volume turned down. As Rizzuto practiced in his Hillside, New Jersey, den, he thought broadcasting was cinch. That was before he became Mel's assistant.

"I didn't realize he was a perfectionist," Rizzuto says.

Rizzuto compared working with Mel to playing under Joe McCarthy, the manager who would chew someone out in front of the rest of the team to ensure that the guy didn't make the same mistake twice. As Rizzuto mispronounced words (saying "Ath-EL-letics" instead of "Ath-LET-ics," "Cuber" instead of "Cuba" and "root" instead of "route") and blurted out calls before umpires actually made them, Mel sometimes corrected his partner's mistakes on the air. "It bothered my mother," Rizzuto says, laughing. Rizzuto got upset, however, when Mel asked him to stop using the expression "Holy cow," which Cardinals broadcaster Harry Caray had already popularized in baseball circles. Mel talked to Rizzuto about "Holy cow" as a favor to Caray, who complained to him that Rizzuto had stolen the saying. "That's not yours," Mel told Rizzuto firmly. Rizzuto, a proud, pint-sized man who became an American League MVP after a Giants coach told him he was more apt to be a shoe-shine boy, wouldn't budge. He told Mel he had used the expression as a kid growing up in Brooklyn before he even knew who Harry Caray was.

"Mel," Rizzuto said, "I can't stop doing something that keeps me out of trouble when you might want to say something mean."

Mel could think of plenty of derogatory things to say about Rizzuto, the most difficult partner he ever endured. He always cringed when, right over the air, Rizzuto read from his list of friends celebrating birthdays. Even with the bases loaded, the Scooter might say "Happy Birthday" to Joe in Hoboken or Jane in Hackensack.

"That was not my way of doing things," Mel said. "I was used to network stuff on CBS. You just don't do that kind of thing. It was his own style. It took a while for people to get adjusted to that style, which is not the normal way of doing a game. We all like to have a little fun here and there depending on the game, but we never had a list of birthdays. The game was primary. Let's put it that way. To Phil, the game was secondary. That's not a criticism on my part. I just mean that is his style."

The Scooter also developed a habit of ducking out of a broadcast early to beat traffic or to play golf. "Where you going?" Mel would ask when the Scooter stood up in the booth. Mel never knew. During one of their very first games together, Rizzuto decided to go home after the Yankees and Tigers entered extra innings.

"And now to take you into the 10th inning, here is ..." Mel said, looking around. "Here is ..."

Rizzuto was listening to Mel as he drove across the George Washington Bridge.

If he stayed for an entire game, Rizzuto would rush home to his wife, Cora, right after the final out was recorded. Mel's previous partners had often remained for a while to talk about the game or to go over how they handled the broadcast.

"But Mel, we can't win a ballgame," Rizzuto would tell his exasperated partner.

To Mel, his work was his love and his life. To Rizzuto, it was just a job that he never took too seriously. At the expense of talking about a game, the Scooter would discuss the Italian dish Cora had prepared for him the previous night or his fear of lightning and the wasps that buzzed over his head in the broadcast booth.

As he digressed, the Scooter would utter plenty of malapropisms. He told WPIX viewers in 1961 that Mel was out "enjoying the holiday" on Yom Kippur, the Jewish Day of Atonement. Rizzuto's commentary was usually much more harmless.

"Old Mr. Moon, lookin' down on us," he said while broadcasting a 1960 Yankees-Senators game over the radio. "Boy, he is bright now that it is gettin' dark. Watchin' the ballgame for nothin.'"

When he talked about the game, Rizzuto shared an intuitive player's perspective. He would tell listeners how Hank Bauer's bunt failed because the outfielder was holding the bat too tightly or that Mickey Mantle was a great two-strike bunter. No matter what Rizzuto said, though, his charming, innocent, unsophisticated manner endeared him to most Yankees fans. So did Rizzuto's raw Brooklyn accent as it uttered "Clete Boyah" and "Orlando Cepader." The accent, though, made Rizzuto feel insecure working alongside the sweet Southern sounds of Allen and Barber.

"I was very nasal then," he says. "And I would breathe when you're not supposed to breathe. I finally went to opera singers and asked them how I could get rid of this. And they helped me tremendously. I wouldn't dare ask Mel or Red."

Rizzuto always thought Mel picked on him, and he rebelled. He bought a toy clicker and clacked it when Mel snapped at him in the booth and he took bathroom breaks that lasted two or three innings. Barber had much less tolerance for such childishness than Mel and would go out of his way to try to embarrass Rizzuto on the air. He asked questions he knew would stump the Scooter. *What states border Nevada? What is Michigan's state rock?* Or, in his calm, irreverent way, Barber would scold Rizzuto's syntax. When the Scooter shared with listeners that he craved a "pizza pie," Barber would say, "Pizza means pie."

Barber and Mel found new respect for one another while working with Rizzuto. The Scooter served as proof to them that broadcasters should attend college and season themselves further through a series of jobs in their field before covering major sports teams. Ex-athletes like Rizzuto, Allen and Barber felt, only denied professional broadcasters like Jim Woods of jobs.

"I doubt I'd have had the same opportunity to make it to the top of my profession if I were breaking in today," Mel told *TV Guide* several months before he died in 1996. "Too many top positions are handed to ex-ballplayers."

By the late 1950s, the exodus from the field to the booth had already begun. Rizzuto and Pee Wee Reese, his former Brooklyn counterpart at shortstop, were broadcasters, as was ex-Dodgers pitcher Rex Barney. Dizzy Dean preceded the three in a baseball booth and Sandy Koufax would follow them.

By 1964, CBS news essayist Eric Sevareid had come up with a term to describe how ex-athletes were filling jobs that qualified broadcasters once held: "Creeping Rizzutoism." Sevareid coined the phrase while responding to a decision the Yankees, NBC and Major League Baseball's Commissioner's office made to select Rizzuto to the 1964 World Series broadcast team in favor of Mel.

By 1965, another ex-ballplayer, Joe Garagiola, would have Mel's full-time job.

CHAPTER 16

TV Talk

It was the bottom of the eighth inning of Game 3 of the 1961 World Series. The Cincinnati Reds' Wally Post was at the plate. The Yankees' Luis Arroyo was on the mound. Mel was at the microphone. At least NBC's viewers thought he was.

"Saw him hit a ball in St. Louis that hit the scoreboard," said Joe Garagiola, cutting in on his partner with an observation about Post, a six-foot, 200-pound strongman. "And with Jay Hook, an engineering student, and Charlie James, a graduate student, they figured it out with Newton's Law and calculus and everything else and it was 539 feet. How's that for gettin' the dope right now?"

"They got the square root of that," Mel responded playfully.

The two partners had planned to go back and forth like this. Traditionally, each Series broadcaster called half a game. But in 1961, Mel did all the play-by-play and Garagiola contributed commentary wherever he saw fit. When Garagiola broke in on Mel, he broke new ground.

"We found Joe Garagiola's constant interrupting of Mel Allen on the TV annoying," wrote *Long Island Star-Journal* sports columnist Lou O'Neill after the Series. " ... 'Twould have been better if Joe had come on at the end of each inning."

During the 1965 season, Red Barber's face would turn the angry color of his hair as he worked with Garagiola on Yankees broadcasts.

"It was the first time in my life that I had sat in a radio booth with a fellow who moved in on my broadcast," Barber recalled later.

Two decades later, Garagiola freely infringed upon Vin Scully on NBC's major league *Game of the Week*. By this time, he had helped to carve out a new position in the broadcast booth: the sports broadcasting analyst or color man.

The color man violated the sacred, one-on-one relationship that a sports broadcaster once shared with his listener. In the radio days before television, the listener more carefully considered the announcer's words, working with him to picture an event in his head. "Army will defend the goal to your right as you look at your radio dial," Mel would say if he was calling a football game. Imagining the game through Mel's words, the listener tensed as Mel called each play, leaning forward to hear every last detail that would paint a richer picture.

By the 1961 World Series, the listener could sit back in an easy chair and watch his television. The colorful screen enabled him to follow a game even if he half-listened to Mel and Garagiola. As the listener relaxed and reclined, sometimes he dozed off.

"There's one!" Mel shouted, jarring him awake after Roger Maris had blasted a ball off the Reds' Bob Purkey to begin the ninth inning of Game 3. "It is deep to right field! And that ball is going, going … it is gone! Roger Maris gets his first hit of the Series, and you could tell as it left the bat that it was gone. And the Yankees lead 3-2."

As a television announcer, Mel tried to only offer tidbits that complemented the screen. If he had called Maris's shot for radio, he probably would have told his listeners how Maris powered the Purkey pitch 20 rows up into the stands at Crosley Field and then hurried around the bases with his head down. He might have mentioned how Purkey had hung a pitch to Maris. But his audience could see this. Viewers had watched the pitch from an angle behind Purkey's shoulder, thanks in part to a 1959 meeting between Mel, Ballantine advertising manager Len Faupel and WPIX television officials. The men decided to plant a camera beyond the center field wall, which produced the over-the-pitcher's-shoulder angle, and NBC soon adopted the idea.

Mel sparked another monumental television innovation on July 17, 1959, as he worked a Yankees-White Sox game for WPIX, during which the Yankees' Ralph Terry took a no-hitter into the ninth inning. After Chicago's Jim McAnany singled to left field off Terry to break up the no-hit bid, Mel called down to television director Jack Murphy in the control room to see if he had "taped" McAnany's hit using WPIX's cutting-edge recording technology. Murphy had, and WPIX showed the first instant replay. Viewers saw McAnany's hit drop in front of Yankees left fielder Norm Siebern.

Mel often contacted Murphy during games with ideas for camera angles he thought would improve the WPIX broadcasts. Mel asked for a shot of a third baseman playing in for a bunt or of commotion in the left field bleachers at Yankee Stadium. "I'll take responsibility for it," Mel said of the left-field fracas, which turned into a full-fledged fight among beer-swilling customers on a sweltering day.

Umpires stopped play as fans flailed at one another with folding chairs that were being used to accommodate an extra-large crowd. "I would have been remiss for lack of reporting if I had ignored it," Mel said later.

Though an old radio guy at heart, Mel recognized the power of the television. "TV has been the greatest boon to major league baseball since Babe Ruth," he said in October 1960. Mel credited television with garnering the game millions of more fans, including multitudes of housewives who tuned in during the day. With an ever-increasing audience in mind, Mel had suggested the new broadcasting strategy to Garagiola for the 1961 Series.

"I decided to make my announcing job this year a team effort with Garagiola," he said in October 1961. "I hope I didn't talk too much for TV, but we figured that when 80,000,000 people are watching there are many in the audience who are not familiar with the players."

From the beginning of his Yankees career, Mel had always faced the complaint that he was too talkative. As he worked a Yankees-Red Sox game at Yankee Stadium in 1948, a wire foul-up hooked a man attempting to make a phone call into Mel's radio broadcast. "Oh shut up, Mel Allen," he said upon hearing Mel's voice.

Mel got some more scattered complaints from fans that he talked too much from 1948 through 1951when he worked a simulcast, meaning his Yankees broadcast was piped to both radio and television listeners. He also simulcast Washington Redskins games in 1952 and 1953. Simulcasting was a no-win situation for a broadcaster. Either he talked too much or he didn't talk enough. Mel often chose to be more verbose. "I think silence lessens drama," he said.

Mel liked to have a constant conversation with his listeners. Tuning in to one of his radio or television broadcasts, fans might immediately hear: "Seventh inning, one away ... New York five, Pittsburgh four, it's the first of the seventh. Bobby Richardson on deck ... Pirates got two runs in the first, two in the second, the Yankees one in the fifth and four in the sixth, with homers by Skowron and Berra accounting for four of the runs driven. Mantle's single drove in the other ... " Mel briefed the game like this numerous times during a three-hour broadcast, giving his late listeners a chance to catch up.

Mel always called games with millions of uninformed listeners in mind. When situations arose that he felt were abstract to the casual fan, he explained them: "For the benefit of those not so familiar with the game, the infield fly rule states that, with first and second base or first, second and third occupied and less than two out, a ball which in the judgment of the umpire ..." And on and on he would go. Mel would carefully clarify his statements over the air, which also contributed to some drawn-out descriptions.

New Yorker television critic John Lardner pulled one of Mel's monologues from a mid-1950s Yankees game: "By sending Mize to the bat rack, Stengel may have kept Boudreau from replacing Brown, because—You see, Collins is a left-handed hitter. That means that Mize, being a left-handed hitter—Well, we've got a right-handed pitcher in there now, but if Boudreau had called in a southpaw—Of course, Collins is a left-handed hitter, too. But what this might mean—Well, of course, it may mean nothing at all."

Lardner noted that Mel stuck in the statement during a lull in the action, "while the rival managers were stopping to think." During such dead moments of ballgames, Mel often injected corny language and drawn-out descriptions to fill the empty airtime. This was an old radio trick.

"McDougald's not playing is no evasion," he told Home of Champions Network listeners during a 1958 Yankees-Senators game. "He's sitting on the bench because of a knee abrasion. But may still see action the second game on this Washington invasion."

Mel wasn't quite done.

"I was just tryin' to rush the sprouting of corn," he said. "I love it with butter."

Corn sustained Mel's Fox Movietone News career for nearly two decades as he narrated shorts on offbeat sports like bobsledding ("it takes nerve to swerve around a curve") and skiing ("the difficult slalom, one place when you definitely need to zig and zag around the flag, and that's no gag"). When Mel described a New Jersey baby-crawl race, he called it "no mere child's play" and, when one infant plopped over on its stomach, he exclaimed, "Oh my tummy, Mummy!"

Mel never goofed around like this amid tense moments of ball games. However, as a crop of so-called television "experts" arose with the new industry, they hammered him for what they thought was excessive talking. Through the 1950s and mid-1960s, sportswriters would run excerpts of what they saw as Mel's abominations:

International Falls is the coldest spot on earth. Temperature-wise, that is.

We have now reached that stage of the game where every pitch must be considered by the pitcher with the utmost care. In other words, there is no room for margin of error.

Frank Robinson is known as a fastball hitter. This is not to say he doesn't hit other types of pitches, but he hits the fastball best.

You'll notice the Minnesota defense is a modified Tennessee, an overshifted 5-4, or Oklahoma, with ends and tackles shifting, linebackers playing opposite the fullback and halfbacks coming up close.

TV critics especially assailed Mel's football work. The technical nuances Mel knew about from pregame meetings with coaches had once provided masterpieces over the radio: "First down and goal to go on the nine for Wisconsin, leading Purdue seven to six, two minutes to go in the third period, single wing over to the right. The ball comes back to Ameche, goes off right tackle, to the FIVE on a hard drive! … Lamar Lundy, the left end for Purdue, making the tackle, helped out by Phil Ehrman, who plays the left linebacker spot."

Mel liked to include every name he could with plays, in case players' parents were listening. "We'll call men who make a tackle, but all the boys take a part on it," he would say.

To many television critics, he was being a windbag. In November 1952, *The New York Times'* Jack Gould wrote that Mel spent "a couple of hours straightening out the quarterbacks of Army and Navy in Philadelphia." Earlier that year, Gould wrote: "Whether it is football or baseball, Mr. A. [Allen] could endear himself to a few million sports fans by a very simple expedient. Mel, for heaven's sake, don't talk so much."

Five years earlier, Gould had selected Mel to be a member of the *Times'* "Radio Honor Roll" and hailed him for his "fresh and distinctive work." By the early 1960s, many TV critics found Mel anything but that.

In a 1962 profile on Mel entitled "Baseball's Babbling Brook," *Sports Illustrated's* Huston Horn wrote: "Sober, industrious and otherwise well-adjusted men have been known to fall into gargling, sputtering rages as, sitting helplessly before their TV sets, they feel themselves assaulted by Allen's tedious, drawn-out explanations."

Two years earlier, in another long piece on Mel that *Look* magazine called "Baseball's Most Controversial Voice," writer Bill Davidson quoted Yogi Berra as succinctly saying in response to a question about Mel: "Too many words." When asked some 40 years later if he remembered his statement, Berra offered this wisdom: "What sports announcer don't talk too much? But he had a voice you could listen to."

Through the mid-1960s, Mel still steadily cleaned up on his annual "best sportscaster" awards. He finished atop categories like "Favorite TV Sportscaster" and "Best Sportscaster on TV" for publications like *TV Radio Mirror, Radio-Television Daily, Motion Picture Daily* and *Television Today,* all of which sought input from United States television editors, critics and columnists.

"He still talks too much, but who's better?" Wayne Oliver of the Associated Press wrote in 1954.

But Mel wasn't satisfied with his accolades. Writers' chastisements bothered him so much he would lie awake at night trying to figure out how to balance the right amount of chatter with the television screen. When writers interviewed him, he would joke about the difficulties with "knowing when to shut up."

"Look, Ben," he told the *Daily News'* Ben Gross in 1957, "If anyone can show me a happy medium between talking too much and talking too little, I'll be happy to adopt it. I'm not that stubborn; but so far no one has been able to come up with such a compromise formula."

Mel wrote countless opinion pieces in publications from *Sport* magazine to *The New York Times* addressing his toils with transitioning from radio to television.

"You may be sure that the announcer is not in love with his own voice, but rather is eager to help in presenting a full and accurate account of the event," Mel wrote in a letter "to the Radio-Television Editor" that *The New York Times* published in 1952.

Instead of talking about what was obvious to his viewers on the monitor, Mel liked to describe what viewers couldn't see. While calling the sixth inning of Game 7 of the 1955 Series for NBC, Mel noticed that Brooklyn left fielder Sandy Amoros was playing the left-handed-hitting Berra close to center field, ceding the pull hitter almost all of left. Mel mentioned Amoros's position and told his viewers to watch for Berra to slap the ball to left. Berra did, slicing it down the line in fair territory near the corner. On the run, Amoros snagged the ball with his outstretched glove hand, then threw back to shortstop Pee Wee Reese, who fired to Gil Hodges at first to double up the Yankees' Gil McDougald and squelch a Yankees rally. The Dodgers took the game and the Series.

But NBC officials criticized him for describing things fans couldn't see on their screens. This technique was distracting, they said. "With complaints coming in, with people telling you that you talk too much, you begin to think well, why not sit there and say, 'Ball one, strike one,' and let it go at that," he said later. Out of frustration, Mel experimented with talking minimally on both radio and television broadcasts in the late 1950s and early 1960s. During his baseball games, viewers and listeners could practically hear fans shift in their seats as Mel stayed silent for stretches of 15 to 20 seconds. Mel let the crowd's cheers color the dramatic moments on games and, when he spoke, offered minimal play-by-play and commentary.

Mel still received criticism that he talked too much.

※※※※※※※

As Mel worked the first inning of Game 2 of the 1958 World Series, an NBC executive handed him a wire from a fan.

"Quit yapping, you Yankee lover," it read. "You're talking too much. Let me just watch the game." Mel slumped in his seat before glancing at the telegram again. "Dad gum," he said, cupping his hand over the television microphone. "Why, that son of a buck sent it two hours before the game ever started."

Millions of fans despised Mel no matter what he said. Not because they thought he blabbed too much or not enough in the booth, but because he was their closest tie to a relentless winning machine.

By May of 1961, Mel had broadcast an estimated 10,000 hours as a sportscaster. He had called more than 3,200 major league baseball games and more than 300 college or professional football games. He had handled more than 100 World Series contests, the majority of which involved the Yankees trampling a hapless foe like the 1961 Reds, which the Yankees dumped in five games.

"In New York, Mel's like the drinking friend who takes home the town drunk," said Lindsey Nelson, Mel's sportscasting comrade. "Since the anti-Yankees aren't able to change the team, they hit the nearest thing—Mel Allen—with a rolling pin."

The same year Nelson made that comment (1962), he became a member of the inaugural broadcasting team for the expansion New York Mets. New York had been without National League baseball since the end of the 1957 season, when the Giants and Dodgers fled west. The Yankees immediately tried to lure the city's baseball fans to Yankee Stadium by telecasting 140 of their 154 games in 1958. But displaced Dodgers and Giants and fans would have rather jumped off the George Washington Bridge than pay to see the Yankees. The Yankees' attendance actually dropped by almost 70,000 fans in 1958. New York was always more of a National League town. Giants and Dodgers fans lived and died with their clubs, while Yankees fans were more apathetic after an onslaught of winning.

In his 1967 book, *The Decline and Fall of the New York Yankees*, author Jack Man compared a Yankees fan with a zoo spectator. "You don't go to the zoo because you love the lion," Mann wrote. "The lion is powerful and cruel and swift and lithe and terrifying and fascinating. You don't root for the lion because you can tell at first glance that he doesn't need support. ... You come to see the lion because he *is*."

New York's National League-starved fans, who gave the Mets an instant fan base, loved their new team for what it wasn't. The 1962 Mets didn't win, but sure lost colorfully. They kicked the ball all over the Polo Grounds in setting the standard for baseball futility with a 40-120 record.

"Can't *anybody* play this here game?" asked Casey Stengel, the Mets' first manager.

This was the very Casey Stengel the Yankees had cruelly cast off. New York baseball writers who had witnessed that carnage rushed back to Stengel's side as if their prodigal son had returned. When the 1963 Mets recorded their 13th win to surpass the Yankees' 12, the *Journal-American*: "More Wins Than Yanks ... 'Break Up the Mets.'" The headline played off the words on a banner a fan displayed at the Polo Grounds, but "Break Up the Mets" was also a battle cry for New York writers and fans alike who were sick of seeing the Yankees prevail.

"Rooting for the Yankees is like cheating your buddy at cards," wrote the *Journal-American*'s Jimmy Cannon. "You win, but it ain't no fun."

✿✿✿✿✿✿

The Yankees were still New York's more popular attraction by the end of the 1963 season, when they outdrew the Mets by nearly 230,000 fans. While the Mets finished at the bottom of the National League in 10th place, the Yankees won the American League pennant by 10 1/2 games. The Yanks, who had beaten the San Francisco Giants to win the 1962 World Series, traveled coast to coast again in 1963 to take on the Los Angeles Dodgers.

Armed with Sandy Kaufax, Johnny Podres and Don Drysdale, the Dodgers drove to a 3-0 Series lead. The left-handed Kaufax, who recorded 15 strikeouts in Game 1 at Yankee Stadium, had a 1-0 lead in the seventh inning of Game 4 at glittering new Dodger Stadium when he faced Mantle with one out. The Mick, who hobbled to the plate on legs that had endured more than a half-dozen injuries, caught up with a Koufax pitch, pulling it to deep left-center field.

Up in the booth, Mel tried to yell but his voice cracked. He had a recurring nasal condition and had shown signs of laryngitis during the Series. A doctor had told him to restrain his voice over the air.

"That's like taking Man O'War and telling him, 'I just want you to jog in the Kentucky Derby,'" says Vin Scully, Mel's NBC television partner for the Series.

As Mel broke into a home run call on Mantle's blow, a glob of fluid had dripped down onto his vocal chords. He said later this felt like someone had placed a hand on his throat. The ball was "going ... going ... gone" and so was Mel's voice. Scully took over the microphone as Mel rushed out of the booth for some hot coffee and lemon juice. An inning or so later, Mel was back. "In the first half of the ninth inning," he rasped before a long pause, " ... the Dodgers out in front 2 to 1. Bobby Richardson the batter. Struck out, doubled to center and grounded to short."

The voice, scratchy and shaky, was almost unrecognizable. "The Dodgers on the verge!" Mel croaked as he tried to elevate his voice. "Ball one," he said, the sizeable frog lingering in his throat, "low and inside. Good fastball. A one and one count."

"That's enough," whispered Tom Gallery, NBC's sports director.

"Wait a minute," Mel said.

"One ball, one strike ... " he said hoarsely.

Two and a half decades later, Gallery recalled having to grab Mel with both hands and lift him away from the microphone and out of the booth.

"Two and one the count to Bobby Richardson," Scully said, taking over again, "and Mel, we all understand ... just hang right there."

Scully called the rest of the game as Koufax pitched the Dodgers to a 2-1 win and Series sweep. Some sportswriters believed that the Yankees' crushing defeat had been the cause of Mel's bout with speechlessness. The *Daily News'* Dick Young said that Mel had had an "emotional crackup" over the air.

"They said he had laryngitis, but if it was, it was psychosomatic laryngitis," Young wrote. "Mel Allen couldn't believe that his beloved Yankees were losing four straight to the Dodgers. His voice refused to believe it, and therefore he could not describe it."

This was a preposterous claim considering that Mel had remained collected to call the Brooklyn Dodgers' Game 7 defeat of the Yankees in the 1955 Series at Yankee Stadium and Bill Mazeroski's Series-ending shot that sunk the 1960 Yankees.

"I had people trying to tell me that Mel was so depressed, that's why he couldn't finish," Scully says. "I spent the whole off season telling people, 'No, I was there. The spring in the wire tore loose on Mantle's home run.'"

Even after Scully had twice relieved Mel on NBC's telecast in 1963, Mel still returned to wrap up the Dodgers' decisive victory. "In a moment we'll review the highlights of the game for you," he said amid the roars of Dodgers fans. His voice still sounded coarse, but it was steady. A hint of the homespun heartiness and Alabama drawl were threatening to emerge.

"Home runs by Howard and Mantle accounted for two of the runs and an error by Pepitone and a sacrifice fly gave the Dodgers the winning run and a sweep in four games, the first time the Yankees have been swept in four straight," Mel said. "And that's the way it went today at Dodger Stadium, as the Dodgers are now the world champions!"

❅ ❅ ❅ ❅ ❅ ❅ ❅

The 1963 Series marked a climax to physical exhaustion that plagued Mel throughout the regular season. In the spring, Mel had developed the flu but continued to work. Weary with a high fever during a Yankees road trip in early May, he took an antibiotic and got into bed at Detroit's Statler Hotel. Hearing a knock on his door, Mel rose suddenly and, feeling woozy, collapsed. He hit his head, causing a slight concussion and opening up a wound that required four stitches.

Mel spent a week away from the broadcast booth as he recovered at Detroit's Harper Hospital. But upon his release, he accelerated in earnest back to his everyday pace. At 50 years old, he tried to keep up with the same ambitious schedule he undertook as a 35-year-old. When he developed more fevers and a series of viruses, Mel couldn't easily shake them because he wouldn't adequately rest. By late summer, he had begun to lose his voice.

"The vicious cycle of fear-pressure-weakness-ego had him in its grip," Red Barber observed.

Mel thought slowing down would only hinder his career. He sensed a swirl of discordant forces around him every time he walked into the Yankee Stadium broadcast booth. Barely anyone who worked for the Yankees in 1939, the year Mel started broadcasting the team's games, was still around by the early 1960s.

Ed Barrow, Larry MacPhail and George Weiss, three high-powered men and staunch supporters of Mel's, were long gone. Weiss had once completely controlled the Yankees' radio and television broadcasts. But haggling with officials who worked for the Yankees' sponsors and the William Esty Company, the advertising agency that handled the sponsors' accounts, diverted Weiss from his true passion: player personal. Before he left his Yankees general managing post in 1960, Weiss had handed his authority over the broadcasts back to the William Esty Company.

A William Esty representative would sit in the broadcast booth and closely watch Mel, making sure he read his commercials for Ballantine and Camel cigarettes, the Yankees' two principal sponsors since 1956, exactly as they appeared on his scripts. For one game, the agency sent a kid right out of college to monitor Mel. The fresh-faced rep didn't like the way Mel cut short or skipped a commercial in order to wrap up a big inning.

"Ballantine says this one's on the house as we review the scoring," Mel would say in these instances. Ballantine officials liked this tactic because Mel would still manage to pitch their product. Not knowing Ballantine OK'd this tactic, however, the new agency rep yanked Mel by the shoulder. Mel pushed the kid's arms away as he continued to talk to listeners over the air. Fiery Larry MacPhail would have clutched this whippersnapper by the collar and booted him from the booth. But Mel didn't have many Yankees allies to protect him like that anymore.

Instead, Mel saw some of his booth mates pass Rizzuto player notes that made the Scooter sparkle over the air. They wouldn't share the same information with Mel. Instead, an assistant television director had Western Union create false telegrams and have them delivered to Mel for promotion over the air. One of the telegrams charged that the Yankees were anti-Semitic because they didn't sign Hank Greenberg. Mel took the bait and read the telegram, then spent half a game explaining how the anti-Semitism charge was unfounded.

On another occasion, after Mel asked a cameraman to hand him something, the same assistant TV director said aloud, "God Damnit. Why doesn't he get his ass out of the chair and go get it himself?" This guy would hover over Mel during games along with other directors, producers, engineers, technicians, coordinators and sponsor and agency reps. They gave orders to him in person or, if they were in the control room, into his headset or earpiece. They pointed at his monitor to make sure he was talking about what they thought his audience needed to hear. Mel yearned for the days when radio was king, when he could just clutch his large desk microphone, survey the field and go to work.

As Mel became increasingly frustrated with working in the Yankees' booth, his father and sister noticed a change in his personality. Mel wasn't as good-natured as he used to be.

"He would play with the kids and there came a time when he would rather not be bothered with 'em," Esther recalls. "Maybe he was unhappy."

Mel began to act much more irascibly. On live television, he told off a kid who tried to snatch his hat across the broadcast booth's railing. On live radio, he yelled at a heckler. "Come down here and say that!" he screamed in the middle of a 1960 postgame radio roundup.

"As he got older, he had a tendency to get a little testy," recalls Bob Wolff. "I think he became wary of people, wary of the front office, wary of things."

Wolff knew Mel from his days covering the Washington Senators from 1947 through 1960. He also would see Mel while working on weekend major league games for NBC from 1962 through 1964. During that time frame, Wolff remembers running into Mel at a newsstand at a Yankees road site.

"We're gonna take you today, Mel," Wolff recalls the vendor saying.

"What makes you think so!" Mel snapped back.

"Come on, Mel," Wolff thought to himself. "It's just the guy at a newsstand making conversation with you."

Mel could get especially irritable during a game. When he thought statistician Bill Kane was daydreaming, Mel would sometimes whack him over the head with his scorecard. Mel felt Kane couldn't do his job adequately despite repeated instructions. Kane, who joined the Yankees in 1961, was the team's first statistician to work under Mel whom Mel didn't interview himself. Kane was public relations director Bob Fishel's choice. Fishel hired Kane with the intent of farming him out to help with pressroom duties.

Working for Mel alone was tough enough. Not only did Mel demand perfection, but he expected tasks to be handled a specific way. Mel expected Kane and his other statisticians to keep score and up-to-the-minute statistics, watch the out-of-town ticker and follow his words closely to ensure he wasn't making any mistakes.

Like any broadcaster, Mel occasionally slipped up on the air. During a football game, the sheer momentum of one of his bombastic calls could carry his voice into the end zone before a ball carrier. Or Mel might blare "and the score, Pittsburgh 14, the Steelers 7" while trying to keep up with furious on-field action. Perhaps Mel's most infamous error came as he called Yogi Berra's sixth-inning, three-run homer during Game 7 of the 1960 World Series against Pittsburgh. "There's a drive hit deep to right field but it is going to goooooo foul and out of play," Mel told NBC viewers before catching himself. "It is all the way! Excuse me!" he shouted. "All the way for a home run! [Right fielder Roberto] Clemente never moved over, and we thought the ball was curving foul."

Mel thought Sam McDowell was pitching for the Indians as he worked the first game of 1963 doubleheader in Cleveland. Jack Kralick, another left-hander, was actually on the mound. Indians manager Birdie Tebbetts had written McDowell's name on the lineup card he posted in the dugout before Game 1. After Kane had relayed that information to the broadcast booth, Tebbetts changed his mind. Around the third inning, Kane realized that Kralick was pitching. Mel, who was calling the game on radio, and Rizzuto and Jerry Coleman, who worked it for television, had been telling their audiences the pitcher was McDowell, though Kralick was a noticeably shorter pitcher with much better control.

Kane, who had gone from college student to a major league statistician in just a few years, needed a couple of innings to muster the courage to speak up. He mentioned the error to Rizzuto and Coleman, who both giggled. Then they got silent. Who was going to tell Mel? Rizzuto and Coleman certainly didn't want to, so they appointed their poor statistician to do so. When Kane whispered the news into Mel's ear, Mel shot his head upward. "I don't think he came down for two minutes," Coleman says.

When he came down, he tossed books and pencils in Kane's direction.

"I thought he was gonna throw Bill Kane off the deck," Rizzuto recalls.

Some Yankees players and officials thought Mel was overly cruel toward Kane, who had fought polio as a child. Kane walked with a limp and one of his legs was disproportionately thinner than the other. "Why is Mel jumping on this kid?" Bobby Richardson asked Larry one day. But Mel would ride anyone for making mistakes in his booth, including his own brother.

"He always thought the next person could do what he did if they would focus and concentrate and listen," Larry says.

That person could also be his 13-year-old nephew, Andy, who was running a high fever after a mid-1970s trip to an amusement park.

"I'm gonna throw up," Andy told his uncle upon entering their Connecticut home.

"You can do that later," Mel said.

Mel sent Andy to the closet and made him shut the door. He asked the boy to recite his upcoming bar mitzvah speech while facing the coats.

I will extol thee, my God, oh king, and I will bless thy name forever and ever and ever ...

"I can't hear you," Mel said.

"Of course you can't hear me, I'm in a Goddamn closet," Andy mumbled to himself before going on.

"I was having vertigo," he recalled. "I was nauseated. I was in a cold sweat."

Even when he was healthy, Andy would have rather been playing ball. But that could wait. The bar mitzvah was looming.

"He sent me to a speech pathologist when I was in third grade," Andy says. "Well, realistically, my speech was probably fine. But for him, I think he thought everybody should be up here, and I was talking like a child."

Uncle and nephew practiced the bar mitzvah speech day after day.

Great is the Lord, and highly to be praised. His greatness is unsearchable.

"That was beautiful," Mel said during one rehearsal. "The way you read that was just right. Just remember, just think of what you're reading, not just the words."

The two began to read lines back and forth, Mel reciting to Andy in his naturally loud voice.

THE LORD UPHOLDETH ALL WHO FALL, AND RAISETH UP ALL WHO BOW DOWN.

Andy responded meekly.

The eyes of all look hopefully to thee, and thou givest them their food in due season.

"Why can't you say, 'AND THOU GIVEST THEM THEIR FOOD— THEIR FOOD!—IN DUE SEASON?' " Mel asked.

They went back and forth some more, Mel often stopped to nitpick, having Andy enunciate, emphasize and pause. "OK … go on," Mel would say eventually.

Our God and our … wait. …

"Well, what are you gonna do when you get up," Mel said. "You gonna stop to say, 'Wait?'"

Andy read the speech cleanly and demonstratively to his audience. Uncle Mel, who was sitting in the front row, cried. Joy isn't exactly the emotion Andy rekindled at age 42 when he listened to an audiotape of him and Mel rehearsing.

"It sent chills up my back," he says of the tape. "Even listening to it now, I'm still like, 'I don't know what he wants me to do.'"

CHAPTER 17

Off the Air

Mel could make rain delays interesting. Many Yankees fans cherished him most when he chattered on and on as the drops fell. Instead of switching to reruns of *F Troop* or *The Honeymooners*, as WPIX might do in later years, the station would just turn on Mel. He would purse his lips, look at the upper deck and vault viewers into baseball Heaven with his Yankees yarns. He interviewed players and sportswriters and put a stopwatch on the grounds crew to see how long it took them to roll the tarpaulin over the infield. He could spend an artful 20 minutes discussing the tarp alone.

The Yankees and Ballantine, their primary sponsor, loved the way Mel meandered during rain delays. He retained viewers—and potential customers—who might otherwise turn off their televisions.

But by the mid-1960s, those who ruled the team and the sponsor wondered if Mel's long-windedness had begun to grate on their fans. They feared that the mere sound of Mel's words irked a public that was growing more and more loathsome of the Yankees juggernaut.

In 1964, the Yankees won the American League pennant but lost the popularity battle to the last-place Mets, who outdrew their cross-town rivals over a full season for the first time. The Yankees attracted only 1,305,638 fans to Yankee Stadium while the Mets lured 1,732,597 to Shea Stadium, their new Queens home.

Across the Hudson River at Ballantine's headquarters in Newark, New Jersey, sales were slumping. Western breweries like Miller and Coors were entering Ballantine's regional market and dealing at discounted rates. Ballantine once dominated the East through ties with individual taverns. But it always brewed all its beer in Newark and couldn't compete with larger breweries that had branched out to smaller affiliates around the country.

Looking to assess blame and find a quick fix for their ills, Yankees and Ballantine executives glared at Mel, the voice and face for a baseball team and a beer.

"One of the complaints would be he talked too much," says Len Faupel, Ballantine's advertising manager at the time. "I don't say that that was unfounded, but I say that that was exaggerated totally." Faupel conducted surveys that conclusively proved that beer drinkers loved Mel and his down-home delivery.

"From a marketing perspective, he was one of the best in the business," Faupel says.

The charges that Mel was too chatty mostly trickled in from what Faupel calls the "country club crowd." When he heard the complaints, aristocratic Yankees co-owner Dan Topping, a member of that country club set, began to scrutinize Mel. "Topping had an attitude about who he thought his audience was," Faupel says. "And he was wrong."

As Topping listened more intently to Mel, he heard a slightly different announcer than the Mel Allen of the 1950s. His voice was still strong and resonant, but his tone was a little weaker, his pace a little slower. His broadcasts also took on more of a drawling quality.

"You know when it comes to having a favorite team, that's all part of the game," Mel said to begin a between-inning commercial during a 1960 Yankees game. "Each person has a preference. And I'm sure that, naturally, all you people have a preference to the type of glass you like your beer served in. Some folks don't care, some do. I like one of those big ones—I give up! Well, getting away from the fireworks for something that cools you off—the Crisp Refresher—I think the kind of glass you use is a matter just of personal taste, but what counts is the real taste in the glass. And that's where Ballantine comes in. It delivers top taste and refreshment in any glass. The Crisp Refresher. That golden Ballantine is mighty refreshing. And when it comes to flavor, Ballantine's the light beer with true lager flavor. It proves a beer can be truly light and still give you all the downright delicious lager beer flavor you want. That's the reason Ballantine beer is the Crisp Refresher. So enjoy the one beer that tastes great anytime in any glass. Enjoy light, delicious Ballantine beer. The Crisp Refresher."

On and off the air, Mel was a chatty guy. He loved to talk. Sportswriters knew they might be in for a 30-minute discourse if they engaged him.

"Mel is an articulate man," Jimmy Cannon observed in 1961. "His hellos are longer than the Gettysburg Address."

When *The New York Times'* John Drebinger saw Mel appear in the Yankee Stadium press room, he would turn down his hearing aid in plain view of his peers. When Mel's voice thundered above everyone else's as it told old Yankees tales, Drebinger would bang on the device, which had a volume control at mid-chest, and crack, "All I ever get on here is Mel Allen." But these jabs were good natured.

Leonard Koppett, who wrote for the *Herald-Tribune*, *Post* and *Times* over his New York sportswriting career, especially loved to needle Mel during Yankees losing streaks.

"He was very enthusiastic, very warm, very much a big Yankees fan without any decrease in his professionalism," Koppett said in 2002.

Bob Dolgan, a young Indians beat reporter for the Cleveland *Plain Dealer* when he met Mel in the early 1960s, was struck by how such a mega-celebrity could be so approachable. "He'd always be around to talk," Dolgan says. Dolgan was similarly startled when he attended one of Mel's speeches at a downtown Cleveland luncheon in 1963.

"It became apparent that he had nothing prepared," Dolgan recalled in a late-1970s column. "He began a rambling discourse that was charming at first. But then he began droning on and on, with no focus to his speech. The businessmen in the audience, who had to get back to work, began coughing. Allen kept talking. Fifteen minutes later people began walking out. Allen continued, oblivious to them. By the time he finished, about an hour later, half the audience must have been gone."

Dolgan ran into Yankees manager Ralph Houk in the visitor's dugout at Cleveland's Municipal Stadium a few hours after the luncheon. Houk laughed as the reporter approached him.

"I hear Mel did it again," Houk said.

"What do you mean?" Dolgan asked. "Has he done this before?"

"It happens in every town we go into lately," Houk replied.

✼ ✼ ✼ ✼ ✼ ✼ ✼

Houk's relationship with Mel dated back to 1947, when he joined the Yankees as a rookie backup catcher. "Everybody liked him," Houk says today. "He was a friend of all the players."

Mel also maintained an amiable working relationship with Houk. After Houk rose to Yankees manager, Mel would sit on the bench next to him before games and inform out-of-town writers about Yankees happenings. "I thought he was one of the most secure people in the world," Houk says.

After Houk won three straight Yankees pennants, Topping rewarded him with a promotion to general manager as Roy Hamey retired. Houk's bump upstairs also opened up the managerial spot for Yogi Berra, the chummy retired catcher whom the Yankees could use to generate a fun-loving image of their own to counteract that of Stengel and the Mets. But Topping would fire Berra after the season out of fear that his manager didn't have control over his team. The opposite could be said for Houk, who cast a no-nonsense image as both manager and GM.

"Houk isn't the kind of man you would ever be likely to disregard or even take lightly," Mel wrote in *You Can't Beat the Hours*.

Players noticed that Houk adopted the staunchly bottom-line attitude of the Yankees front office almost overnight after becoming GM. The man with whom they felt comfortable enough to sling back beers was now telling them the Yankees couldn't give them raises. When Houk reported back to Topping, who oversaw daily operations of the team (co-owner Del Webb was focusing on his real-estate development in the West), his words weighed heavily. Topping ran the team from a distance. He surrounded himself with capable people who guided him through his decision making, especially after 1962, when his health began to decline. Houk was one of Topping's right-hand men.

"Houk was a very forceful figure," says Jack Lang, who covered the Yankees for the *Long Island Press* from 1958 through 1961. "When Stengel was gone after 1960, Mel became the biggest name around the Yankees, and Houk didn't like that."

Traveling with the Yankees during his first year as GM, Houk would hear Mel's voice boom and at the back of pressrooms with accounts of Ruth, Gehrig and DiMaggio. After an early-September game at Minnesota's Metropolitan Stadium, Mel was holding court with a large group of writers as they waited for the Yankees team bus. It was a jovial atmosphere in which some were enjoying a beer.

"Mel's voice started to get louder and louder," recalls Maury Allen, who covered the Yankees for the *New York Post* at the time. "Mel went on to such a degree that people would sort of leave the crowd. It wasn't repetitive, but it was sort of a monologue. But when Mel was on, it was pretty much just Mel telling the stories. There were occasions when it would get a little boring."

Maury Allen observed several writers leave the pack. He also noticed that Houk, who was away from the group talking to a waitress, was turning red in the face.

"Houk was in the corner and said something like, 'Goddam Mel,'" Maury Allen says. "I knew Mel was in trouble."

Maury Allen then watched Houk storm out of the room. The message was clear to him: Houk couldn't stand having Mel around anymore. "That one incident put him over the top," Maury Allen says. "He had to go out of the press room because Mel dominated the scene, and that was really the essence of his whole leaving the Yankees, why the Yankees decided that they didn't want him."

Houk alone didn't force Topping's hand to drop the hatchet on Mel. Topping had heard the whispers from Newark that Mel's gabbiness had somehow contributed to Ballantine's financial swoon and from Yankee Stadium that the Yankees weren't drawing and that Mel was combustible in the broadcast booth. Still, as late as summertime, Topping had sent Mel a letter from Florida, where he had a yacht, complimenting his recent broadcasting. Often in sports, such an out-of-the-blue vote of confidence is an ominous sign a pink slip is coming. Indeed, under increasing pressure from several angles, Topping decided to dump Mel.

"I best describe the decision as a marriage that had gone on so long," Faupel says.

Twenty-five years, to be exact.

On September 21, 1964, Topping summoned Mel to his Fifth Avenue office. Mel thought the owner wanted to negotiate new contract, but soon learned the opposite. Mel noticed Topping light cigarette after cigarette as he broke the bad news to him. "He was the most nervous guy I ever saw," Mel said later. With Houk sitting nearby, Topping told the same man who had emceed galas in his honor that the Yankees weren't going to renew his contract. Silent and stunned, Mel listened to the owner. Topping told Mel the decision wasn't based on anything he did, but Red Barber wrote in two of his books that the owner had told him, "I'm tired of him popping off," concerning Mel on the day he dropped the bomb.

Topping said CBS hadn't made his decision, either. The network was in the process of purchasing controlling interest of the team, a transaction it would complete in November. Topping and Webb each kept a 10 percent share of the team and Topping served as Yankees president until 1966. When Topping and Webb had decided to sell most of their stock in the team, they began to significantly cut costs to help make their balance sheet enticing to potential buyers. From 1962 onward, they spent only a fraction of the money on prospects that they had in the past. But purging Mel was not a related cost-cutting measure. CBS has already agreed to purchase the club by the time Topping terminated Mel. The Yankees then signed his successor, Joe Garagiola, to a reported $75,000-a-year deal after Mel had signed a $60,000 contract with the Yankees for the 1964 season. The Yankees retained Red Barber, Phil Rizzuto and Jerry Coleman for their 1965 broadcasting staff. When Topping and Houk talked with Barber on the same day they terminated Mel, they offered him a $5,000 raise for the 1965 season.

After Barber met with Topping and Houk, he flew to Cleveland to fill in on Yankees broadcasts for Phil Rizzuto, who took that series off. When Barber reached the Municipal Stadium booth 15 minutes before game time, he saw Mel seated quietly at his place, staring across the field.

"I don't think he knew I had come in," Barber recalled later. "I don't think he knew where he was. He was numb. He had protruding dark eyes. They were bulging out so far they looked like Concord grapes. He was the saddest-looking man I have ever seen. He was in a nightmare. His look was not frantic, not wild—just sad, numb, deserted. He just couldn't believe it. He was desolate, stricken. ... When airtime came, I touched him on the shoulder, shook him slightly. He looked at me, blinked, turned to the mike, and said, 'Hello everybody ... this is Mel Allen ... '"

When he broadcast his final game for Topping's Yankees, on October 4, 1964, at Yankee Stadium, Mel didn't even begin with his famous greeting.

"And coming on now—sorry he wasn't with us yesterday—one of the few clinchas he's evah missed, the voice of the Yankees, Mel Allen," Rizzuto told Yankees radio listeners.

"Thank you very much, Phil," Mel replied. "Had a football game to do—right now, my little nephew, about two years old, is seeing his first baseball game."

For the next minute and a half, Mel drifted into an unknown area of the airwaves. As a final goodbye, he decided to make himself—and not the game—the subject of his commentary, at least momentarily.

"Hi Andy!" he said to his visiting nephew. "You know, a lot of kids have a lot of fun coming to the ballgame. Does 'em a lot of good. I really think it does. I saw my first game—oh, by the way, hello there everybody … "

Mel laughed slightly but slipped right back into his story.

"I saw my first game when I was about the same age—that's Larry's kid there—when I was about two and a half. But I don't remember it. It was about 1,200 miles from here—it was a Class A league. But my mother remembers it very well because my father had to travel 30 miles from a small mining town where we lived to take me, but he had to tend to some business, so he told my mother. He was a great baseball fan.

"What business he had to tend to, he tended to in a hurry, 'cause that night, we came back, Mom was undressing me, putting me into bed. She said, 'Did you have a good time traveling with daddy today?' I said, 'Yes.' And I started talkin' about having peanuts, soda pop, and she knew what had happened … "

"Well, we're all set to go," Mel continued, after pausing for several seconds. "I knew that the clinching would take place the day that I had to do my first football game—if it took place, that is."

New York had won the American League pennant the day before. During the hangover game, Bob Sheppard's voice echoed off tens of thousands of empty seats, announcing the names of Yankees backups and prospects who filled in for resting reserves: Pedro Gonzalez, Elvio Jimenez, Archie Moore, Mike Hegan, Jake Gibbs. Mel spoke slowly and sentimentally as he broadcast.

"Hector Lopez, playing third base, where he has, on occasion, performed," he said. "The delivery is swung on and fouled back, one and two. … I remember one day Hector had in Kansas City—and he remembers it well, too. There were several balls that, uh, were hit to him at third. This is when he was playing with Kansas City. More properly, I should say, they were hit through him at third base … the pitch to Wagner, swung on, beautiful changeup, strike three … It was one of those days, though, where everybody did things wrong. It was so bad that, 15 minutes after the game was over, Lou Boudreau, who was then managing, brought the whole ball club back out onto the field and—particularly Lopez—and gave him battin'—or, rather, fielding practice."

Mel seemed a little lost, somewhere between his glamorous past and uncertain future, but not exactly in the present.

"We are awaiting the arrival of the Indians' catcher, Duke Simms," he said to begin the bottom of the first inning. "A tisket, a tasket, he's lost his big catchin' basket. But he'll be up in the minute. … You know, with Gibbs on deck, it reminds me, that there've been very few catchers in the history of baseball that every hit second. One of them was Mickey Cochrane. … That's about as far back as I go without doing some research. I only got to see him play a coupla games— that was before I got into this business—but, I do know that he hit number two in the order."

Mel seemed remarkably spirited for a man who was broadcasting his own funeral. "Always at the end of the year, we like to express our appreciation to many people," he said at the beginning of the third inning. He offered thanks to Topping, Webb, Houk and, by name, other Yankees executives, scouts, secretaries, receptionists and stadium administrators and accountants. After he called Luis Tiant's first major league home run, Mel continued.

"As he trots around the bases, we'll continue to trot around our bases of thanking folks who've worked hard around here," he said. Interspersing more play-by-play as his list grew, Mel thanked Yankees ticket vendors, switchboard operators, mail clerks, doctors, trainers, clubhouse attendants, batboys, press box workers, Western Union operators, Stadium Club officials, the WPIX crew and "the fine men in blue who maintain order outside."

Mel's tribute lasted an entire inning. "That takes care of just about most everybody, but not everybody," he said. "Always miss a few. Without these people, you don't do your job."

Because Mel and Topping had agreed to be quiet about his dismissal until they could work out a mutual statement that suited both of them, fans listening to Mel didn't know he was saying goodbye. But Barber did. Shortly after the Ol' Redhead took the radio reins from Mel in the top of the fourth, he paid his longtime partner a subtle pat on the back.

"Curve, swung on, there's a high popup into short right field," Barber began, "there's Gonzalez out underneath it and heee ties a record. Three putouts in an inning. Isn't that somethin'?"

Barber paused for a split-second.

"How 'bout that," he said gleefully.

✼ ✼ ✼ ✼ ✼ ✼ ✼

Although the Yankees had discarded him, Mel admittedly "sort of took it for granted" that he would be calling the 1964 World Series between the Yankees and St. Louis Cardinals. He had a cordial relationship with Commissioner Ford Frick, who made the final decision about Series announcers. He also had a "principal announcer" stipulation in his 1964 Yankees contract. But as he prepared to pack for St. Louis, Mel realized that nobody, either from Frick's office or the Yankees, had contacted him about the Series. That's because Frick had chosen Rizzuto as the Yankees' Series representative.

"In keeping with your established precedence most respectfully request your granting me as contractually stipulated Yankee principal announcer for 1964 equal consideration with St. Louis Cardinals principal announcer for World Series broadcasting assignment," Mel wrote in a wire he sent to Frick's Rockefeller Plaza office in the wee hours of October 5. Mel wired a similar plea to Topping. But the decision was final. Frick didn't like to overrule a team's recommendation, and Topping had chosen Rizzuto.

Rizzuto joined NBC's Garagiola, the Cardinals' Harry Caray and the Red Sox's Curt Gowdy on the Series team. The previous time the Yankees played in a Series and Mel wasn't behind its microphone had been 1943, when he was serving in World War II.

"I was quite shocked and disturbed when I tuned in the first game and discovered that you were not covering the Series," Bob Prince wrote to Mel in a letter dated October 9. "I don't blame you for feeling hurt over this turn of events. I just wanted you to know that I was sorry to learn of this, and I think it's pretty small of some individuals to flagrantly overlook the use of the 'Voice of the Yankees.' I shall never forget the great help you were to me in the 1960 Series and will always count you as my personal friend."

When fans mailed their grievances to the Yankees over neglecting Mel, they got a standard company line. In a mass-produced response, Houk diffused the responsibility in selecting team announcers among NBC, Series sponsor Gillette, the commissioner's office and the Yankees and said the team was invoking a new policy of using fresh announcers in the Series.

"There had been many requests in years past to change announcers for Series games," Houk wrote. "Had we been able at the time to foresee the number of Series in which the Yankees were going to be participants, we most surely would have suggested rotating the Yankee 'voices' on Series telecasts and broadcasts. ... We acknowledge that Mel has been an outstanding baseball announcer for a quarter century, but changes are inevitable for varying reasons that can be justified."

The Yankees gave similarly vague responses to local and national reporters. Unsatisfied with the answer, writers sought out Mel.

"I've been in this business long enough not to be surprised at anything," Mel told *The New York Times'* Val Adams for an October 7 story.

As writers sniffed around the situation, they correctly determined Mel might be out of the Yankees' booth entirely. The phone at the Bedford Village house began to ring off the hook. One reporter, John Cashman of the *New York Post*, showed up at the front door. In an October 9 story, Cashman recorded Mel rooting for the Yanks as he watched the Series on television.

"Atta boy Philly," he shouted as New York's Phil Linz homered in the ninth inning of Game 2, which the Yankees won 8-3 to even the Series at 1-1.

"I'm very happy they won," Cashman quoted Mel as saying. "I hope they win the Series. I have no reason to do otherwise."

Before Game 1, Mel had wired to the team: "You are a great group of friends and a great team that deserves the richest of rewards." Mel told them that his mother Anna's coronary condition kept him from wishing the Yanks "the best of success" in person.

Somehow, Mel hoped, there was a shot at regaining his job.

"I still don't know anything about all this," Cashman quoted Mel further. "But I'll tell you one thing. I'm certainly going to see somebody in the next few days and find out what the hell is going on."

Cashman, like every reporter in the country, didn't know Mel's fate. The *Post* writer mentioned a report to Mel that Garagiola would replace him in the Yankees' booth.

"Today it's Garagiola," Mel reportedly responded, "yesterday it was [Tigers broadcaster] George Kell. What I'd like to know is where the dad-gum all this stuff is coming from. Don't you think they [the Yankees] would tell me something if there was anything in all this?"

As reporters hounded him during the 1964 Series—he found the pressure so taxing that had to leave his house for long periods of time—Mel would tell them he hadn't heard anything from the club about his not returning in 1965. This was what Topping had requested until Mel and the team could put together a mutual statement about his future. Mel wired Topping, Houk and publicity director Bob Fishel in St. Louis in hopes of hastening that process.

"Dear Dan," wrote in a wire to Topping on October 7. "Pressures from press upon me and probably on you require mutual attitude in statement to protect good will between us personally and also Yankees."

Mel finally talked to one of the three men, Fishel, on October 9. Fishel had tried to call Mel back before that, but Mel's Bedford Village line has been busy as he fielded calls from reporters.

"I want everything to remain on a friendly basis," Mel told Fishel. "I have been misquoted. I made absolutely no statements. They tried to pin me to the wall."

"Any employment statement should not come from me," Fishel told him. "I think it should be your privilege."

"I do not think any employment statement should come from me or you," Mel said. "I think the boss is the one who should indicate a joint statement of continuing friendship. I have a career to protect. I do not want any bad publicity for anybody. I know no reason for it and it will not do anybody any good."

Mel and Fishel were both unmarried men who buried themselves in their work and fell in love with the Yankees. They had once considered one another close friends, but Mel's Yankees dismissal put a visible strain on their relationship. When freelance writer Clark Whelton approached Fishel for a statement about Mel's discharge for a 1976 magazine piece, Whelton saw that the matter still pained the public relations man. Fishel told Whelton that the Yankees had had no choice but to make the move.

"He went out of his way to tell me Mel had been suffering from some sort of wandering," Whelton recalls. "He said, 'Didn't you ever notice the way he changed? Don't you agree?' The answer was, 'No, I don't agree.' It never occurred to me that there was anything wrong."

Millions of fans felt the same way as Whelton. From the time the Yankees announced that Rizzuto would be their 1964 Series announcer in early October, through the flurry of newspaper reports that circulated over the next two months that Mel was out and up to the Yankees' official public announcement confirming the speculation on December 17, thousands of vengeful letters flooded Yankee Stadium. The letters that weren't addressed to Yankees brass read, "Dear Mel," even if their authors had never met him before.

"Pardon the informality, but 'Mr. Allen' just sounds too detached for someone I think of as a friend," typed a man from Ithaca, New York.

"I became a Yankees fan first because of you and second because of the team," wrote a woman from Madison, New Jersey.

"Say it ain't so, Mel," said a man from Asbury Park, New Jersey. "The winter will never end if Mel Allen isn't there next March to say, 'Hello everybody, this is Mel Allen from Fort Lauderdale, Florida.'"

"The Yankees may have a new man saying words to describe ball games, but the 'Voice of the Yankees' will not be there," wrote another from Carlstadt, New Jersey. "I only hope the men who made this awful mistake could read this letter as I know there are many thousands like me who would like to tell them in words I cannot put in this letter."

"The apparent firing of Mel Allen is completely unjustified and nothing short of a disgrace," grieved a guy from New Haven, Connecticut. "For the truth is, as every sports fan knows, whether he's a Yankee fan or not, Mr. Allen is the best in his field."

"If they did fire you, don't regret it, because they don't deserve you," penned a woman from Waterbury, Connecticut.

The Waterbury woman told Mel that even her husband, a Red Sox fan, "was shocked at your leaving and was the first to say that no one could call a game better than you, and any team that dropped you would be 'crazy.'"

Mel even received numerous nods from his so-called enemies who were nauseated by decades of Yankees winning.

"I loved hating you win!" wrote a Giants fan. "I enjoyed your comments— and loved to talk back to you."

"Firstly, I'm a Yankee hater, but this fact doesn't distort my recognition of great talent," penned another man from Clarks Summit, Pennsylvania, "and unlike some of my friends, I've never felt that I dislike you just because you happen to broadcast Yankee game. I can tell that your heart is in what you do."

Fans believed in their own hearts that Mel was still the same Mel, despite the mystery drifting around his name as a result of the Yankees' public silence. "I believe that the fans in general are entitled to an explanation," wrote a man from New Haven, Connecticut, in a letter addressed directly to Topping.

With even the venom-spitting, anti-Yankee fans—people whom the club's executives thought it could lure through the turnstiles with a new voice—now defending Mel, the front office became frayed.

"In the near future we will want to announce our plans and we are hoping that you would have a method of making the announcement that would best serve your purposes," Topping wrote to Mel in a letter dated November 4. "However, we will not be able to wait much longer before we complete and announce our plans for 1965 and we do not want to do anything to hurt your position. I am hoping that you and Bob can work out a mutually satisfactory announcement that will serve your purpose, if you feel such an announcement would be beneficial. As you know, Mel, we appreciate your long and devoted service to the New York Yankees and we hope that this has been as valuable to you as it has been to us."

Mel and Fishel met at New York's Savoy Plaza hotel to draft that announcement. Fishel and the Yankees hoped Mel had a statement prepared that the Yankees could use as a basis for their own.

"I have no announcement to make," Mel said. "I wasn't charged with anything."

So the Yankees decided to sit on the news of Mel's dismissal. There was no press conference to announce the move, no second Mel Allen Day the following season to give fans a chance to fuss over him and for Mel to say one final goodbye.

"They didn't want a controversial environment where he would say, 'I've been loyal to the Yankees, why aren't they loyal to me?'" Maury Allen observed.

Berating the Yankees, however, had never been Mel's intent, a sentiment he expressed in an October 5 letter he had mailed to Topping:

> Dear Dan:
> I have spent my adult life as announcer for the Yankees except for a turn in the army, and they have been both golden and glorious years of dedication to a sport, to a team, and to employers who have been unsurpassed in their generosity, understanding and patience. I only wish I could further express my personal and professional attitude in the championship manner of those whom I was so privileged to represent on the air from the front office to the field of play.
> In a relatively short time I have lived a lifetime of wonderful personal associations and unprecedented baseball history. I regret that all the best things in life must come to an end, but I am proud though that you have been and still are my fine friend. I could never have achieved the stature of those whose numbers 3, 4, and 5 have been retired, but like them and their teammates I have learned much from my exalted experience. I too am proud to have been a Yankee.
> Whatever may have brought about the multiplicity of changes, as you told me, plus the fact, as you stated, that my option was the first to come up and, therefore, was among the first to be affected, but not fired, I appreciate so much your graciousness in granting to me the consideration in bowing out gracefully.
>
> With best wishes and greatest thanks, I shall always remain
> Your friend,
> Mel Allen

A "multiplicity of changes" became apparent on December 17, when the Yankees held a showing for media members of the 1964 Series, which they lost to the Cardinals in seven games. This exercise, held at Toots Shor's was a usual ritual, but the Yankees also showcased an unusual side.

"We're trying to change the image of the Yankees," Houk told the assemblage. "We're not a bunch of stuffed shirts."

Houk announced that the Yankees would allow fans to bring banners into Yankee Stadium in 1965, just like the fun-loving Mets did across town. Houk also introduced the new face of these suddenly cuddly Yankees.

"We are very happy to add Joe Garagiola to our top-notch team of broadcasters," Houk said. "Joe has developed into an outstanding sports personality in New York and around the country, and we are confident that Yankee fans will enjoy his warm, personal interpretation of the game."

Garagiola had grown up on St. Louis's Hill, an Italian section of town. Unlike his childhood friend, Yogi Berra, Garagiola had been a marginal major league catcher. He played for the Cardinals, Pirates, Cubs and Giants. But his career took off when—using a shtick of baseball one-liners and anecdotes—he became a broadcaster for the Cardinals and then NBC.

"The days with the Pirates, I'll never forget them," Garagiola told everyone at Shor's. "We once lost 112 games. We had a rainout and held a victory party."

The Garagiola Show had also performed on NBC's *Today* and throughout his book, *Baseball Is a Funny Game*, which at the time was baseball's all-time bestseller.

"He had a lifetime batting average of .257, but talked like a guy who never hit under .450," columnist Barney Nagler of New York's *Morning Telegraph* wrote about Garagiola's performance at Shor's.

The media ate Garagiola up. The Yankees hoped he would distract them from their other announcement, which they casually handed out on a slip of paper: "After 25 years of happy association, Mel Allen's departure is deeply regretted by us. Mel's mellifluous voice has become known not only as the voice of the Yankees but of all sport fans in this country. We extend affectionate wishes to him in his growing activities and we shall always cherish our friendship for him as a great sportsman, whose vivid descriptive powers and personality has made its own Hall of Fame mark on baseball tradition."

Some writers had known for months that Mel was finished with the Yankees, publishing articles speculating that Garagiola, Kell, Gowdy, New York football Giants broadcaster Chris Schenkel and others might be his successor. But December 17 marked the team's first public acknowledgement of the matter.

"There is no point in going into any details as to why we made the change," Houk told reporters. "I can see no reason for embarrassing Mel or anyone else. We just thought that a change would be beneficial."

As Mel had recognized in his October 8 letter to Topping, he was one of the first the Yankees clipped in the sweeping image change.

"I place the Yogi Berra and Mel Allen incidents in the same category," Houk would tell reporters along a meet-and-greet caravan through Connecticut with Garagiola and new manager Johnny Keane in early 1965. "We made decisions that we felt were best for all concerned, Mel and Yogi, the public and for the good of the Yankees."

As manager, Berra had led the 1964 Yanks to a 22-6 September that won the AL pennant by a game over the White Sox. But the club fired him and replaced him with Keane, the Cardinals' skipper in 1964.

"I'll have to make excuses for the film you're about to see," Houk said before running the World Series reels at Shor's, "but at least we got the winning manager."

Like U.S. Steel, which was running an advertisement in publications picturing several smiling, ordinary-looking Americans that read, "These are *our customers*," the Yankees sought to erase a decades-long aura of being cold, insolent and corporate with a facelift and a few more jokes. Fans weren't buying the act.

"I am sorry, Mr. Houk," wrote one woman from Brooklyn, another among the masses protesting Mel's axing, "but the Yankees made a terrible mistake which they will regret for a long time."

PART IV

REDEMPTION
(1965–1996)

CHAPTER 18

Missing

With Houk and the Yankees officially moving on from Mel on December 17, 1964, New York's dailies, which had carefully reported on Mel's fate beforehand, decisively trumpeted the news.

"Yanks Pick Garagiola—Mel Out," the *World-Telegram & Sun* ran in a headline across the top of his front page. The *Post* pictured Mel wincing on its front. On its sports page, the *Herald-Tribune* pasted an equally unflattering shot of Mel looking bewildered underneath the headline, "Yanks Ax Allen."

Two months earlier, when the *Post*'s John Cashman had visited Mel in Bedford Village with an accompanying photographer, the paper had depicted Mel on its front page sitting in the den, staring at his large television set that broadcast the 1964 Series he couldn't cover. The camera angle caught Mel looking bleary-eyed, as if caught in a trance.

Mel wasn't just a man who had merely lost his job. "He gave the Yankees his life," Red Barber once said, "and they broke his heart." The orbit of Mel Allen, a man who never married and lived with his parents, revolved around his job with the Yankees. "It's something I loved," Mel told the *New York Post*'s Leonard Shecter for a December 18, 1964 story. "I don't know how the hell it will be this summer without it."

Even a handwritten note from idol Joe McCarthy ("Dear Mel: the Yankees will never be the same without you," it read) only temporarily soothed Mel's pain. For years, he would constantly ask friend Curt Gowdy how the Yankees—*his* Yankees—could dump him. "Mel, you gotta forget it," Gowdy would reply. "There's nothing you can do about it now." Gowdy was so enraged with the Yankees' handling of his mentor that he called Houk and other Yankees officials and asked for an explanation. "They wouldn't give me a straight answer," he says.

Mel would never publicly bad-mouth the Yankees. In fact, he called Garagiola to congratulate him on his new job. It was the first such call Garagiola received. "It's the best job in the world," Mel said to his successor. "I know you'll do well. "Just be yourself, and I wish you the best of luck."

It was hard for Mel to be angry with the Yankees, or anyone associated with them. They were his team, and would remain so for the rest of his life. "I have the friendliest of relations with the front office," he would tell assemblages at his speaking engagements eager to find out what had happened with the club. For the rest of his life, Mel always maintained he didn't know. "If I knew, hell, I'd be glad to tell 'em why, so I'd at least get people off my back," he said in his waning years.

In early 1965, Len Faupel, who had just left Ballantine, which was teetering on a financial collapse, asked Mel to lunch. As Ballantine's advertising manager, Faupel had always tried to maintain a business-first relationship with his colleagues, but he considered Mel a friend and he wanted to explain why the Yankees let him go.

"He could never understand what happened," Faupel says. "Explaining it was too simple to understand. You take a man with that kind of talent and they let him go, the simple answer wasn't good enough. So you take the rumors: He talked too much and the drinking thing."

Seeing him hold a glass of Ballantine to his lips in commercials for all those years, fans assumed Mel was a big drinker. And when some listened to him gab on NBC's weekend news program, *Monitor*, an off-the-wall 1960s show that called for its hosts to cackle and kid, they swore they heard him slurring. But Mel was born with a deep Southern accent and, after studying speech at the University of Alabama, learned to enunciate clearly so that his audience would understand each of his words.

"I think that people would mistake that for struggling with drinking," Faupel says. "And that was not true. I never saw him as a drinker at all. And we were in social situations. Nothing ever got in the way of his professionalism at the ballgame."

But because the Yankees didn't publicly reveal why they dropped Mel, silence led to speculation. Rumors swirled through the broadcasting industry that he was a drunk, mentally ill, a dope addict and a loan shark. These charges were never printed, so Mel didn't issue a public denial of them.

The Hartford Times however, did report on January 31, 1969, that Mel had had a major operation at the Mayo Clinic in Rochester, Minnesota, and his condition was listed as "critical." Mel had had surgery all right. On Long Island. For hemorrhoids.

"We had to laugh," his sister Esther says of the erroneous report.

Intrigue about Mel also flourished because his network television duties almost entirely dried up for a decade and a half after the Yankees dismissed him. With his friend Tom Gallery gone as NBC's sports director after 1963 and the more youthful Lindsey Nelson waiting his turn, NBC had dropped Mel as voice of the Rose Bowl in January 1964. Mel covered college football for NBC in the fall of 1964, but after the Yankees dumped him and didn't say why, the network became leery. So did much of the broadcasting industry.

"It was as if he had leprosy," *Sports Illustrated*'s William Taaffe reflected later.

Reporters hesitated to report a reason for Mel's Yankees demise because no one knew exactly what had happened to him. "We didn't know, and didn't work hard enough to find out," the *Daily News*' Vic Ziegel, who covered the team in 1964, admitted decades later. Had reporters looked a little closer, they would have seen that Mel was regularly making speaking engagements ("I never went to so many," he said in the winter of 1965) and working weekly on *Monitor*. He attended Old Timers' Day at Yankee Stadium—the club at least let him come back to that—and had the crowd eating out of his hands at the microphone just as he had during his prime. When Mel introduced the Mick on Mickey Mantle Day in 1969 at the Stadium, it was hard for some to tell who got the bigger ovation.

But Mel's work at Yankee Stadium was strictly per diem. He had much more time to spend at home, where he might adjourn to his room and close the door. After 1965, he lived in two separate houses in suburban Connecticut with Larry, Margie, Carolyn and Andy.

"Was he a little depressed?" says Andy, today a Birmingham internist. "I suspect when he'd go in his room and close the door and not want to be bothered, he probably was. I don't doubt it a bit. And I'm sure if they had some of the antidepressants they have now, it may have been a good thing. But I don't know that. I was a little boy."

Andy remembers Uncle Mel emerging from his room and taking him everywhere: to his Little League games (Mel would stand behind so not to make his nephew nervous); to the Little League World Series in Williamsport, Pennsylvania, on a puddle-jumper plane during a terrible thunderstorm ("He was white as a sheet," Andy recalls) or maybe just to the newspaper store down the road on Sunday morning.

He was like a second father to Carolyn, too.

"My friends would come in and he would sit at the table and they would ask him questions," she recalls. "He always had time. The funny thing is, he would go away, and he'd come back and you'd say, 'Where were ya?' 'Um, I had an event to go to.' And you'd say, 'Well what was the event?' And you'd find out later that he was at the White House with the president."

Lyndon Johnson commended Mel in Washington for his work as part of a delegation of major league stars including Stan Musial, Hank Aaron, Joe Torre, Harmon Killebrew and Brooks Robinson who enlivened American troops in remote outposts in Vietnam during an 18-day trip in November 1966. Raised in the solid South, Mel voted for Democrats like Johnson but was always pro-establishment. He could never understand why his other nephew, Billy (who had become "Bill" as an adult) hotly contested the war. Mel would even lecture his nephew about the evils of Communism. He wanted to be a role model for his nephew Bill and his sister, Risa, who lost their father to lymphoma in 1974.

Mel was closer to Andy and Carolyn than Billy and Risa because he lived with Larry's kids.

"He was very involved in our lives—probably more than most uncles are," Risa says about Mel. "Sometimes it was a good thing, sometimes it wasn't. Sometimes I felt like I had two dads. I know that a lot of my friends—they had uncles and they hardly even knew them. There was never that kind of closeness that there was with our family."

When Anna died of a blood clot in 1965, after the funeral procession circled the driveway in front of the Bedford Village house to give Mom a final look at her home, Mel moved his father and Easter, their live-in housekeeper, in with Larry's family in Connecticut. The idea was that everyone could help take care of Julius, who had several health issues.

"That extended his life," Margie says. "Mel didn't want to put him in a nursing home."

Julius died of colon cancer in 1974, just five weeks before Esther lost her husband. Esther sold her house on Long Island and moved to Florida.

"Whatever you do," Mel told her, "I just want you to know that home is where I am."

☆☆☆☆☆☆☆

In 1965, Mel took a part-time job broadcasting the lame-duck Milwaukee Braves over a series of Southeast stations. The Braves were paving the way for their move to Atlanta in 1966. Mel flew out from New York for weekend games, working more than 70 radio or television broadcasts. He had no intention of making this a permanent gig. He just hoped that he could kill off all those rumors about him by proving he could still perform.

"Let me say that all of us in the Braves organization are delighted to have you on the team and we are most impressed with the job you are doing for us on Atlanta radio and TV," Braves vice president John J. Louis, Jr. wrote to Mel in a letter dated May 14, 1965.

After catching a Braves game in April 1965, *The New York Times'* Jack Gould, in the past a harsh critic of Mel's long-windedness, found him "in good voice."

Mel worked a similar part-time arrangement for the Indians in 1968, flying in and out of New York to Cleveland for games. The Indians finished 16 1/2 games behind first-place Detroit, playing in front of some scant crowds. During a dull Indians-Twins game, Mel filled time by rattling off some names of Minnesota lakes. He got onto the subject of Lake Superior, which just happened to be the setting for Henry Wadsworth Longfellow's poem, *The Song of Hiawatha*. Then, in front of dumbfounded partner Harry Jones, he began reciting several stanzas of the poem. *By the shores of Gitche Gumee, by the shining Big-Sea-Water …*

Mel enjoyed doing the Braves and Indians jobs, but his heart was elsewhere. As he worked the last day of the 1965 season, he had bumped into Johnny Blanchard, once a Yankees outfielder and backup catcher extraordinaire who now played for the Braves.

"Jesus, Mel," Blanchard said. "I know what happened to me, but I can't understand you. You were as much a part of the ballclub as anybody."

"I don't know, John," Mel said to Blanchard, "I don't know."

"Oh bullshit, Mel," Blanchard said. "They don't dump you after all these years and not give you a reason."

"This is God's truth, John," Mel told him. "I don't know what happened."

Blanchard was bitter himself that the Yankees had dropped a surprise trade on him to the Kansas City Athletics toward the start of the 1965 season. "We were just a bunch of numbers to them," he said about the Yankees. But thoughts of those same Yankees kept Mel from accepting a job offer from A's owner Charlie Finley to become the full-time voice of the new major league franchise in Oakland, California, in 1968.

"He would not leave New York," says his sister, Esther. "He would not be defeated."

Shortly after the Yankees had washed their hands of Mel in 1964, before the rumors about personal problems overtook Mel's image, Mel was an instant candidate to join the broadcast staff of the upstart Mets. On November 3, 1964, the *Daily News* ran a cartoon in which Casey Stengel's face appeared on the Statue of Liberty. Swimming toward him in the water were caricatures of Mel and Yogi Berra on a plank emblazoned with a Yankees "N.Y." Berra took a job as a Mets coach after the Yankees fired him in 1964, but Mel never made it ashore to Shea. The *Long Island Press* had run a story on November 23, 1964, announcing that the Mets had called a press conference for that day to unveil Mel, but the event never occurred. Before he could sign Mel, George Weiss, who had become the Mets' president, had to seek the permission of officials with the team's sponsor, Rheingold beer, a key regional rival of Ballantine's.

"He can open his mouth and say 'Rheingold,' a thousand times a day," Weiss was told, "but every time he does it people still are going to think 'Ballantine.'"

Losing Mel's voice didn't help Ballantine, either. The company lost $6.5 million in 1966. After Carl W. Badenhausen retired, Ballantine actually had tried to revive itself with Mel's voice and face—the same ones the company thought hindered it in the 1960s—on television commercial spots in 1971. "There's more than memories behind Ballantine," Mel said in one ad after pouring a beer. But Mel couldn't save Ballantine. It closed its Newark brewery and sold off to Falstaff Brewing Company the next year.

Yankees prosperity was in the past, too. Almost on cue with Mel's release, the team had slipped into a slump that lasted over a decade. Since Weiss left the club, the farm system had grown barren as the major league core of Mantle, Maris and Ford aged. The season after firing Mel, the Yankees finished sixth in the American League, ending a streak of five pennant-winning season. In 1966, they finished 10th, dead last in the AL.

"The only time they looked like the Yankees to me is when Frank Crosetti ran across the field to coach," Garagiola says.

CBS, which knew little about owning a baseball team, was more concerned about Yankee Stadium being freshly painted and its pipes working for paying customers than wins and losses. And, of course, the network wanted to exude that new, friendly Yankee way.

"Availability," said Michael Burke, who took over as team president in 1966 after Topping and Webb sold off their shares, "is the operative word. There was complacency in the Yankee organization. Yes, some part of it may have 'filtered up' from the success on the field. This is only human nature. But I feel that if there is to be a different climate, it must come through me, and it must be genuine. I do believe that we can change that climate—not immediately, of course, but in a relatively short time. I would say that the haughty, cold, remote Yankees are a thing of the past."

So were large Yankee Stadium crowds. Only 413 showed up on a rainy September day in 1966 at a stadium that sat over 74,000. Burke was attending his first game as Yankees team president. Barber, who was broadcasting for WPIX, immediately noted that the fan turnout was the smallest in Yankee Stadium history and demanded that a cameraman pan on the empty seats and on Burke, who was sitting alone. Perry Smith, the Yankees' vice president for radio and television, repeatedly denied Barber the request.

Four days later, Burke told Barber he was gone. The Ol' Redhead had become increasingly contentious with Rizzuto and Garagiola in the booth, and the camera incident had sealed his fate. But Burke didn't tell him that. All he said was: "We have decided not to seek to renew your contract."

Soon after Burke broke the news to him, Barber was in the office of his agent, Bill McCaffrey. "I'm not going to have happen to me what happened to Mel Allen," he told McCaffrey. Barber asked McCaffrey to inform the appropriate New York sportswriters of the news and to tell them to call Barber in his hotel room at the Hilton on 53rd Street in Midtown, where he stayed during the regular season.

"I'm going to have this thing out, and I'm going to have it out right now," Barber told his agent. "The Yankees have dismissed me. The move is now mine, not theirs. They have no more moves in my life."

Barber went back to his room and fielded phone calls all afternoon.

"I'm at liberty, but I never felt better," Barber told *The New York Times'* Val Adams. "My best years are ahead of me. I want to broadcast in baseball on a job where I am welcome."

✳ ✳ ✳ ✳ ✳ ✳ ✳

In the ensuing years after the Yanks got rid of him, Mel bought a Canada Dry bottling distributorship in Stamford, Connecticut, which he and Larry ran. He made frequent appearances for the soft drink company at store and restaurant openings. When Mel sold the distributorship, he continued his public relations work for Canada Dry and bought a country music radio station near Birmingham, which Larry managed while Mel remained in the New York area.

Mel always left the business side to Larry because he didn't care for financial matters. "I've never made any investments," he once said. "I'm not a gambler."

During his early years in New York, Mel used an accountant he had met through Ralph Edwards. But the guy didn't do him any good because Mel didn't know he was supposed to check in with him.

"Why is Ralph making so much and I'm not?" he asked the accountant.

"You never asked me," the man said.

It wasn't until the twilight years of Mel's life that he found someone who invested his money wisely. Even by 1965, Mel put his luxurious Bedford Village house on the market for a mere $75,000. Today, the home is worth millions. In that house, Julius once found a six-month-old check for $800 that Mel had forgotten to deposit.

Mel always said he would have covered sports for free had he been financially able to do so. During the decade and a half after the Yankees released him, he usually accepted whatever sports broadcasting gigs were offered to him. He did weekend sports reports for NBC's New York television affiliate, handled the Little League World Series for a Sacramento radio station, provided commentary for track and field's Millrose Games at Madison Square Garden for New York television and continued with sports-related radio commercials and voiceovers.

He taped three and a half-minute segments for a syndicated radio series called *Wake Up the Echoes in Sports*, a title taken from a line in Notre Dame's football fight song. He did two-minute segments for *Memories from the Sports Page*, a radio program broadcast to nine major U.S cities in which Mel took past personalities, events and stories and touched them up with personal experiences.

"Babe Ruth, in the minds of most folks, was America's greatest sports hero," Mel began one *Memories* episode. "Babe had a lot of great days, but there was one day I'll never forget. It was a day of sadness—a day of glory, too. It was Babe Ruth Day at Yankee Stadium."

So many great sports moments were still fresh in Mel's mind, and he shared them with anyone who wanted to listen. One taker was Bob Berger, a college-aged intern at Miami radio station WINZ in 1977. WINZ hired Mel to broadcast University of Miami baseball and football games that spring and fall. "He was a hero," says Berger, who had grown up a Yankees fan in the Washington Heights section of Manhattan. Berger delighted in striking up conversations with Mel at his home number.

"He was a guy who, in many ways, still lived in the past," Berger says. "You couldn't have a conversation with him without him bringing up Joe DiMaggio or the Yankees. People working with him really had no respect for the guy. They had grown up in different places, probably in many ways they were jealous. 'I'm on my way up in this business; this guy's a has-been.'"

This Miami experience was extremely distasteful for Mel. He could service-ably call games but he was now a 64-year-old man who announced against the Mel Allen of old. That Mel was not only younger and sharper, but he hadn't faced questions about what had happened to him for so many years.

Mel and Miami mutually parted ways after the football season, but Berger, today a Sporting News Radio personality, was left with cherished memories. A whole new generation of young baseball enthusiasts would soon have them, too.

CHAPTER 19

T.W.I.B.

By the 1970s, baseball no longer ruled the American sports scene as it had in the years following World War II. A television-watching sports culture had emerged, and, thanks to the handiwork of a father-son team, the National Football League was dominating the medium.

Ed Sabol and his son, Steve, turned a small, suburban-Philadelphia outfit into a public-relations brainchild known as NFL Films. Since 1967, pro football fans had been able to tune into a weekly show to see highlights of their favorite teams. With all the footage NFL Films collected, it had become a multimedia empire, light years ahead of baseball.

"Baseball had kind of been living in the Dark Ages in comparison to the NFL," says Geoff Belinfante, then the head of an advertising agency contracted to sell major league baseball.

Major League Baseball's marching orders to Robert Landau Associates, Belinfante's company, were straightforward: Take us to the NFL's level. Joseph Reichler, an executive for Major League Baseball Promotion Corporation, had an idea of how to do so. NFL Films used the almost supernatural voice of John Facenda, a former Philadelphia sportscaster, to sell its product. When Facenda bellowed, "the frozen tundra of Lambeau Field," fans shivered in their living room easy chairs. Reichler thought baseball needed its own vintage voice to sell its product.

As a baseball writer for the Associated Press from 1943 through 1965, Reichler had met many of the game's famous voices, but one name stuck out in his mind: Mel Allen. Reichler recalled how Mel still drew the biggest rounds of applause at baseball writers' dinners and at other banquet circuit events.

"I knew Mel hadn't done anything on a national scale for a long time—in a way, he was like a golden flash from the past," Reichler told Curt Smith for the book, *Voices of the Game*. "But quality is quality, I knew the voice, and I figured, 'Hell, if he was great in the forties and fifties, the early sixties, why wouldn't it work again? Why couldn't fans love him now?'"

Reichler called Mel, who perked up at the interest. In the spring of 1976, Reichler had Mel re-narrate 10 World Series highlight films as well as AL and NL season-in-review films for 1975. Members of the team assembled to produce this series, called *This Is Baseball*, found Mel a little testy and uneasy working with a young staff. He also had trouble pronouncing words and reading everything on his script in his allotted time frame. But the voice still spoke magic. As it thundered through Grand Central Station alongside Jody Shapiro, who would produce the first episode of *This Week in Baseball*, as the two men walked to one of Mel's first tapings, Shapiro sensed they had something.

"It took me an hour and a half to get through Grand Central because people kept on talking to him," Shapiro recalls.

After having *This Is Baseball* produced, the sport's executives pushed for a weekly baseball show, and Mel seemed the obvious choice to host it.

"What better name, what better person to give a new baseball show legitimacy than the man who had done so many World Series for so many years?" Belinfante says. "Mel was a big star and he gave us the legitimacy we needed to make a go with *This Week in Baseball* in world of syndication that was tough for us to break into."

One major issue remained: Pro football played a mere baker's dozen games a week, but there were 70 weekly baseball contests. NFL Films could send two or three film crews to every single game and then have time to get their film back to Philadelphia to prepare it for their weekly show.

"There's no way you could economically do that with baseball," Belinfante says.

There was no *proven* economical way to do it. Sony had introduced a 3/4-inch tape recorder designed for recording programs off television. A 3/4-inch recorder became the standard VHS model, but at the time, the half-inch recorder revolutionized the news gathering area of broadcasting. Baseball's young staff had the radical idea of using this 3/4-inch tape recorder to capture every baseball game in TV remote trucks outside all 26 major league stadiums.

"The format of choice of the time in the broadcast business was two-inch [tapes]," Belinfante says. "There were a whole lot of people in the television business who didn't think we could pull off what we were intending to pull off.

Baseball applied its idea in the spring of 1977, and the footage recorded using the half-inch technology became the basis for *This Week in Baseball*, which debuted that June. As games were collected from around the country, the tapes were shipped back to the New York City area, where the television show was produced. For the first time, fans got a heavy dose of baseball highlights, especially from out-of-town games. In these pre-*SportsCenter* days, fans saw few highlights beyond their local TV sports reports until *T.W.I.B.* arrived. The early *T.W.I.B.* episodes were highlight-heavy, recapping the big series of the week game by game, sometimes even pitch by pitch.

By 1979, the show had already soared to become sports' highest-rated syndicated series, broadcast in most major markets in the country on well over 100 stations. Up until 1989, *This Week in Baseball* ran right before *Game of the Week* on virtually every NBC affiliate.

"Week in, week out, fans set their Saturdays by it like clockwork," Reichler said. "In the East, 1:30 it was Mel, two o'clock the game."

Mel's friendly Southern tones were back on the national airwaves on a full-time basis and *T.W.I.B.* fans were treated to the same expressions their fathers had heard. As Mel endured for three decades as the show's host, his calls seemed lifted from the past:

"Going, going, it is … gone. It's a winner!" he roared while narrating a Darryl Strawberry game-winning homer.

"Kansas City's Steve Hammond, outstanding in the stands, a Royal sensation. How about that!" he purred to describe a diving catch.

Around the country, children rushed to finish their Saturday chores so they could hear the calls.

"I didn't care if I missed the Saturday afternoon game as long as I could see *T.W.I.B.*," says Jeff Noricks, a baseball fan who was born in 1973 and grew up in Detroit. "It was the highlight of my week if my Tigers were profiled."

In Nashua, New Hampshire, Mark Robert, who was 10 when *T.W.I.B.* first aired, yearned to see highlights of his Red Sox.

In Bloomington, Illinois, Rick Campbell, who is 10 years older than Robert, watched for footage of his Cardinals. "I used to live for that show," Campbell says.

And *T.W.I.B.* fans lived for listening to that folksy voice.

"San Francisco's Robby Thompson thinks he has a stolen base. And he does, plus a little egg on his face … Uh oh," Mel lamented as Thompson stole second base, then get tagged out trying to go to third after an infielder duped him.

Mel's light-hearted jests helped sell perhaps the most popular segment of the show, which was devoted to goofy plays.

"I often joked that the bloopers in *This Week in Baseball* pay the rent in my house," Belinfante says. "We did a whole lot of home videos with bloopers that people still love to this day."

T.W.I.B. employees, who spent some 250 hours a week sifting through game footage to prepare for each episode, found Baltimore Orioles outfielder Pat Kelly closing his glove too early and watching the ball bounce over the fence for a home run. They discovered Chicago Cubs third-base coach Peanuts Lowrey tackling player Bobby Murcer as Murcer ran through Lowrey's stop sign. They drudged up other footage of players running into each other, tripping over bases or watching helplessly as the San Diego Chicken stole their hat.

"Have you heard the song, 'We Won't Get Fooled Again?' Well, Ozzie Guillen hasn't … look," Mel said as Guillen fell for the hidden-ball trick on two occasions in one season.

Mel could rhyme or speak with a British or French accent, spouting "tres bien" or "mon dieu" amid a blooper.

"He had an ear and he had the natural delivery of a real thespian of an actor," says Mark Durand, *T.W.I.B.*'s first writer. "He could have been on Broadway."

Durand was in the studio for those first few tapings when Mel labored through his scripts. But the writer noticed a distinct difference in Mel's clarity when kids started to come up to him on the street and ask him about the show.

"That really meant something to him," Durand says. "This is a different generation. I think that that just flipped a switch and lit a fuse. Whatever problems or issues or difficulties he might have had were gone completely."

After a series of bloopers, Mel confidently called a heroic salute to the week's fielding gems. "New York Met catcher Gary Carter," he said as Carter, pictured from behind, tumbled over a wall behind home plate going after a popup. After Carter made the catch, he sprung up and displayed the ball. "Got it!" Mel said, going on to the next play in the same breath.

Says Belinfante: "For 20-years plus, there's a whole generation of people who grew up not knowing that Mel had been a play-by-play broadcaster of some note. We reintroduced Mel to a whole new group of fans, and he was very grateful for that."

After Mel signed off ("That's all for now, folks," he would say. "See ya next week on *This Week in … Baseball.*") and the credits rolled, fans saw another montage of highlights, these in slow motion. Pete Rose dove headfirst while stealing a base. Fernando Valenzuela's glanced skyward in mid-windup. Kirk Gibson gave heavy high-fives at home plate. This closing sequence had an accompanying instrumental score that gave kids around the country goosebumps. The tune was a piece of stock music called *Gathering Crowds,* which was available to all TV producers.

"I would get people all the time who'd say, 'I want to use it as my wedding theme,'" Belinfante says.

Episodes of *T.W.I.B.* routinely played in stadiums across the major leagues and on television sets at the Baseball Hall of Fame in Cooperstown, New York. As the show swept across the big screen at Dodger Stadium, Vin Scully's head shot up to look at it.

"When Mel was hired to do the show I thought, 'Well, who better to do it?'" Scully says.

❁ ❁ ❁ ❁ ❁ ❁ ❁

Curt Gowdy, who had remained in touch with Mel over the years, was pleased with his friend's new fame. But Gowdy also thought about how the voice had once announced the World Series and the Rose Bowl. Now it was calling bloopers.

"Mel, what the hell are you doing this show for?" Gowdy asked his friend. Mel grew solemn.

"Curt," he said slowly, "don't ever get out of baseball. I'll do anything to stay in it."

Since his departure from the Yankees, Mel had filled in on a few weekly network major league games, but he had become a mere blip on baseball's landscape before he began doing *T.W.I.B.*

"A lot of people didn't know that Mel was even alive," says Warner Fusselle, a former *T.W.I.B.* script editor who also served as Mel's backup voice.

Grateful for a second shot, Mel made *T.W.I.B.* the highlight of his week. He looked forward to the tapings, which were held in various recording studios throughout the New York City area. The night before, he would stay at fancy Manhattan hotels. During the show's inaugural season of 1977, he would have breakfast with his old Yankees statistician, Joe Gallagher. Gallagher was now a TV man, and the creators of *T.W.I.B.* brought him in to steer the fledgling show and its autumn announcer through its first season. After Mel and Gallagher ate, they would walk to the recording studio, which in 1977 was on Third Avenue in Midtown. On the street, people would stop him almost with the regularity they used to 30 years before.

"That gave him great pleasure," Gallagher says.

T.W.I.B.'s creative staff of fresh-faced 20-somethings were similarly smitten with Mel. When Belinfante shook hands with Mel after the broadcasting legend agreed to do the show, he thought of rushing home from school on fall afternoons to catch the end of World Series games. Now here he was a producer of an all-baseball television program. He had the chance to instruct the voice behind those World Series telecasts of his youth.

Belinfante and Fusselle, who were in their early 30s during *T.W.I.B.*'s initial seasons, were the elder statesmen on the show's first creative staff. "We were a bunch of kids," Belinfante says. Says Fusselle: "Geoff Belinfante was the only one with any kind of experience. The rest of us just came in off the street."

Fusselle had read in a newspaper that Mel was to broadcast college baseball games at the University of Miami in the early spring of 1977. He taped some of them off the radio, thinking this would be his last chance to hear the great Mel Allen do baseball. Fusselle, a native of Gainesville, Georgia, had been a broadcaster for the Triple-A Richmond (Virginia) Braves and for the American Basketball Association's Virginia Squires. He was out of work after the ABA merged with the National Basketball Association, so he got in his car and blindly drove north. When the highway divided and he had a choice of taking the left lane to Trenton, New Jersey, or the right one to New York, Fusselle just happened to be in the right lane.

When Fusselle arrived in New York, he went all over the city looking for work. He checked out Madison Square Garden and baseball's office of the commissioner. The baseball people sent him to go see Larry Parker, who was then the executive producer of a new show called *This Week in Baseball*. Parker hired Fusselle in July 1977, initially on a temporary basis to serve as a backup announcer for Mel. He was paid $200 a week. Fusselle's first day on the job coincided with one of the worst blackouts in New York City history.

"I was in the Times Square Hotel," Fusselle says. "I cried that first night. I just looked around and the plaster was falling off the ceilings, and the blanket had cigarette holes. It was terrible, but it was the only thing I could afford. I said, 'I can't believe I'm going to have to be in this room the whole week.' I lived in that room for three and a half years."

Fusselle's rudimentary first assignments for *T.W.I.B.* included picking up highlight videos that had been shipped from Philadelphia and Baltimore by train at Penn Station. He also drove to New York's airports, where the rest of the tapes were flown in from other major league cities.

"I did this because I had a car," Fusselle says. "I was part secretary."

As Fusselle sat in on the first tapings of *T.W.I.B.*, he realized his radio background would be helpful to the show. He watched Durand standing in the cramped sound booth with Mel, tapping him on the shoulder to indicate when to read. Fusselle suggested using a green light, which would flash on and off to cue Mel. Fusselle also thought the scripts should be doubled-spaced and written in pencil, so that they were easy to edit on the fly.

"We had to invent how this stuff was done," Fusselle says.

Fusselle didn't take a day off during his first three weeks with *T.W.I.B.* But over that time, he was making himself indispensable. He was eventually hired as a full-time script editor. He began to write the tease, the 60-second, highlight-laden introduction to the show that Mel read as the catchy *T.W.I.B.* theme song played. This musical selection was called *Jet Set*, a sprightly, upbeat tune. *Dunnt-dunnt, Dunnt-dunnt. Dun dun … dun dun dun dun …*

Fusselle and *T.W.I.B.*'s other scriptwriters and editors would routinely pull an all-nighter before taping day. Writing the tease could take as long as five hours, as Fusselle agonized over each pun or pop-culture reference to preview the week's show.

In one memorable tease from 1982, relief pitcher Rollie Fingers was pictured lying asleep in a cot in a firehouse while wearing his Milwaukee Brewers uniform. The setting played off the baseball nickname of "fireman" for a team's top reliever, who often enters a game with his team in a jam and requiring him to put out metaphorical flames. In the *T.W.I.B.* tease, a phone next to Fingers rang, and he answered with a sleepy, "Hello?" The screen paused.

Well hello there, Mr. Fingers, this is Mel Allen. Hold on now, baseball's got your number.

Jet Set's jingle began as highlights interspersed with Mel's narration.

Dial M for Milwaukee: Long distance information from Harvey's Wallbangers. Person to person. (This introduced a segment on the surging Milwaukee Brewers, managed by Harvey Kuenn. The team was nicknamed "Harvey's Wallbangers.")

The Fenway area code: Please deposit the ball over the wall. (This introduced a segment on a Red Sox-Angels series with a highlight of the Angels' Rod Carew hitting a home run.)

Philadelphia calling: A first-place busy signal—the next-best thing to being there. (This introduced a segment on the Phillies hanging around in second place in the National League East.)

Call back, Atlanta: The Braves reverse the charges. (This introduced a segment on the Braves, who won 10 of 11 games after losing 19 of 22.)

Mr. Brock, this is a re-recording: Rick the Quick's no phony. (This introduced a segment on Rickey Henderson breaking Lou Brock's single-season stolen base record.)

The screen panned back to Fingers in bed.

"Right. Be there in a flash," he said.

Fingers, clad in his Brewers uniform and a fireman's helmet, rode on the side of a fire truck as it left the station.

Off the hook to hook and ladder, let the Fingers do the talking and answer the call on This Week in Baseball.

Week to week, the tease carried a specific theme such as water, school or The Beatles. After Fusselle finished each tease and did a final edit to each script in the wee hours of the morning, he would crash, sometimes on the studio floor, until it was time to tape.

When Mel arrived, the next set of challenges began, as he and the young *T.W.I.B.* staffers often clashed, albeit lovingly.

"Mel was not the kind of guy you would hand a script and say, 'Mel, just read it,'" says Joe Lavine, a *T.W.I.B.* producer in the early 1980s.

During his heyday, Mel would write and edit his own scripts for Fox Movietone News. With his newfound friends, he wanted to go over each word and point of emphasis, too.

"There were times when I wrote 'laugh' in parentheses," says Jim Rogal, a *T.W.I.B.* writer in the mid-1980s. "He would either completely ignore it if he didn't find it funny or laugh when I didn't write it in."

Mel and the young staff would play these games weekly.

"I don't like this 'O-for-4' about Pete Rose," Mel would say. "O is a letter, not a number. Can I say, 'Nothing-for-4?' And the word, 'collar.' How many people listening will know that word?"

"Everyone knows, Mel," a producer would reply.

"I'm not sure they do," Mel would persist.

"It's a good word, Mel."

On the next take, Mel would deliberately drop the word. Mel would sometimes win these jousts, other times he wouldn't.

"Not too many fancy phrases, or anything like that," Mel once said to script writer John Bacchia.

Then Mel saw Bacchia's handiwork.

"Goddam blandest script I ever saw!" Mel growled.

After a contentious taping session, Mel would sometimes turn to a writer and say, "Ah, don't worry about it. I was practicing my law."

As the writers learned about Mel's style, they began to write to it. Fusselle would polish scripts down to Mel's last "hmmmm" and "How about that!"

Then the only dicey issue became tailoring the day around Mel's personal quirks. He would arrive at the studio and need to "get the frogs out." That could entail singing or, as former producer Bob Bodziner recalls, using devices "that looked like they were from 1930," such as a "ball that squirts stuff in to your throat."

Mel's mannerisms only became an issue because he came to the office once a week, and everyone collectively had to meet a deadline.

"There was a list of people you weren't supposed to mention during the voicing," recalls Heather Mitchell, a *T.W.I.B.* associate producer in the early 1990s. "Babe Ruth, Lou Gehrig, Joe DiMaggio ... "

The confining nature of a script and a timed show, however, prevented any "wandering," as Mel liked to call his wordy explanations for things. Mel could just play to his main strength: His voice.

"Most play-by-play guys couldn't pull off reading a script with any sort of resonance," Bacchia says. "He had that ability. He could read copy, and give it some flair and feeling."

As he narrated the *T.W.I.B.* scripts, Mel would punch the air and contort his face. He would pretend he was doing live games.

"I think that play-by-play was his first love, but he began to realize that this was where his life had led him," Belinfante says. "As he grew older, I think he appreciated being around the younger people. I think in an odd way, it kept him young and it kept him going in his later years."

After the day's taping was over, the youthful *T.W.I.B.* staffers loved to hear Mel's stories. They might be about how he finished his day's work at Yankee Stadium and walked across the bridge and into the Polo Grounds just as Ralph Branca delivered his infamous pitch to Bobby Thomson in 1951. Or how the sickly Lou Gehrig lavished praise upon his work. "His Lou Gehrig story would make you cry," Fusselle says.

"The guy that you heard on *T.W.I.B.* was the guy that we knew," Belinfante says. "We knew him as a warm human being, and we wrote our scripts to make him a better, likable, warm person."

Mel always seemed happy with the modest salary the people at *T.W.I.B.* paid him. He had an agent at the time named Frank Paige, but pay-related issues between he and Belinfante, who rose to became the show's executive producer, were always done one on one and sealed with a handshake. Sometimes finances would allow Mel a small raise, other times they wouldn't. Belinfante can't remember Mel ever complaining about his paycheck.

"Thanks for the opportunity," Mel would always say in his Southern drawl, more pronounced in conversation than on the air.

Over the years, as Mel and the staff worked on their 29 episodes, their relationship grew stronger. Mel would gladly agree to do extra narration on home videos that the makers of *T.W.I.B.* produced, such as seasons-in-review and collections of memorable bloopers and plays. Belinfante would field calls requesting Mel for commercials and voiceovers, and he would share *T.W.I.B.*'s fan mail with the announcer.

"We were always very protective of Mel," Belinfante says. "We treated him the right way over the years."

Discussing Mel several years after the announcer's death, Belinfante carries a sad expression on his face. He talks fondly of his *T.W.I.B.* years, repeatedly calling them "the good ol' days."

"He would like to spend time here," Belinfante says from his desk at the offices of The Phoenix Communications Group in South Hackensack, New Jersey. Phoenix produced *This Week in Baseball* during the final 10 years of Mel's life.

The show endured many behind-the-scenes transitions. In 1978, after *T.W.I.B.*'s first season was deemed a success, Major League Baseball Promotion Corporation purchased the assets of the show away from Robert Landau Associates. Belinfante and the rest of the *T.W.I.B.* staff became part of Major League Baseball Promotion Corporation.

But bottom-line baseball commissioner Peter Ueberroth cut off the *T.W.I.B.* subsidy in 1986, and Belinfante scrambled to start a new independent company to produce *T.W.I.B.* Phoenix became that company, and Belinfante made the *T.W.I.B.* staff employees of Phoenix.

There were other setbacks. The *T.W.I.B.* staff coped with the death of Joe Reichler, the brains behind the original show, in 1988. The next year, NBC dropped baseball's *Game of the Week*, and *T.W.I.B.*'s viewers struggled to find the show on television as it ran at new times.

The show moved from the archaic videotapes of the late 1970s to satellite production. It also transitioned from being highlight-heavy to doing more interviews and features. Through all this change, however, fans still connected with the show because it maintained its cheery face and jolly voice. Even after enduring heart surgery in 1989, Mel never deserted his surrogate family, and *T.W.I.B.* persevered.

"We truly considered ourselves blessed to be working with Mel Allen," says Roy Epstein.

CHAPTER 20

Father's Day

In the mid-1950s, Mel fielded a blind phone call from an assistant football coach at Northwestern. The young man had met Mel while Mel covered one of his weekly games for NBC.

"You don't remember me, do you?" the coach said to Mel.

He wanted to get into sports broadcasting and sought Mel's advice. Mel talked to him for about 45 minutes and set up an interview for him at NBC.

"He didn't know me from Eve," George Steinbrenner says today. "He cared about the little guy. I tried to never forget it."

When Steinbrenner acquired the Yankees from CBS in 1973, he immediately wanted to know what had happened to Mel Allen. He made Mel feel welcome anytime at Yankee Stadium and honored him at its most exalted events. Amid the unveiling of a renovated Yankee Stadium in 1976, Steinbrenner asked Mel to be one of the day's four most honored guests during the opening pitch ceremonies.

"Your devotion and loyalty to the Yankees for many years have been without comparison," Steinbrenner wrote to Mel in a letter inviting him to the affair. "It is just one small way we have of saying thank you from all of us for all you have done and meant to the Yankees and New York City as well."

Mel framed the letter and hung it the wall of his Stamford, Connecticut, home, where he lived at the time.

"What a man you are," he wrote in a response to Steinbrenner.

The two men had started a friendship that would last until Mel died 20 years later.

"He extended his hand to me and I never forgot it," Steinbrenner says. "I did nothing for him that he hadn't done for me. Bringing him back was just a small thing."

Steinbrenner extended Mel virtually an open invitation to watch games in his private box at the Stadium, one time with his friend, Richard Nixon. The owner, criticized for a quick temper and short patience with managers, never had a single issue with Mel.

"George is a great humanitarian," Mel once said. "You can't help but like him."

The Yankees' owner made Mel a trusted advisor on personnel moves. "Whatever he said, I tried to do," Steinbrenner says.

During the late 1980s, Mel recommended to Steinbrenner a throaty announcer with whom he had worked a Yankees postgame show on New York radio station WMCA in the mid- to late-1970s. Steinbrenner hired John Sterling as a Yankees radio announcer in 1989 and Sterling spiraled upward in acclaim as he detailed the rise of new Yankees dynasty in the late 1990s.

Before Steinbrenner crowned Sterling, however, he invited Mel back into the Yankees' booth to call the team's cable telecasts on New York's SportsChannel in between tapings for *This Week in Baseball*.

For 40 games a year from the late-1970s through mid-1980s, Mel again became the voice of the Yankees. His return to the booth coincided with the arrival of the Yankees' first two World Series titles (in 1977 and 1978) since Mel had left. He hadn't missed anything but Yankees hardship.

By July 4, 1983, however, the club's fling back atop baseball had ended. The Yankees lineup showcased Butch Wyneger, Steve Kemp and Roy Smalley. But on this day, Steinbrenner's birthday, Mel would remind Yankees fans of the team's heroic past as he called Dave Righetti's no-hitter of the Boston Red Sox, New York's such no-hitter since the Don Larsen masterpiece of 1956.

"And all set to articulate the description of the game in his best Independence Day voice, none other than Francis Xavier Healy, on SportsChannel!" Mel said to introduce his partner.

A former major league catcher, Fran Healy once compared calling a game with Mel to getting a Ph.D in sports broadcasting. Mel initially didn't appear so professorial, though, on this 94-degree day. After mentioning a Yankees sponsor, Sealy mattresses, he said to Healy, "I'd like to be stretched out on one of 'em now in the air conditioning."

Mel then ducked out to get a snack as Yankees broadcaster Bill White relieved him.

"See you a little bit later, Coach," he said to Healy.

While Mel was away from the booth during the Righetti game, Healy told viewers: "Righetti has held the Red Sox hitless through three ... check that, through four." Such loose chatter stopped when "The Master," as Healy termed Mel, returned to the booth in the top of the sixth, when Healy's Ph.D program was revisited.

"There have been five hits in this ball game, for any of those who have turned in late, and the Yankees have had 'em all, leaving one conclusion," Mel said.

"You're not superstitious," Healy replied.

"It's something I learned from fellas like you who played baseball," Mel said. "That's a dugout tradition, not a superstition."

Mel turned back to field and announced Don Baylor's solo home run that gave New York a 2-0 lead: "There's a drive ... if it stays fair ... it is going, it is going, it is gone!"

Mel continued his lesson with Healy.

"Fran," he said, "when you were talking about this bit of superstition, when you say that there have been five hits, six hits and the Yankees have had 'em all, there's only one conclusion: The other side has not had any. The expression that you do not use stems from an ancient baseball dugout tradition. A lot of people through the years have begun to think that was something initiated in broadcast booths, but it isn't. As you know, you've caught no-hitters. It's just those three words: He's pitching a ... you know. It's just out of respect to those guys in the dugout. They do it, so you do, but you don't keep from reporting it."

"That's right," Healy said.

The television screen flashed to the scoreboard.

"As you look at the scoreboard, it tells the story," he said.

"Under number 'H'," Mel added.

The zero remained in that column when Mel faced the Red Sox's Wade Boggs with two outs in the ninth inning.

"This crowd is standing!" Mel said. "This crowd is wild! The Yankees are leading, 4 to 0, and Wade Boggs, one of the top hitters in the American League, standing between Dave Righetti and a pitcher's dream.

Righetti wasted a fastball outside to the left-handed hitter.

Outside—ball one. Three-sixty-one is what he was batting going into this game. Wade Boggs—Dave Righetti trying to get him out. Two out.

Righetti fired a strike over the outside corner.

And there's a strike and it's one and one and this crowd is roaring! There's [Yankees manager] Billy Martin, nervous, everybody on the bench is nervous, even on the Red Sox bench—they're trying to break it up. Dave Righetti, under the toughest sort of pressure. Will he get it?

Boggs waved at a slider low and away.

Wade Boggs swings and misses! Strike two! One strike away for Dave Righetti. This crowd is going nuts! And there's [Red Sox manager] Ralph Houk looking on. Everybody in Yankee Stadium is standing and roaring. The Red Sox, trailing, 4 to 0, a runner at second.

Boggs fouled off a pitch.

Out of play beyond third. Dave Righetti, who has permitted only three Sox to reach base, all on walks, has got just about as tough a man to get out as the Red Sox could put up at the plate. It's the ninth inning, one ball, two strikes, two out. Hoffman on second.

Righetti missed with an outside pitch.

Boggs takes just outside, ball two. The deuces are wild! Two balls, two strikes, two out. Billy Martin, anxious. The crowd is standing, 40,000-plus people standing and roaring, and Righetti trying to get Boggs ...

Boggs swung and missed a low slider.

And he gets him! A no-hitter! A no-hitter! A no-hitter for Dave Righetti! How about that!

The call was classic Mel. He maintained not mentioning the no-hitter before the feat was accomplished, yet he masterfully set up the situation for fans tuning in late.

During Boggs's at-bat, he methodically outlined other crucial details—two outs, a runner on second, Yankees lead 4-0, Boggs was hitting .361. And after Righetti whiffed Boggs, Mel rode the exuberance of the crowd like a wave.

"And there's former vice president Nixon applauding from the stands," Mel said. Realizing his momentary lapse—that Nixon had later been *President*—he quickly muttered, "Former President."

Mel had been a little lost in his past on this day. (Ralph Houk was even managing the Red Sox from the visitor's dugout.) But the Righetti no-hitter, broadcast on replay after replay around the country, re-invigorated the image of Mel Allen in the present.

"If baseball is back, Mel Allen must be, too," William Taaffe wrote in a 1985 *Sports Illustrated* article. "The voice is rich, thick and Southern, to many the most recognizable in baseball. When you hear it, it's summer again, a lazy July or August afternoon with sunlight creeping across the infield. Like the game itself, Allen is timeless."

Sportswriters, now seeing that nothing was wrong with Mel after all, began to jump back on his bandwagon. Dick Young, who accused Mel of coming down with a case of "psychosomatic laryngitis" while losing his voice as the Yankees got swept by the Dodgers in the 1963 World Series, called Mel "the most remarkable comeback man of all" in a 1984 column.

"That wonderful voice," wrote Young, who had moved over to the *New York Post* from the *Daily News* by then. "It still sings."

Mel was not only heard on Yankees telecasts and *This Week in Baseball*. He once again became a mainstay on radio and television commercials. Whenever a baseball-related videotape needed a background voice, whether it was a World Series recap or a how-to about baseball card collecting, Mel was again the automatic person to ask. He made cameos in movies, his voice calling Yankees games during a summer at the beach in the 1950s-era 1984 movie, *The Flamingo Kid*, and facing the camera as himself in 1988 cops and robbers spoof, *The Naked Gun: From The Files of Police Squad!*

The ultimate example of Mel's re-emergence in pop culture came when he doubled as a rapper—as in a singer of rap music—in a 1980s song entitled *Baseball Dreams* by a group called The Naturals. The song began normally enough, with Mel saying, "Hello there everybody," but an 1980s bee-bop beat ensued and the song rolled downhill from there: "Here's the windup, the pitch, the count, 3-2. He swung that stick and that ball flew; man alive, what a drive, a grand slam homer, that ain't no jive."

✿✿✿✿✿✿✿

On August 7, 1978, shortly after his ascendancy back into the national eye as the host of *T.W.I.B.*, Mel and Red Barber became the first two broadcasters honored by the National Baseball Hall of Fame. They received the Ford C. Frick Award, named for the former commissioner who was also a sportswriter and sports broadcaster.

"I'm very happy to say that this decision when it was made was made in alphabetical order," Mel told the crowd in Cooperstown, "because the old Redhead, there was nobody ever greater. He should have been here first."

After Mel's acceptance speech, Esther, who witnessed Mel's enshrinement along with Risa, Larry and Andy, ran into Barber.

"I just can't get over it," he told her. "I wouldn't have done it."

In public, Mel and Barber always tried to be civil with one another. Privately, their sentiments differed.

"Mel Allen had developed a habit of walking into the play-by-play booth at the last minute. I mean the very last minute," Barber wrote in *The Broadcasters*. "At the Stadium, his brother Larry would have his scorecard in order, waiting for him. On the road, Mel often penciled in the batting orders while announcing the first inning. I never asked him why he cut it so close, but I sensed he felt it gave him 'an entrance.' Mel would just suddenly appear out of nowhere. His chair would be empty ... then he was in it ... 'Hello everybody ... this is Mel Allen ... '"

When Esther read that passage, she ran into Mel's bedroom in their Greenwich, Connecticut, townhouse. Mel was reading the newspaper on the bed.

"Why don't you do something about people who do this to you?" she demanded.

After Esther read Mel the passage, he started to laugh.

"Let me tell you something about Red Barber," he said, "Did you see him say anything good about anybody else in that book?"

"No, I didn't," she answered. "Mel, I don't know. If somebody did that to me, I would call him up on the telephone and I would tell him what I thought of him."

"Ah, forget about it," Mel said.

He could have this calming effect on his sister. The two had moved in together in the late 1970s, and, though they fought, they had usually made up and gone on to some other activity until the next dispute. Mel would head to a ball game, Esther would take to the golf course.

"I always called my mother and uncle 'the oddest couple,'" Risa says. "But it made a lot of sense. He was a bachelor and was getting older. My mother was single. They had their own lives. It was companionship and I guess that's a nice thing, rather than being lonely."

Esther cared for Mel around the clock after his 1989 five-vessel heart bypass. Noted surgeon A.D. Pacifico performed the procedure at the University of Alabama at Birmingham. Andy, who attended UAB for medical school, suggested Pacifico and Robert Bourge, the head of transplant at UAB, to his uncle.

"Uncle Mel," Andy told him, "you'll get the best care."

Mel communicated with the doctors from the New York area as he drifted about the banquet and speech circuit. Since his first Yankees life, he had never really let up on his speech load.

"I've got about seven or eight speaking engagements," Mel told Pacifico during one conversation. "I thought I'd come down after that."

"You better get down here tomorrow," Pacifico replied.

Mel did, and the surgery laid him up for weeks. Esther came down from Connecticut to help Larry and Margie care for him at their Birmingham home. When Andy saw Uncle Mel after the surgery, he said to himself: "That's my grandfather in bed there." Mel had his hairpiece off (Mel had worn one since the early 1960s) and was noticeably gaunt.

"He went from this big, hulking guy," says Bob Bodziner, his *T.W.I.B.* producer, "and he turned into a little old man. It looked like he aged 20 years."

After Mel's surgery, Esther monitored his diet religiously. When Mel would go to *T.W.I.B.* tapings, he would request only a lettuce-and-tomato sandwich on white bread and a 7-Up. In these years between the surgery and his death, Mel had a pacemaker and was treated for an aortic aneurysm, congestive heart failure, hypertension and colon bleeds. But he still worked.

He reported to *T.W.I.B.*'s studios in New Jersey each week and on April 30, 1990, WPIX honored him as baseball's first seven-decade broadcaster. Mel wasn't calling games regularly anymore, but producer Marty Appel had offered Mel the opportunity to do a little play-by-play.

Mel walked into the booth at Yankee Stadium wearing a gray suit and his trademark fedora.

"Here he is, a Hall of Famer, Mel Allen," Phil Rizzuto said on the air as Mel joined he and partner George Grande.

Rizzuto, who had remained a Yankees broadcaster since Mel left the booth in 1964, put his hand on Mel's shoulder. The two good-naturedly reminisced about their previous seasons together while looking at some old photographs, which flashed on viewers' screens. Rizzuto pointed out Jerry Coleman in a picture of the team's 1963 announcing crew.

"Jerry joined us," Mel said to Rizzuto, "then you really could go home early."

Rizzuto laughed aloud.

"The only voice of the Yankees," Rizzuto said. "Any time anybody else gets introduced as the voice of the Yankees, I get angry."

Mel chuckled. Then Rizzuto looked at him and said, "The greatest voice still. You should still be back broadcasting, Mel."

Mel remained silent. Soon, Yankees public address announcer Bob Sheppard asked fans for a "warm Yankee Stadium greeting" to honor Mel.

The crowd was sparse, for the Yankees were well on their way to a last-place finish that season, but it gave Mel a hearty ovation. Surprised, he slowly lifted his body off his chair and smiled uneasily. He clenched his hands and waved to fans in triumph.

✶✶✶✶✶✶✶

During Mel's final years, Fusselle began to fill in for him more and more as the host of *T.W.I.B.* But Mel had just worked an episode in May 1995 when he woke up in the middle of the night to go to the bathroom and passed blood. He felt woozy the next morning and called his doctor, who advised him to go to the hospital.

Mel was placed in intensive care at a Connecticut hospital, where doctors tested him and gave him several medications in an attempt to halt some persistent bleeding. "I lost a hell of a lot of blood," he told the New York *Daily News'* Bob Raissman. "I don't know if they were kidding or not, but they said I lost half my blood."

As Mel lay in a hospital bed for nearly two weeks, he watched television reports of Mickey Mantle's failing health. Mantle had undergone a liver transplant, and Mel felt a bond with his old Yankees buddy as they both withstood difficult times. Once both young and strong, they were now old men fighting for their lives.

"A lot of things began occurring to me, including where it all began for him—the get-go—in 1951," Mel told Raissman, recollecting spring training of that year. "The big story was Mickey Mantle. I closed my eyes and could just see the expression on Casey's [Stengel] face when he raved, 'That boy hits balls over buildings.'"

Two months after Mel's stay in the hospital, Mantle was dead. And when the Mick went, he seemed to take some of Mel with him. It was just one more Yankee he had seen at his youthful best who had aged and died.

"What can I say?" he told Raissman. "It's sad—very sad."

Mel narrated a Mantle tribute episode of *This Week in Baseball* that ran on August 18, 1995. The show was meant to eulogize Mantle, but it gave the grave impression that Mel was saying goodbye himself. At the beginning of the episode, not only were viewers presented with images of a boyish Mantle, but also one of a young Mel in a fedora.

As the old version of the announcer spoke, his voice seeped sadness. "Good old number seven," Mel said softly as highlights from Mantle's career played. Film rolled from Mickey Mantle Day, which Mel emceed on June 8, 1969, at Yankee Stadium. At the end of the show, producers allowed Mel to give his personal tribute.

"You know, for those of us who were fortunate enough to watch Mickey Mantle play every day from his days as a 19-year-old rookie, it sure is a time of special sadness, but it's tempered by wonderful remembrances of his Hall of Fame achievements," Mel said, his voice cracking. "On a personal note, I sure consider myself mighty fortunate to have been behind the microphone for most of Mickey's career, and to have had the chance to watch this magnificent man play baseball."

Viewers then heard old calls from Mel of Mantle home runs:

"In comes the pitch, Mantle swings … there goes a long drive, going to deep right field, it's soaring up high, it's going, going, it's gone! A home run for Mickey Mantle."

"From us all, Mickey, thanks," Mel said. "You'll always remain in our minds and in our hearts."

Mel finished that season with *This Week in Baseball*, but it turned out to be his last. He had hoped to return, so the producers decided to bring the show back for a 20th season.

Mel turned 83 in February 1996, and soon after that, he attended the dedication of Legends Field, the Yankees' glamorous new spring training facility in Tampa. He and Esther had spent the winter in Tampa, where they rented an apartment. That winter, Esther had called Larry and Margie, who now lived in Montgomery, Alabama in their retirement, to tell them she had put Mel in the hospital again, this time for exhaustion related to his heart condition. "He overdid it and he needed to rest," Esther says. She needed help caring for Mel, so Larry and Margie came down.

By June 9, Mel was feeling better. He welcomed author Richard Ben Cramer, who was researching a biography on Joe DiMaggio to his townhome in Greenwich, Connecticut, and the two spent the afternoon together traveling to Chicago's Del Prada Hotel in overnight Pullman cars and in Mel's midnight-black Cadillac, which he used to cart DiMaggio around. After a while, Cramer, who had grown up listening to Mel in Rochester, New York, while lying on his mother's cool linoleum floor on sweltering summer afternoons, just stopped taking notes.

"His voice was perfect," Cramer says. "It was just perfect."

Cramer stayed for hours listening to Mel and the other sounds of summer: The neighbor's lawnmower, the bird chirping, the slight breeze rustling in.

"He was in perfect shape," Cramer says. "I can't tell you how perfect. I thought, 'This is great. He's gonna go on forever.' And the next week he was dead."

The following week, Belinfante invited Mel to The Phoenix Communications Group's offices in the shadows of New Jersey's Meadowlands. Belinfante wanted to test Mel's voice and gauge his energy level to see if he could count on him for the upcoming season.

Mel arrived at the Phoenix offices on Wednesday, June 12. It was widely known he had been sick, so Mel's trip to the studio was an event.

"I remember when he came in, everybody just crowded around him," Fusselle says.

Mel did a trial run through a *T.W.I.B.* episode. The old intonation and nuances were there, but the voice's resonance was missing. Belinfante decided Mel wasn't quite ready to do a live show again, but gave him some VHS tapes and scripts of prior episodes on which to practice.

"Just use your instinct, use your voice," Belinfante told his show's heart and soul.

Mel and Belinfante drove down the street to a restaurant for lunch. Like just about everywhere in the New York area, Mel was a celebrity at the place they chose, which showcased a baseball he had signed. As they entered, an elderly hostess fawned all over him. As Mel and Belinfante ate, they chatted about the current baseball season. Before they parted, the two agreed that Mel would return to Belinfante's office to try out his voice again on June 26.

Belinfante told him he wanted Mel back on *T.W.I.B.*

"Let's wait and announce it after the All-Star Game—then you can come back strong," Belinfante said.

"Whatever you say, Coach," Mel replied.

❊❊❊❊❊❊❊

On June 16, Father's Day, Mel got up about 10 o'clock in the morning, unusually late for him. Esther fixed him cream of wheat and toast.

"Breakfast is so late this morning," she said. "Do you want to eat lunch? I'm gonna fix dinner tonight."

Mel didn't know whether he would want lunch.

"Well, you let me know if you want lunch," she said.

Mel eventually went back upstairs to his room. Esther never heard from him about lunch, and he wasn't bashful about letting her know when he wanted it. In his bedroom, Mel watched the Yankees hold off the Cleveland Indians 5-4 at Yankee Stadium. A Yankees revival was beginning. After several years as an also-ran, the team would win its first World Series title in 18 years that October. But Mel wouldn't see it.

Around five o'clock, Esther began to prepare dinner. She started making veal chops, which she didn't fry for fear of Mel's health. She broiled them with a coating of flour and seasoning that she put on instead of salt and added just a little oil, so the chops wouldn't burn. Esther's son Bill called and they chatted for a few minutes. As they talked, Esther heard Mel walk to the bathroom in his bedroom. She never heard him walk back to his bed.

Around 6:30, she yelled upstairs, "Mel! Dinner's ready!"

No response.

Esther went upstairs, knocked on his door and got no answer. She saw Mel wasn't in bed. "Mel? Mel?" she said as she walked into his bedroom. When she turned the corner into his bathroom, she saw him on the floor. He wasn't moving.

Esther rushed over and saw that Mel's eyes were open but expressionless. She knew immediately that he was dead, but she didn't want to believe it.

"Mel! Mel! Wake up! Wake up, Mel!"

She tried to shake him. Mel was much larger than her, so he didn't move. Esther got up and raced to the phone to call 911.

"My brother is expiring on the floor of the bathroom!" she screamed. "Please hurry!"

She gave the operator her address, slammed down the receiver and ran back to Mel. She tried to wake him again. She then ran downstairs and outside and saw no one, though it was still daylight. The ambulance and police car arrived almost immediately.

"Upstairs," Esther said, "in the front bathroom."

A policemen came back downstairs to tell her what she already knew about Mel.

"Is there anybody in your family that you want me to call for you?" the policeman said.

"I have to tell his brother," Esther said. "He's in Alabama. He's so far away."

"Have you got his number?" the policeman said. "I'll call him for you."

Esther couldn't remember Larry's number. Then she couldn't find it. She gave the policeman her telephone book and he found the number.

When Esther called Alabama, she was so hysterical Margie could barely understand her. When Margie relayed the news to Carolyn, who also lived in Montgomery, she crumbled to the floor. Just earlier in the day, Carolyn had told her kids, Aaron and Anna, that they needed to make sure and call Uncle Mel on Father's Day.

❄ ❄ ❄ ❄ ❄ ❄ ❄

Mel's death had likely stemmed from a heart arrhythmia.

"He was rallying and planning to go back to work," Esther told *The New York Times'* Richard Sandomir the day after he died.

New York's *Daily News*, *Times* and *Post* billed Mel's death on their front pages. The *Daily News* and *Post* played the story up more than Michael Jordan leading the Chicago Bulls to their fourth NBA title in six years.

"Mel Allen, Voice of the Yankees, dies," read the letters across the top of the *Daily News*.

The Birmingham News plastered its headline across the top of its sports page, "Mel Allen, voice of the Yankees, son of Alabama, dies."

Curt Gowdy, who was in Paris, was surprised to see the news. New York sports radio station WFAN called him and asked him to come on the air. Gowdy gabbed about his colleague, mentor and friend for an hour.

Back in New York, Fusselle also worked the talk-radio circuit.

"I thought of Mel's life as a real celebration of greatness," Fusselle says. "I didn't get sad until a month later. I went on all these shows and said all these great things."

The next night at Yankee Stadium, Bob Sheppard was on the public address system as a picture of Mel's smiling face flashed on the jumbo screen above center field. Yankees players bowed their heads, wearing black armbands in memorial.

"May we ask you to spend a few moments in silent prayer as we remember Mel Allen," Sheppard said to the crowd.

After the silence, a tribute to Mel played on the big screen. An interview of him that was conducted late in his life was shown.

"You still get letters from people, and so many people say, 'I grew up with you,'" Mel told the crowd. "I grew up with you, too."

Up in the radio booth, Yankees play-by-play man John Sterling dedicated the evening's broadcast to Mel, "the once and forever voice of the Yankees."

On June 19, more than 600 mourners paid tribute to Mel at Temple Beth-El in Stamford, Connecticut. Among them were George Steinbrenner and a line-up of Yankees greats, including Joe DiMaggio, Yogi Berra, Whitey Ford and Rizzuto. But none of them spoke at the pulpit. Esther wanted the funeral "simple, thoughtful, religious."

Arthur Richman, an advisor to the Yankees and Mel's friend of 60 years, eulogized Mel as "a wonderful, warmhearted soul who never tried to impress anyone with his importance."

In his own eulogy, Rabbi Joshua Hammerman said, "Mel Allen's life was one, long, extended, exhaustive, exhilarating, triumphant prayer."

Metropolitan Opera singer Robert Merrill, the longtime voice of the national anthem at Yankee Stadium who used to give Mel tips on how to conserve his voice, sang *America the Beautiful* as Mel's casket was carried from the synagogue. Mel was buried at an adjacent cemetery next to his parents.

For years, Mel had said a memorial prayer for them at Stamford's Congregation Agudath Sholom. Rabbi Joseph Ehrenkranz had become friendly with Mel as he attended his synagogue and remembered the announcer's story-telling ability fondly.

"When he came in for service, he would talk baseball with everyone." Ehrenkranz says. "His friendliness was unmatched. He loved people."

Ehrenkranz, a Newark, New Jersey, native, grew up following the minor league Newark Bears, then the Yankees' top affiliate. Of course, he also heard Mel's voice on the radio and cherished their one-on-one conversations. However, what truly impressed the rabbi about Mel was something the announcer never told him: that Mel would take World Series films to seminarians studying for the priesthood at North American College in Rome.

Ehrenkranz found this gesture extraordinary.

When Mel died, Ehrenkranz wanted to recognize his interfaith achievements. He suggested to Cardinal John O'Connor, the archbishop of New York, that his Center for Christian-Jewish Understanding, which is based out of Sacred Heart University in Fairfield, Connecticut, sponsor a tribute to Mel at St. Patrick's Cathedral in Manhattan.

O'Connor knew Mel had been a friend of Cardinal Spellman. Spellman had even arranged seating for Mel and his parents to meet the pope on one of their visits to Rome as a thanks for the announcer's work with the seminarians. When Ehrenkranz asked O'Connor about a St. Patrick's tribute to Mel, the cardinal simply replied: "Done."

O'Connor admired Mel, too, for his ability to "bring alive a sense of goodness" through his descriptive broadcasts. Plus, O'Connor loved how Mel succinctly referred to St. Patrick's as "the Yankee Stadium of churches."

On November 4, 1996, New York was still reveling in the Yankees' come-from-behind World Series triumph over the Atlanta Braves. But for about an hour, the city paused to remember a man who, as his friend Arthur Richman said, was probably looking down on the Yankees during their triumph.

The Mel Allen Memorial Tribute honored a Jewish man at the grand Fifth Avenue stage of Catholicism.

"Mel was an ambassador of good will long before the word ecumenism entered our vocabulary," Ehrenkranz, who presided over the service, told the crowd of over 1,000.

Sportscaster Suzyn Waldman, a pioneering woman in a male-dominated field, gave impassioned renditions of the national anthem and *America the Beautiful*. Waldman had once introduced herself to Mel at a press conference at Yankee Stadium.

"Hi, I'm ... " she began before Mel interrupted.

"Oh, no no ... I know who you are," he said.

After the two chatted for a while, Mel told her, "Ms. Waldman, you have an intrinsic love for this game and I love listening to you, and don't let anybody stop you."

"He was a lovely man," Waldman recalls today. "I never forgot that he was so kind to me at a time when most people weren't."

O'Connor, Gowdy, Richman and Marty Glickman, a classic voice of the NBA's New York Knicks and the NFL's New York Giants and Jets, also spoke glowingly of Mel at the podium at St. Patrick's.

"I always respected his ability to respect the opposition," Glickman told the crowd. "Sure, he rooted for the Yankees, but he rooted for Ted Williams."

Ehrenkranz also read a letter to the crowd from Ralph Edwards who fondly recalled the days he and Mel shared an apartment while starting out as young broadcasters in New York City. Edwards couldn't make the memorial because of ill health, but Berra, Rizzuto and Don Dunphy, who called Yankees games over the radio while Mel served in World War II, all attended, as did many friends, relatives and walk-ins off the street.

One of them was Bill Ries, a former neighbor of Mel's in Connecticut.

"Oh, he could tell stories," Ries told *New York Times* sportswriter Richard Sandomir, who covered the memorial. "He came to dinner once, and he talked so long the turkey or the duck burned."

While Mel's funeral was a sad occasion, there were fewer tears at the St. Patrick's tribute. It was much more of an upbeat affair. It was a chance, nearly five months after Mel's death, for those who loved and admired him to recognize the man and his achievements.

As Ehrenkranz had begun the memorial by saying, "Hello there everybody," Gowdy put closure on the life and career of his good friend.

"Goodbye everybody," Gowdy said to the crowd, "this was Mel Allen. A giant in our business and one of the most decent men you'll ever meet in your life."

EPILOGUE

Just listen for a minute. You'll probably hear the expression, "How about that." Someone might have a hangnail. Or have left the house without an umbrella, only to discover rain outside. Mel wouldn't mind such abuse of his most famous three words. He never thought they belonged to him.

What would bother Mel would be the broadcasters who blab "How about that!" after a team goes ahead 3-2 in an NBA game. As they utter them, they deepen their voices and concoct a contrived exterior of emotional angst. They inject filler phrases like "trifecta" and "tater." They babble that they've never seen anything so "unbelievable" before.

"The trend today seems to be to put yourself first and the event second," Mel said about the state of his industry as early as the 1970s. "Any reporter's job is first to report."

Mel would shudder while reporting on today's sports world. A steroid scandal surrounds the game he loved. The banned drug and other performance-enhancers may have aided players in pummeling the home run record he saw Roger Maris attain through sheer will. The players have reached the postseason on teams that didn't even finish first in their own division, let alone their own league.

On the broadcast side, Mel's old show only recently stopped using a claymation "Mini-Mel" to spout "How about that!" as viewers watched the week's best plays.

"We went too far with it," admits *T.W.I.B.* writer Jeff Scott, a holdover from the Mel Allen era. "It's tough to carry on that tradition. He was the show."

There are some more tasteful memories of Mel still around. Yankees radio broadcasters John Sterling and Charley Steiner proclaimed "Ballantine blast" in 2004 after Yankees home runs. The beer, which Falstoff has revitalized, can be found at some food and beverage stores, too.

"Do you think about Mel?" I asked Steiner during the 2004 season.

"All the time," he responded. "How many people are so identified with a beer and a ball club? One or the other is impressive. Here's a guy from Alabama who conquered and, in many ways, defined New York."

In 1998, George Steinbrenner enshrined Mel in Monument Park beyond the outfield wall in Yankee Stadium. Larry and Esther were on hand to unveil the first such Yankees tribute to a non-playing broadcaster.

"Mel would never believe this," Larry said to me in his Alabama home as we watched footage of the occasion.

When Larry speaks in his warm Alabama drawl, you're almost sure his brother is somewhere in his house. Mel is alive and at the microphone, wearing a fedora and a loose-fitting, short-sleeve dress shirt, in a painting that hangs on Larry and Margie's wall. Larry walks past the picture dozens of times daily, donning a Yankees hat. He hardly ever takes the cap off, except to put on the crimson-colored one that he wears as he attends every Alabama home football game in Tuscaloosa. When Larry is at home, he and Margie drink Canada Dry Ginger Ale.

"It's the best," Margie says, as if still helping her husband and brother-in-law pitch their product.

Margie talks in a maternal tone, her Connecticut accent overtaking some Southern sounds she has acquired after nearly 30 years of Alabama living.

Esther, who still lives in the northeast, also has both Connecticut and Alabama in her voice, although her accent points due South as she recalls tales from West Blocton, Johns and Cordova.

"I can't tell you about our family in three minutes," she jokes. "I need at least five minutes."

Three minutes was all the time Esther had at Aaron Bern's Bar Mitzvah. Aaron's mother, Carolyn, asked her great aunt to speak about family heritage. Esther gave a brief family tree and mentioned how Wolf Israel helped form and foster the family in Alabama. She also mentioned how Mel brought her parents, Larry and herself north and then how Larry, after marrying Margie and raising two children—including Aaron's mother—in the North, came South again. Knowing Aaron was an avid sports fan (he's now a member of the University of Indiana's football team), she left her grand-nephew with one final thought.

"After going over your family history, I found that we, as a family, could stand to have an All-American football player or a great baseball player," she said. "How about that?"

INDEX